COUNTERPART

COUNTERPART

A South Vietnamese Naval Officer's War

Kiem Do and Julie Kane

Naval Institute Press

ANNAPOLIS, MARYLAND

The names of certain persons in this book, both Vietnamese and American, have been changed to protect their identities.

Library of Congress Cataloging-in-Publication Data

Do, Kiem, 1933–

   Counterpart : a South Vietnamese naval officer's war / Kiem Do and Julie Kane.

     p. cm.

   ISBN 1-55750-181-5 (alk. paper)

   1. Vietnamese Conflict, 1961–1975—Personal narratives, Vietnamese. 2. Do, Kiem, 1933– . 3. Vietnam (Republic). Hải quân—Officers—Biography. I. Kane, Julie, 1952– . II. Title.

DS559.5.D6 1998

959.704'3'092—dc21   98-12206

Printed in the United States of America on acid-free paper ∞

05 04 03 02 01 00 99 98   9 8 7 6 5 4 3 2

First printing

To our parents
Mr. and Mrs. Do Van Sach
Edwin Julian and Nanette Spillane Kane

A hundred years: in the span of one lifetime,
Talent and destiny are apt to clash.
It's like the changing mulberry field:
The things we witness make us sick at heart.

Nguyen Du, The Tale of Kieu

Acknowledgments

The authors wish to thank the following persons for providing information, critiques, or encouragement for this book:

Richard Armitage, Bernard Cavalcante, Victor Croizat, Thomas Cutler, Timothy Curren, Thom Le Do, Mark Gatlin, Betty Glancey, Vicki Holley, Wayne Holley, Cindy Kane, Edwin Kane, Helen Kane, David Madden, Edward Marolda, Brenda Mitchell, Dana Nelson, Maurice Shine, Harry Trumbore, Mike Walker, Thomas Wasson, and Reginald Young.

Abbreviations

AGP	Motor Torpedo Boat Tender
ARL	Repair Ship, Landing Craft
ARVN	Army of the Republic of Vietnam (South Vietnam)
ASPB	Assault Support Patrol Boat
ATC	Armored Troop Carrier
AWOL	Away without Leave
CAP	Combat Air Patrol
CCB	Command and Control Boat
CIA	Central Intelligence Agency
CIC	Combat Information Center; Commander in Chief
CNO	Chief of Naval Operations
CO	Commanding Officer
DAO	Defense Attaché Office
DER	Radar Picket Escort Ship
DLG	Guided Missile Frigate
E-Plan	Evacuation Plan
HQ	Hai Quan (meaning "Vietnamese Navy"—identifier used as prefix to hull numbers on all VNN ships)
LCM	Landing Craft, Mechanized
LCU	Landing Craft, Utility
LCVP	Landing Craft, Vehicle and Personnel
LSM	Landing Ship, Medium
LSIL	Landing Ship, Infantry, Large

LSSL	Support Landing Ship, Large
LST	Landing Ship, Tank
MRF	Mobile Riverine Force
MSC	Minesweeper, Coastal
MSF	Minesweeper, Fleet
NVA	North Vietnamese Army
PBR	Patrol Boat, River
PC	Submarine Chaser
PCE	Patrol Craft, Escort
PCF	Patrol Craft, Fast (Swift boat)
PGM	Patrol Gunboat, Motor
PRC	Personal Radio Communications
PX	Post Exchange
R&R	Rest and Recuperation
ROTC	Reserve Officers Training Corps
VC	Viet Cong
VNAF	Vietnamese Armed Forces; Vietnamese Air Force (South Vietnam)
VNN	Vietnamese Navy (South Vietnam)
WHEC	High Endurance Cutter
WPB	Patrol Boat
XO	Executive Officer
YOG	Gasoline Barge

COUNTERPART

Prologue

It was sometime between noon and sundown on 29 April 1975. Capt. Do Kiem, deputy chief of staff, operations, of the Vietnamese Navy, ducked into his office on the third floor of Saigon Naval Headquarters to slump for a minute in his big chair. The electricity was out. Through the open window he could hear the loud, insistent throbbing of helicopters and the *pop-pop-popping* of small arms. Charred scraps of paper fluttered from the U.S. Embassy smokestack like clouds of black butterflies.

He picked up the hourly CIC report tablet and glanced at it: "River assault unit at Long An bridge evacuated; ARVN 21st Division in disarray; last naval coastal group at Phan Rang under heavy attack; Vung Tau–Saigon bridge destroyed to stop advancing troops. . . ." He sighed, put the tablet back on its rack, and massaged his temples.

It still didn't seem real that the South's army had given up fighting or that President Minh had warned the naval CNO that further bloodshed would be pointless. In less than twenty-four hours the war that Captain Kiem had been fighting all his adult life would be over—and his enemy would be the victor. But unlike the South's army, the navy still had a choice: they didn't have to surrender. They didn't have to hand one of the top ten navies of the world to the enemy, making North Vietnam—with its laughable "mosquito navy"—a major sea power overnight. There was still a way to get their blue-water fighting ships and up to thirty thousand sailors and family members out of the city and out of the country. They had a plan: a secret

"Evacuation Plan." The order had gone out an hour ago. The ships were loading.

It was a good plan, Captain Kiem told himself, rummaging through his Samsonite briefcase in search of a cigarette. Richard Lee Armitage, Kiem's old buddy from his years as commander of IV Coastal Zone, had flown back into the country to help Kiem come up with the plan—at a time when everybody else was flying out. The husky, blond American hadn't changed a bit from his old days in U.S. Naval Intelligence, even though he lived in Virginia now and had five or six kids. He still looked like Marlon Brando, and he still had guts. But Kiem wished he knew where Rich had flown off to that morning. It sure would be easier with him around.

His eyes moved to the small, framed picture on his desk: his wife, Thom, a former beauty queen at her French high school in Da Lat, and their three little girls, aged eight, six, and two. He'd been meaning to bring in a picture of their two boys, aged sixteen and twelve, but it was too late now. Suddenly his confidence faltered. He'd had plenty of chances to put Thom and the children on a charter flight out of the country, as late as last week, before his last U.S. Navy "counterpart" had fled the country—but Kiem's Confucian upbringing hadn't let him do it. If his men could have had the same privilege, then sure—but, of course, they didn't. Now, with his family's fate tied to his own and that of the Vietnamese Navy, Kiem wondered if he'd done the right thing. Even by his most optimistic projections, the E-Plan's odds of success were about one in five.

There was a knock, and Kiem reached for his Smith & Wesson .22 revolver. It was his aide, Lieutenant Su.

"Excuse me, sir," said the lieutenant, "but there was a call while you were out. A colonel from the Four Party Joint Military Commission, speaking with a heavy accent. 'Borck' or 'Borek'—some Polish or Hungarian name beginning with a B. He wouldn't leave his number. Said he had an important message for you and that he might call back later."

"What the hell?—" said Kiem. He didn't know a soul on that worthless commission charged with monitoring the terms of the 1973 Paris "peace" agreement. That lying, two-faced German Henry Kissinger had set it up as a sham, just before selling out South Vietnam to the communists. If the Four Party Commission had a message for him, they could stick it, as far as Kiem was concerned. A message to surrender, most likely. Fuck the bastards.

But what if somebody on the other side is trying to get in touch with me? Kiem thought suddenly—because, even though he'd risen to be third in command of the navy of the South, Captain Kiem was from the North. He'd been born in Hanoi forty-two years before and had lived there till the age of twenty-one, when he'd left to start school at the French Naval Academy—never to see his family again, as it turned out. Did somebody up there know who he was and what he was doing? If so, then who? One of his brothers—Nam, Lam, "Frenchy," or Trung? One of his two half-brothers by his father's other wife? Tuong, his best friend from the French Naval Academy, who'd defected to the North at the beginning of the war? An uncle or a cousin? And what could they possibly want from him now—to stay behind so he and they could meet?

Well, it was too late now. He'd chosen his way, and he was going to finish it, dead or alive.

"Thank you, Lieutenant Su," he said. "It was probably nothing."

Then the phone rang, and Captain Kiem reached for it.

W O O D

I am a reed, but a thinking reed.

Blaise Pascal

CHAPTER 1

Heads French Indochina

Brevie Named Governor-general in Colonial Shakeup

New York Times, 9 August 1936

When Do Kiem was five years old, his grandfather, Mr. Do Van Soc, began to plan his own funeral. Mr. Soc was seventy-five years old and in robust health, as far as anyone could tell. He was the Phu Tai village schoolteacher, and Kiem was one of his students.

Every day for several weeks Kiem's grandfather would hitch up the skirts of his long, blue scholar's robe, climb on his horse, and roam the countryside in search of the perfect grave site. The choice of the site was extremely important. When a man was buried properly, his family would prosper; but when a man was buried carelessly, his family would come to ruin.

The site that Mr. Soc finally chose was on high ground and open to the river and shaped like one of the Buddhists' sacred animals: *kim qui*, the golden tortoise. Mr. Soc was very pleased with his choice, although no one would have guessed that by looking at his face. A pair of wire-rimmed glasses hid his eyes, just as a black turban hid his forehead, a white mustache hid his upper lip, and a gray goatee hid his chin. He was very fierce-looking. All of the schoolchildren of Phu Tai, except Kiem, were afraid of him.

"Very well," said Mr. Soc. He pulled a hand-drawn map from his saddlebag and marked the spot with an X. Then he set about designing his coffin.

The coffin was to be made of *lim* wood, the most precious timber in all of Vietnam. The wood was so hard it took two men grunting and straining at opposite ends of a handsaw to cut it. They labored for nearly six months on the patio behind Kiem's grandfather's house, under the overhang from the palm-thatched roof.

The parts of Mr. Soc's coffin, glued with tree sap, fit so snugly together that the carpenters didn't need to use nails. The black lacquer finish had also oozed from a tree's veins; it was rare and expensive, but its fumes were harmful to living things. One of the maids passed too close while it was drying and came away half her face scorched bright red.

When the lacquer had dried, the carpenters began gilding the lid and the carved Chinese characters at head and foot that meant "long life." Kiem crept out on the patio while they weren't looking and snatched a square of gold-leaf tissue. Then he took it down to the bathing pond to gild the flat rocks that lay beside it. Under the surface of the water, carp flashed gold and red-gold. The whole world gleamed.

When the coffin was finished, it just sat out on the back porch, waiting. On nights with a full moon, the villagers of Phu Tai would stop by to admire it, but on other nights they just went straight to bed after dinner, because kerosene lantern fuel was expensive. "Are you sick, Venerable Teacher?" they would ask.

"Do I look sick? What a silly question. A glass of wine, gentlemen?" Kiem's grandfather was referring to *van dien*, the French-produced rice wine that was really more like harsh brandy, which the French "protectorate" government forced every village to buy according to a quota system.

One day, playing hide-and-seek with some other village boys, Kiem opened the coffin's lid and climbed in. The lining was padded silk, so comfortable that he yawned and dozed off. He had guessed that they would be too frightened to look for him in there, and he was right. When he woke up and cracked the black box open like a mussel shell, they ran off screaming in all directions. *What were those sissies so afraid of?* A coffin was for when you died, like going to sleep at night. Daddy had nearly died. And silkworms died.

Kiem's mother raised silkworms so that she could make cloth for the family's good clothes. First she paired the breeders, which she had saved from the last crop, and dropped them into cups: the little male, whose wings fluttered constantly, and the larger and more sedate female. The male mated with the female and then died; the female laid her eggs on a square piece of fabric, and then she died too. A little while later the eggs hatched into tiny worms, no bigger than a comma on this page. Kiem and his Uncle Thinh, who was also five years old, had the job of picking mulberry leaves to feed them. They had to be very careful to wipe the dew from the leaves so that the worms wouldn't get diarrhea.

At first Kiem and Thinh tore the leaves into itty-bitty pieces. But the worms grew fatter and hungrier every day. After ten or twelve days the boys merely ripped the leaves in half. After twenty days they dumped them in whole, and the worms made a constant racket with their chomping, like rain drumming on a roof. Kiem's and Thinh's legs began to ache from rushing around plucking leaves fast enough to satisfy the hunger. The only times they got a break were when the worms slowed down their eating in order to molt, splitting their skins open and slithering out of the crack. They were delicate then: one fly could kill a hundred of them. Kiem and Thinh would drape mosquito netting over the worm beds and keep the brazier well stocked with coals.

Soon the worms were as big around as a boy's little finger. Pale green in color, they began to turn a lighter and lighter green until they were almost transparent. Then the color inside turned from pale green to blonde. Silk began to dribble out of their mouths.

Kiem's mother showed Kiem and Thinh how to shape a bundle of dried broom into a wreath. "This is to help them make their mutation," she said; "watch." She dropped a worm on the wreath. It reared its head and looked around as if remembering something. Then it crawled up into the foliage, selected a spot, and began to wrap the silk around and around itself, until the cocoon was two fingers wide. Soon the house was as thick with branches as a forest, each wreath ornamented with hundreds of cocoons. Inside the house it was all golden, as if gold rings and bracelets were growing on trees.

"It's so pretty," Kiem's mother said, "but we can't let the caterpillars hatch, or they'll eat their way out and ruin the silk. Help me pick out the biggest, strongest, glossiest cocoons to save for breeding. We'll need two dozen pointed ones, and two dozen oval ones." Pointed ends meant males inside, and rounded ends, females.

When that was done, it was time to harvest the unlucky ones. Kiem's mother built a cooking fire and dumped the first batch into a vat of boiling water, shoving them underwater with a poke of her chopstick to kill the larvae inside, then nagging and prodding at a floating cocoon until its tag-end of silk thread came loose. Untangling the thread, she twisted it with four or five others into a firm strand. Then she wound the strand around a bamboo spindle, grafting a new cocoon on each time a thread ran out. When a spindle was fat with silk, she carried it outside. Soon the brick courtyard was covered with spindles drying in the sun.

When Kiem got bored with hopping over spindles—unwinding one as

far as he could and then twisting it back up so his mother couldn't tell—
he'd go wandering out back to the comb-shaped garden formed by a
dozen strips of land sliced by irrigation canals. Areca palm trees bordered
each comb-tooth along the water, and in between the double rows of
betel nuts sprawled mangoes, guavas, pineapples, star fruit, oranges,
grapefruits, and far less interesting lemons and vegetables. The smell of
ripe fruit sugared the air, so sweet that not even the garden crabs could
resist it. Using their big claws to grasp the hull, they would drill with a
small claw until they pierced through to sweetness. After a few days the
drilled spot would turn soft and rotten, and the crab would skulk back to
dig out the meat. If Kiem and Thinh spotted a fruit with a telltale hole in
it, they would carry it to their grandfather and beg permission to eat it.
Then they would cut out the rotten part and split the good part between
them. Now and then they tried to fake the mark of the garden crab, but
Mr. Soc was never fooled. He would look up from his sheaf of funeral
plans—how many pigs to feed the mourners, where to pitch the sleeping
tent, what sad songs the hired musicians should play—and shake his head.

Every year, with the same shake of his head, Kiem's grandfather would
decide who could and couldn't be admitted to his old-style village
school. In early spring the hopeful parents would form a line outside his
house, clutching a live rooster or basket of fruit or bunch of fish under
one arm and a small boy under the other. Those "goodwill gifts" were
Mr. Soc's only pay, so he could accept or reject students at his whim. It
was a great honor to be selected by him.

When he had finished choosing his students, Mr. Soc would arrange
them in a seated circle: about twenty boys ranging in age from four to
ten. They would steal nervous glances at the bamboo rod lying in the
dirt beside their teacher. Its name was "Long One." Five knots spanned
its length like the knuckles of a hand, one for each of the five elements
that moved the world: metal, wood, water, fire, and earth.

"Very well," Grandfather would announce, "we will start by reciting
the 'Three Thousand Words': *Thien, troi; dia, dat; cu, cat; ton, con.* . . .
Follow along with me."

"*Thien, troi; dia, dat,*" the boys would begin chanting. The first word of
each pair came from *Nom,* their ancient scholarly language, written in
Chinese characters. The second was from the language of everyday
speech. *Thien* and *troi* meant "heaven," "sky," "God"—whatever dwells
up above. *Dia* and *dat* meant "soil," "ground," "dirt"—whatever dwells

on the surface of the earth. Then *cu* and *cat*, "to lift up," and *ton* and *con*, "to remain."

The words weren't arranged in any particular order according to meaning, but their sounds were patterned to aid the memory. Rhymes and rhythms helped the reciter get all the way to the end without encountering Long One.

Mr. Soc would show the students how to form the Chinese character for *thien*, and they would copy it in the dirt in front of them with sharpened sticks. Then he would show them how to write the Vietnamese word, *troi*, and they would copy that, too. They weren't allowed to use paper yet, because characters came from the heavens, and it would have been a sacrilege to crumple them up and throw them away.

"*Le ciel*," Mr. Soc would say to Kiem alone. "*La terre*." Kiem didn't understand why he was being singled out, but he knew better than to ask a question. It didn't matter whether or not he understood: the important thing was to memorize, because one day in the future he would find out the meaning. "*Quan, su, phu*," the boys' parents were fond of saying: "king, teacher, father." Obey the father first of all, and the teacher over the father, and the emperor above the teacher. *Obey without question.*

At the end of every school day Mr. Soc would quiz them orally on what they had learned, then pull out two tubes of red and black ink-powder. Kiem would get a red dot on his forehead—meaning he'd learned his lessons well—but the circle around Thinh's mouth would always be black. Kiem would wait until the older boys were out of sight and then catch up with Thinh's sad shuffle. Thinh knew that his mother, Madame Thin, would be upset with him when he got home. Madame Thin was Mr. Soc's concubine. She'd been a maid in the house before Kiem's grandmother died.

Meanwhile, through a dry and a rainy season, under sunlight and moonlight, the coffin just sat out under the eaves, waiting. At last, on the very day he completed his funeral plans, blowing on the last wet ink-strokes to dry them, Mr. Soc gave a satisfied nod and dropped dead, surprising everyone but himself.

Contacted by telegram, as Mr. Soc had requested, his former students came journeying from all over the country to pay their respects. Some of them arrived in motorcars, parking them at the village crossroads and proceeding up the dirt oxcart path to the farm on foot. Chauffeurs stood guard where the cars were parked, but that didn't stop the village boys from sneaking up behind them and trying to squeeze a horn: *ah-oo-ga!* One lucky boy got to rub the dusty fenders with a soft cloth.

The visitors continued along the trail, bamboo twigs catching at their sleeves on either side, until they came to an earthen wall crowned with shards of jagged glass and to a gate in the wall below the guard tower with its round peephole and pointed roof, like a birdhouse for men. Once through the gate, they followed the sounds of wailing to the Do family's ancestral shrine. One by one they took off their shoes, bowed low before the altar, and cried out: "Ho, ho, ho, Venerable Teacher! I am here to pay my respects to you."

Kiem watched proudly as his father returned every gesture of respect made by the visitors: a bow for a bow, a bent knee for a bent knee. He and his mother and brothers and sister and the rest of the immediate family were sitting just outside the entrance to the shrine, by the closed coffin, moaning as loudly as they could. Thinh was there, too, but not Madame Thin, because she wasn't part of the family. Mixed in with the real mourners were professionals who'd been hired to swell the sound-level. They wailed in rhyme, interpolating the names of family members. Kiem listened for the delicious shock of his own name: "*Kiem . . . Kiem. . . .*" Now and then he sneaked a sideways peek at his three big brothers: Nam, Lam, and Tri, who'd come all the way from Hanoi. He wished that his grandfather's funeral could go on forever.

By the second day, though, Kiem was getting fidgety. It annoyed him that Thinh still had tears dripping down his cheeks and snot pooling above his lower lip. Thinh's lower lip stuck out like the rim of a clay jug. The other boys said that it was to catch all of that milk without spilling it: Madame Thin was still breast-feeding him, even though he was five years old and in school.

At last Kiem's father dismissed him, and Kiem went wandering into the shrine, noticing that the usual clutter of candles, braziers, and ancestor pictures had been shoved back to make room for more offering trays. He shuffled his fingers through heaps of gold paper money, to be burned so that Grandfather would be rich in the spirit world. While his father wasn't looking, he bit into a ripe plum and then replaced it, bitten-side-down, on its brass tray.

He drifted back outside. "*My father, you are all,*" the professional mourners were chanting, "*like the big ripe betel nut in the tree; and when the wind shakes the tree, you must fall down. . . .*"

Kiem moved on to the great bamboo-slatted tent overarching the brick courtyard. Under its canopy guests were squatting on sleeping-cots, nibbling roast pork with their fingers and sipping homemade rice wine. "That's Mr. Sach's fourth son, Kiem," they whispered loudly when they saw him. "So handsome! And tall, like his father." "Watch out! It's risky to call attention to a child's good looks. Here in the countryside we name a good-looking baby *Mud* or *Ashes* so the spirits won't be jealous." "Oh, nonsense! I'm from Hanoi, and I don't believe those foolish old folktales." "Is he in school yet?" "Not primary school, just the village school. Next year, I think." "He looks quick-witted." "Why, you know, the father is one of the smartest men in the country. He won a scholarship from the French to study civil engineering. Now he works for the French government in Hanoi." "Eh, it's a bad thing to leave the ancestors' graves." "Yes, a terrible thing. But the boy's mother stays in Phu Tai." "Eh, it's a bad idea to leave one's husband in the big city." "Yes, he has taken a second wife."

Kiem snatched a piece of bitter starfish from the buffet table and began sucking on it. Then he paused to listen to a three-piece band playing mournful folk tunes, but the horn player shooed him away. "The sight of it makes my mouth water," the horn player said, pointing to the starfish. "I'm blowing all spit and no air."

So the boy wandered down to the firepit, where two red-faced servants were scalding and scraping a pig. "This is the third pig we've slaughtered so far!" one of them bragged. "And you know a pig feeds a hundred people. Here!" He puffed air into the pig bladder, knotted its end, and tossed it in Kiem's direction.

"I'd better not get my clothes dirty," Kiem moped. He was wearing white pants and a long white robe, the same as yesterday, and he'd be dressed in the same clothes for days and days ahead, as far as he knew.

"Foolish boy! Ragged clothes are a sign of respect for the dead. One who's caught up in grief doesn't bother to check his reflection in a mirror."

"Oh, great!" And Kiem raced off to play with his new football.

The coffin had to be buried at noon sharp, the luckiest time of day; so, late in the morning of the seventh day, the funeral procession set off. Two men led the way, carrying a bamboo pole with a white pennant snapping at the top to symbolize Kiem's grandfather's soul. Behind them walked a monk in ceremonial dress, counting his beads with one hand and waving a scepter with the other. From time to time he called out to his assistant—a bald-headed boy-monk about Kiem's age—to shoo the devils from their path with a handful of fake money. Four men followed the monk and boy-monk, carrying the dead man's painted portrait. Behind them marched a group bearing something special that Mr. Soc's former students had pitched in to buy: a black velvet cloth with gold lettering praising their distinguished teacher.

Next came the family members. Men and women alike wore white, the color of mourning. The fabric was cheap, like mosquito netting, and frayed at the edges. The men had belted their robes with lengths of cheap, rough rope and fashioned hats and sandals from banana leaves. The women were wearing tall white conical hats over long hair hanging loose down their backs. "Look," the men's and women's clothing announced, "our grief was so distracting, we just plucked at anything handy to cover ourselves!" Grandchildren wore yellow headbands, great-grandchildren red.

Kiem's father, the oldest son, walked backwards in front of the coffin, pantomiming as if he were trying to halt its steady progress toward the grave. Behind the coffin tramped sons and adopted sons leaning on bamboo walking sticks. "Look," they seemed to be saying, "grief has bent us double; we are weak with grief, exhausted." To their rear marched the entire village, twirling black umbrellas for shade.

Then all of the excitement was over. Mr. Soc's former students climbed into their fabulous motorcars, and the villagers helped push them down the road until their engines caught. Servants knocked down the tent poles and dumped buckets of dirt on the barbecue embers.

That year there were no firecrackers at Tet, the Vietnamese New Year, because the family was in mourning. Nor was there a *cay neu*, a bamboo pole with paper streamers and noisemakers on top to scare off evil spirits while the year was changing from old to new.

Three years later, according to the custom called *cai-tang*, Kiem's family dug up grandfather's bones and washed them lovingly with perfumed water and alcohol. Then they placed them in a simple terra-cotta vessel and reburied them at Tortoise Point, at the most sacred spot in the middle of the tortoise's back. The beautiful black and gold coffin was broken up into boards, some of which were put to use as makeshift bridges across the farm's irrigation canals. Nearly as strong as steel, those lim-wood footbridges may still be there to this day, though everything else survives only in memory.

CHAPTER 2

Reins in Indo-China Wrested by Japan

New York Times, 10 March 1945

For two thousand years Vietnam had been ruled by an emperor and a class of mandarins—scholars who had passed the difficult poetry and philosophy examinations necessary to advance through the bureaucratic hierarchy. Anyone could take the examinations, young or old, poor or rich, and become a mandarin. In a society where change was almost nonexistent, memorization of traditional knowledge was the key to success.

Then, late in the nineteenth century, following decades of armed resistance by the Vietnamese, the French finally succeeded in conquering the country. They took over everything, from the government to the police, and staffed all of the good jobs with French colonials. The annual mandarin examinations continued, but the highest scorers could aspire to be only low-level civil servants under the French.

But just when Kiem's father, Mr. Do Van Sach, was reaching high-school age, he got a lucky break. The French were keen on modernizing the country's roads, bridges, railroads, and ports so they could ship raw materials to Europe, but they couldn't recruit the French professionals they needed to do the job. In desperation they began to round up the smartest Vietnamese schoolboys and send them to civil engineering school. That was how Kiem's father came to win a full scholarship to high school and college.

Math and science did not come naturally to Kiem's father; in fact, his long fingers and red palms revealed a passion for the arts. But he studied very, very hard. The other scholarship student in his class, Mr. Tan, was also very studious. He and Kiem's father lived in the same boardinghouse in Hanoi, and each was scared to death the other would eclipse him with his studying and cause him to lose his scholarship. They had to watch each other all the time. At night they would both stay up late studying and get very tired and want to go to sleep, but then they would look down the hall and see the crack of light from the kerosene lantern under the rival's door, and they would study even harder. Kiem's father confessed to his children that now and then he would turn the kerosene flame down to almost nothing but continue to study, just to fool Mr. Tan into giving up and going to bed.

Kiem's father's graduation picture showed a stern-looking French professor with a long skinny beard and a funny colonial hat, flanked by a dozen Vietnamese students in Western dress. In the place of honor, to the teacher's right, was his favorite student: Mr. Sach. Mr. Tan, the second favorite, stood to the left.

Kiem's father was taller than the other students. He had a fair complexion and fine, handsome features. But physically he was frail, from all that studying. Working as a civil engineer after graduation only made his health worse because he was exposed to the sun and heat and rain and bacteria and insects on primitive construction sites. Still, he was luckier than poor Mr. Tan, who died of tuberculosis just a few years after he graduated, thinking that life would finally begin after all that studying. And they were both luckier than the tens of thousands of Vietnamese peasants who dropped dead working for cruel French bosses on public-works projects or rubber plantations. But Mr. Sach's health continued to deteriorate, and soon after his fourth son, Kiem, was born he was diagnosed as having tuberculosis.

The French authorities begrudged Mr. Sach a bed in one of their own hospitals—his only hope for a cure. Vietnamese doctors treated the spirit rather than the disease: they pounded roots and herbs into crumbly powders or sucked bad blood to the body's surface by cupping a heated glass to the skin. Some of them had even traveled to China to study acupuncture, but few of them knew anything about Western surgery or antibiotics.

The day Kiem's mother left her husband at Lanessan Hospital in Hanoi, she had to watch him stagger across an open courtyard to the contagious wing, carrying a heavy valise in each hand. Halfway across she saw him sink to his knees. "Help him!" she cried through the gate to a Frenchman with a stethoscope slung around his neck. "Help my husband!" The doctor kept on walking. "Help him!" she cried to a pair of housekeepers wielding mops and buckets. They too ignored her. Finally Mr. Sach rose shakingly to his feet.

"If you'd been French, they would have helped you," Kiem's mother accused for many years afterward.

"No, no, not at all! It was because I was contagious, not because I was Vietnamese! It was very hard back then to get personnel to work in the contagious wing. Remember how you had to come nurse me and prepare my meals?"

Mrs. Sach had three older sons and a daughter besides Kiem to take care of, but baby Kiem was her biggest problem. He needed constant attention, and being so young, he was most at risk for catching his father's TB. So Mrs. Sach's mother and father put their heads together and decided that the baby would come live with them in Phu Tai—just for a little while, until his father got better.

How were two old people going to feed a squalling baby, with no wet nurse and no cows? A cow couldn't pull a heavy load or stand all day with its hooves underwater. Only water buffalo could work in the rice fields, and their milk was no good for human babies, only for their own calves. Following the old traditional way, Kiem's grandmother tried chewing her rice until it was a liquid, then spitting it into Kiem's mouth. It worked. The skinny, fussy baby filled out to be a healthy little boy.

Kiem's father's academic honors had made him worthy of the hand of the richest girl in the village, Miss Nguyen Thi Hy, even though he was only the son of the poor village schoolteacher. On her wedding day her parents had given her a huge tract of land. Sharecroppers were to farm it, paying their rent in rice. Although she would be moving to Hanoi to live with her husband, Mrs. Sach would ride the train back to Phu Tai once a month or so to keep an eye on the place: wielding a stick to make sure that the rice baskets were level, balancing the books, that sort of thing.

The arrangement worked well for seven years, but then Mr. Sach's illness made it impossible for his wife to leave Hanoi. Mrs. Sach's family began to worry that the sharecroppers would take advantage of the situation.

Following much discussion the family elders came up with a solution: their son-in-law, Mr. Sach, would have to take his wife's younger sister, Kiem's Aunt Dam, as his second wife. Then Aunt Dam could stay in Hanoi to help nurse Mr. Sach in the hospital, a job anybody could do, and Kiem's mother could return to Phu Tai, where she was needed to assure the family's income. Kiem's three older brothers would remain in school in Hanoi under Aunt Dam's care, but his sister Hanh would come live in Phu Tai with her mother.

Aunt Dam was overjoyed at the prospect of marrying Mr. Sach, who was not only a good provider but handsome and kind. Better to be Mr. Sach's number-two wife than another man's number one, she seemed to think, even though second wives got stuck with the duties the first wife didn't want. Nobody asked Kiem's mother how she felt about sharing her husband with her little sister, who was as glamorous as Mrs. Sach was dowdy—and sophisticated, too, from having worked as a hostess at their uncle's Hanoi gymnasium. So Kiem's father married Aunt Dam, and Kiem's mother moved out to the countryside, and Kiem left his maternal grandparents' care and went to live with his mother on their own farm. Kiem's father made a slow recovery and eventually went back to work for the French government, but his health remained delicate. Two more boys were born to Kiem's mother, and a son and daughter to Aunt Dam. In 1939, the year that Kiem turned six, he moved back to Hanoi with his father and Aunt Dam to start primary school.

Kiem's father's family lived in a two-story house, designed by Mr. Sach himself, on a shady street near the open-air market in the Vietnamese part of town. Mr. Sach and Aunt Dam and the new baby girl slept upstairs, and the rest of the children slept downstairs. Kiem was fascinated by his "new" big brothers, whom he'd seen only during their school vacations in Phu Tai.

Nam, the oldest, was studying to be a doctor, although he couldn't seem to read a medical book without moving his lips. He was skinny and awkward at sports but very generous with his possessions.

Lam, the next one down, had the biggest muscles Kiem had ever seen. He spent most of his spare time lifting weights at their uncle's gymnasium. He wasn't a very gifted student, either, but he was managing to charm his way to a high-school diploma.

Tri was five years older than Kiem, and Kiem's hero. Tri would have been as handsome as a movie star if he weren't always getting into fistfights with French boys, bloodying his nose and blackening his eyes at least once a week. Tri couldn't stand it when the French boys called his friends racist names. But he also had a scholarly side: he could spend hours at a time quietly cataloging his insect collection. Kiem was never so happy as when he could help Tri mount a butterfly with pins and preservative. He followed Tri around the whole time he was home, just hoping for the chance.

Back in Phu Tai till they reached school age were Kiem's two little brothers, Hung, whose fair complexion and almost-blue eyes were the reason for his nickname of "Frenchy," and Trung, a delicate child whose blood didn't clot the way it should. In Hanoi was his little half-brother, Hoan, who was the same age as Trung.

Except for Kiem's half-sister, who was just a baby, Hanh was the only girl in their bunch. She was two years older than Kiem and went to the Louis Pasteur Primary School with him. She was a quiet girl who liked to sew and cook.

With so many children living under one roof, the family had to stick to a routine. In the mornings the school-aged children would hop out of bed, roll up their mosquito netting, and dress themselves. Then Aunt Dam would hand each child a chunk of French bread or bowl of warm rice pudding. "I'm going to school now, Auntie," each one would sing-song, rushing out the door.

After school was out, the boys would linger around the grounds for as long as possible, kicking a soccer ball with friends. Then they'd race home to dinner. "I'm home now, Auntie," they would each cry out, filing through the front door.

When their father had finished eating, the children would ask permission to leave the table, and servants would clear it. Gathering their books, they'd return to their places at the teakwood dining table to study until one or two in the morning. Usually it would be hot, and the ceiling fan would be whirring in the high-ceilinged room with tall windows. Sometimes Aunt Dam would buy a block of ice and set it on a windowsill so that the breeze could blow over it. The boys would be allowed to take off their shirts since the thick flowering vine out front kept strangers from seeing their naked chests.

Through the open windows the children could hear the sounds of street vendors. *Tik tak, tik tak* went the Chinese soup man, banging two pieces of bamboo together. When summoned, he would bring a steaming bowl of soup, then return a half-hour later to collect the empty bowl and his money. Other vendors sang about everything from massages to half-hatched duck eggs. But the children's favorite was the peanut man. He was tall and stooped, with a painted wooden box hanging around his neck. "Roast scented peanuts! Crunchy peanuts!" he would cry. Each time he came down their street, the children would pause in their reading and look each other in the eye. Finally one of them—usually Hanh, who always seemed to have money—would catch up with him, buy a bagful, and dump them in the middle of the table for the others to share.

At some point between midnight and dawn the night-soil collectors from the fertilizer factory would creep by. The French section of Hanoi had trucks to do the dirty job, but the Vietnamese section had only two men pushing and pulling a black-painted cart. Kiem's family's privy was outdoors, next to the kitchen and the ricksha-garage, raised up above the ground with a bucket underneath. The night-soil collectors would un-latch the gate and go down the passageway to fetch the bucket and re-place it with a new one. The children could always smell them going by on their way out. Kiem's family was lucky because their house had a side passageway. Most other families had to let them go directly through their living quarters.

Nam, as the oldest brother, was in charge of supervising the younger children's studies. If an adult passed by the table and a child was missing, it was Nam's job to explain. "Tri is fixing the tire on his bicycle," he might say. "He'll be right back." If Kiem was really floundering with an assign-ment, he might break down and ask Nam a question. But even between brothers, it was a loss of face to admit that you didn't know an answer.

Besides what they were learning in school, Kiem and the other chil-dren were learning many things from their father. Mr. Sach was a thoughtful, scholarly man who liked to quote from literature or philoso-phy to illustrate his point. He quoted from Victor Hugo and Voltaire just as often as from Confucius and Lao-tzu, for he thought highly of West-ern sages, though little of Western politicians. Mr. Sach never lost his temper or raised his voice with the children. He believed in showing them what to do through his example, not telling them what to do. When he was disappointed in a child's behavior, he would look straight in his eyes and speak very slowly, stressing every syllable.

One very hot afternoon Kiem and his father were strolling in the gar-den behind the house. Kiem had been dashing from one curiosity to another—a toad, an anthill—and his legs were getting tired. Without thinking, he plopped down on a marble bench to rest. "Yeow!" he yelled and jumped back to his feet. The bench was so hot it had burned his rear end, right through the fabric of his shorts.

"Sit down on that bench, Son," said Mr. Sach.

Kiem did as he was told.

"Now get up," said Mr. Sach.

Kiem got up.

"Tell me, Son, is that bench still very hot?"

"Yes, sir," the boy said, "it is still extremely hot."

"Then why didn't you yell this time around?" his father asked.

Kiem was dumbfounded. "I don't know, sir," he said.

"Because you knew it was going to be hot, that's why. When you know in advance that misfortune is coming your way, you can prepare yourself mentally, so that you stay in control of your emotions. Always keep your eyes and your ears open. Stay alert to the things that are going on around you and to the things that are about to happen, and you'll always be able to conduct yourself with dignity."

Another time, Kiem had drawn a staircase for an art class homework assignment. He'd always been good at art, and that drawing was his masterpiece: it had shade, light, perspective, everything. But he left it out on the teakwood table overnight. The next morning while everyone was getting ready for school, his little half-brother Hoan got into the ink bottle and dropped a splotch of black ink right on the first step of the staircase.

Hearing the commotion, Mr. Sach came downstairs to see what was going on. Kiem showed him the ruined picture. "It's almost time to leave for school," he sniffled. "I don't have time to do it over."

"Nothing is lost yet, Son," said Mr. Sach. "Use your imagination. What is black and lies on a stairway?"

"A black cat?" the boy asked.

"Very good! A black cat. Now complete the drawing."

It took Kiem only a minute to transform the ink spot into a fat black cat basking in the sun. Later that morning he got an eighteen over twenty on the drawing, the highest grade his teacher had ever given out.

When Kiem came home that evening, he couldn't wait to tell his father the news. Mr. Sach was pleased. "What you have learned today, Son," he said, "is something that has served our people well throughout their history. Turn misfortune into fortune. Always use your head, and there can be no defeat."

At that very moment another chance for the people of Vietnam to turn misfortune into fortune was arising. In the spring of 1940, less than a year after Kiem had returned to Hanoi, Hitler's army invaded France. With their home country paralyzed under the German occupation, the French colonial rulers of Vietnam suddenly had no military muscle to back them up, and the Vietnamese knew it. Bold talk of independence from French rule filled the air for a little while; then, just as suddenly, Japan moved to take advantage of France's weakness by stationing troops throughout Vietnam—a convenient "stepping-stone" to the rest of southeast Asia, which they were out to conquer.

Having just turned seven, Kiem was too young to fully understand what was going on. But he did begin to notice Japanese soldiers milling around the streets of Hanoi, waving their bayonets or stabbing them into sandbags and shouting harsh words at each another. He didn't like them one bit, although some people said they were better than the French because they were fellow Asians.

One evening, just as the children had seated themselves at the teakwood table to study, the front door burst open and a tall, gaunt man with long, greasy hair materialized before them. His eyes glittered like two lumps of coal. "Uncle Tich! Uncle Tich!" Kiem's big brothers cried. They seated him in the family's finest chair, rosewood inlaid with mother-of-pearl; then Nam and Lam went racing upstairs to tell their father. "Father! Father! It's Uncle Tich!"

"That's Father's younger brother," Tri explained to Kiem, seeing the scowl on his face and thinking he must be confused. "He's a nationalist—a real hero. The French locked him up in jail for belonging to the Secret Society—but the Japanese must have let him out. Hooray!" Actually, Kiem had recognized the man's name. He was scowling because he realized there wouldn't be any peanuts that evening, with all of the grown-ups lurking around downstairs.

When all of the welcoming fuss had subsided, Uncle Tich paused behind Kiem's chair and peered over his nephew's shoulder. Kiem's schoolbook was open to a poem about an old man lying awake with insomnia. The old man complains that the night has been unusually long and wonders if daylight will ever come.

"Ah, Nephew!" he exclaimed. "An excellent choice! You see, the old man stands for those who still remember the past of Vietnam. His coughing means that he is still alive, still kicking. The poem takes place at night because our country is in the dark under the French. And when the old man hears a baby cry, it means that the young are beginning to wake up to the fact of our oppression."

"That's enough, Younger Brother," Mr. Sach warned. "Don't be filling the boy's head with dangerous ideas." Only later would Kiem learn that his uncle had been right about the poem. Everyone in Vietnam enjoyed the joke that it had managed to sneak past the French censors into the standard primary school textbooks.

Kiem's father insisted that Uncle Tich move in with them for the next few months to gain back his strength: he had spent sixteen of the last twenty years locked up in La Centrale, the notorious French prison of Hanoi. So Uncle Tich delayed returning home to his wife and daughters in Thanh Ha for a little while.

With Uncle Tich around, the grownups' after-dinner conversation was never boring. Uncle Tich would begin to talk loudly about the Japanese "Greater Asia" movement, insisting that it was their one hope to drive the "white devils" out of the country. Kiem's father would argue back that the Japanese were interested only in expanding their power and territory: "Look at their history, Younger Brother. Remember our emperor, Cuong De, who died in exile in the Land of the Rising Sun, still waiting for help that never came."

The children would have been dismissed from the dinner table by then, but Tri would always find some excuse to hang around and eavesdrop, and Kiem was never far behind his idol.

On the day that Tri came home from school in disgrace—with a note from his teacher explaining that he'd asked to be excused from French class because he "didn't need to learn the language of pigs"—he had even more of a motive than usual to spy on the grownups. After dinner Tri slipped quietly upstairs, and Kiem went trailing after him. The two boys sat on the top step and bent their heads to listen.

"Bro-ther Tich," began their father in a low tone of voice with each syllable stretched out—a sure sign that he was angry: "I have had a lo-ong talk with your nephew Tri this evening."

Uncle Tich mumbled something back.

"'Pigs' is *your* word, Brother Tich. I don't know what you've been teaching the boy, but please: while you're here, don't sow any more hatred in the minds of my children."

"I'm sorry," said Tich, "but with all due respect to you, Brother, I call a pig a pig!" His voice was almost shouting, and Kiem could tell without peeking that his arms were waving in the air and his long hair flying. "What else should I call them, after what they did to me in prison? Forcing me to drink liters of soap water! Shocking my ears and my balls with electric current! Look at me, Brother Sach. I've lost nearly half my weight. My hands shake. I can't hear in one ear, and I can hardly see, and I doubt if I'll ever father children again. You bet I hate those—*pigs!* And I'll hate them and fight them until the day I die."

"I know how you've suffered," said Kiem's father. "Still, I'm asking you to help me. Right now, my children need education, not hate—"

"Sometimes I wonder about you, Brother," cut in Uncle Tich. "Always siding with the French, always defending them. Maybe, under all your fine philosophy, you're just a pro-French intellectual who's a little too satisfied with his social position."

Tri gasped out loud, clapping a hand over his mouth to muffle the sound, and Kiem did, too.

"Brother Tich," said their father, "that is a grave accusation." Kiem could hear the sudden firmness in his tone, though his voice was still level. "You seem to have forgotten, Younger Brother, that I turned down the chance to be classified as a French functionary. I could have tripled my salary and enjoyed all the same benefits as the French. But I refused. Why? Because I love my country. Because I couldn't have served the French interests over our own."

"You could have taken their money and used it to buy guns to kill them with," said Uncle Tich.

"I am no hypocrite," said their father. For a minute or two, there was only silence, and then he continued: "Bro-ther Tich. I admire your beliefs, your courage, your endurance! But my children are young and still easily influenced. All I'm asking is that you give them the same chance you and I had—the chance to get a Western education, to open their eyes to the modern world. Incidentally, Brother, it was Victor Hugo you were quoting just now. He was the one who wrote 'I call a pig a pig.'"

"Why can't we educate our people?" asked Uncle Tich, but in a softer tone of voice. "You and I, Brother?"

"Because education has to come before self-governance, not the other way around. Self-governance depends on civic responsibility, and civic responsibility isn't an instinct—it's something that has to be taught. Ninety percent of our population is illiterate. Ninety percent! Believing in ghosts, in tree spirits, in moon men! Unable to read a newspaper or the printed words on a ballot, unable even to sort what they hear into logical categories—to weigh alternatives and choose wisely. You know as well as I do, Brother, how to govern a people like that: with trickery and deceit. You and your people may start out with good intentions, but pretty soon, along will come a dictator telling himself it's all right to manipulate people because he knows what's best for them. Independence is good, Brother Tich, but freedom is even better. It takes time to build a nation, and the effort has to start from the bottom up, not the top down."

Being so young, Kiem might well have forgotten that night's conversation, but Tri had memorized nearly every word, and he had nobody but Kiem to share the secret and dangerous ideas with.

For awhile at least, the world war raging elsewhere had little effect on the daily lives of Kiem and his brothers and sisters. They went to school, played soccer, practiced their musical instruments. On Sundays they set up their easels in front of Van Mieu, the Temple of Literature, and painted its multiple curving roofs. Once or twice a month they got to go to the movies, Kiem always hoping it would be an American action film and not a stupid French romance or comedy. During school vacations they joined their mother in Phu Tai, fishing, catching butterflies, and flying kites with hollow pipes that made a noise like flutes when the wind blew through them. Another son, Tuan, was born to Aunt Dam, making ten children in all.

But in 1942, after the United States had entered the war, the Americans began bombing Japanese military installations around Hanoi. Over the next year and a half, the bombs kept landing closer and closer, and the air-raid sirens kept wailing louder and louder. Finally, though he hated to interrupt their education, Mr. Sach decided to pull the younger children out of school and send them to live with their mother.

Phu Tai was awfully boring after Hanoi. There was no movie theater, for one thing, and the local children were way behind Kiem in school. In math class, for example, they couldn't be fooled into believing that a plane was faster than a train or even a bicycle. After all, a plane was just a little tiny speck up in the sky! But one local girl, Quy, was nearly as advanced as Kiem, and their rivalry soon blossomed into a friendship. At lunchtime they could usually be found eating or napping together under a shade tree in the yard, and after school, down on their knees together weeding their teacher's garden, since they were the only two he trusted to tend his beloved rosebushes.

Then the rice harvest of 1944 failed, and Quy had to drop out of school to help out at home. In the week before Tet of 1945, many of the small landowners around Phu Tai came to Kiem's mother wanting to mortgage their land to pay off debts. It was a shameful thing to carry a debt into the new year and an unlucky thing to let a debtor into one's house the first week of the new year, so both sides were eager to strike a deal. Behind the small landowners came sharecroppers hoping to secure work for their daughters as cooks or housemaids. Even though she already had more servants than she needed, Mrs. Sach accepted two or three new girls. That way, the girls could get food in their stomachs without a loss of face for their families. To those with no land and no daughter, Mrs. Sach loaned money outright. There was no need to draw up a contract because the pride of the borrowing family was at stake. If the father died before the debt was repaid, the children would pay.

Bad weather had caused the poor rice harvest—a problem that could usually be dealt with by eating last year's rice reserves mixed with sweet potatoes or some other "stretcher." But because of the Japanese occupation, the Vietnamese people had no rice reserves to fall back on now. The Japanese had been hoarding rice for their own troops and forcing many small Vietnamese farmers to plant "cash crops" such as jute or peanuts instead of rice. And the Allied bombing had been disrupting rice shipments from south to north. By March and April, roving bands of emaciated people had begun fleeing the cities for the villages in search of anything edible: roots, tree bark, insects. The countryside turned from green to brown in their wake. One by one, the pet dogs of Phu Tai began to disappear. Many Vietnamese ate dog meat: it was said to be tasty and cheaper than pork. But the dogs to be eaten were bred and raised only for that purpose. Pets were supposed to be off-limits.

Trudging to school in the morning, gathering other children along the way as a rice ball gathers grains of rice, Kiem and his sister Hanh and his brother Frenchy gradually became accustomed to the sight of dead bodies lying in the road. One day they came across a baby crawling in the dirt beside its mother's corpse. Although they knew that it would make them late to school and that they were risking the wrath of their teacher's rattan whip—Long One's cousin—they rescued the baby and knocked on doors until they found somebody to claim it. More children dropped out of Kiem's class each week, until finally school had to be suspended.

By then, Kiem's mother and the two or three other wealthy families of the district had begun handing out food directly. It was not really an organized thing: if one family was dispensing food, then the others would sit back and relax, but if nobody was doing it, then another family would take a turn. Rising at daybreak to help the servants pack cooked rice and salt into hundreds of small balls, Kiem could look outside and see a line of misery stretching all the way to the horizon.

One morning not long after the rice had run out, an old woman clutching a baby and dragging a girl about Kiem's age showed up at the gate. The girl was so thin that Kiem knew without being told that it must hurt her to sit down. Most of her hair had broken off at the scalp, but her black eyes were big and intense, staring through Kiem to a point far away. When she turned her face, Kiem thought he could see a ghost of resemblance. "Quy? Is that you?" he asked. She didn't answer him, but he thought he saw the mother nod her head slightly. "Wait here," he told them in a shaking voice. Perhaps he could give them some raw rice, and the woman could take it home and cook it. So he ran back to the house, scooped some rice into a bag, and handed it to the girl, who might or might not have been Quy.

Before Kiem knew what was happening, the girl had tilted the bag to her lips and begun to swallow. He heard the rice grains click against her teeth like small pebbles. Then, boom! The mother let go of the baby like a balloon, sending him crashing to the ground. With one hand she grabbed the girl's neck and began to choke her. With the other she stuck her fingers down the girl's throat and dug out a few unswallowed rice grains. The woman crammed them into her own mouth, kicking the screaming baby out of her way.

"Hey! Hey!" Kiem was shouting. "If you take it home and cook it, you'll have two or three times as much. . . ." But nobody was listening.

Kiem needed to talk to his father, to make sense of what he'd just seen. He started begging his mother to take him with her on her next trip into Hanoi. She went by train every few weeks to carry food to his father's household. Finally Mrs. Sach said yes.

The smell was what hit Kiem first, stepping outside the Hanoi train station. It was rising from the corpses that seemed to be lying everywhere, like trees blown down by a typhoon, even though Boy Scouts in uniform were picking them up and stacking them in their oxcarts.

Kiem's mother pressed the silk sleeve of her *ao dai* over her nose and mouth as she negotiated with a ricksha driver. Not wanting to be a sissy, Kiem just held his breath as best he could.

Their ricksha had to pass through the Chinese section of Hanoi. As it neared a restaurant, Kiem could smell meat roasting and cooking oil sizzling. His stomach growled, even though he'd eaten on the train. Suddenly three Japanese soldiers came bursting out of the restaurant's front door. He could tell from their loud, slurred speech and stumbling gait that they were drunk. As he watched, one of them leaned forward and began to vomit all over his boots.

Seconds later a swarm of beggars rushed in to scoop up the vomit with their hands and shove it in their mouths. They were pushing and shoving each other, splashing vomit on the soldiers, which made the soldiers curse them and kick them like dogs. Kiem covered his eyes with his hands.

"Why, Father?" Kiem pleaded when at last they were seated together on the marble bench in the withered backyard garden. "Why would a mother drop her baby on the ground? How can a strong man kick a sick man, or two men fight each other over vomit?"

Mr. Sach took a long time to form his answer. "You see, Son," he said at last, "when survival becomes a struggle, a person's focus begins to shift from his country to his community, from his community to his family, and then, at the last moment, from his family to himself. But a superior man never shrinks from his responsibilities. He puts his country first and himself last."

Kiem wasn't sure he had understood his father's answer, but he knew that the main thing now was to memorize the words. One day in the future he would understand their meaning.

CHAPTER 3

Annamese Gird for Battle in Indo-China
Casualties Mount as Rebellion Continues

Pacific Stars & Stripes, 3 October 1945

Two million Northerners starved to death during the famine—
ten percent of the population. Because of Mrs. Sach's rice
reserves, Kiem's family was spared.

But no sooner had the next rice crop ripened and food
become plentiful once again than the Red River delta was swallowed up by a great flood. Once again the Japanese occupation
was making a natural disaster even worse: with the government
in disarray, nobody had been maintaining the French-built
dike system that kept the river from overflowing its banks. The
road from Kiem's mother's farm to the center of Phu Tai lay
underwater. Now and then the bloated body of a pig or water
buffalo went drifting by on the current. The rice fields looked
like a lake, and the courtyard like a rice field. Water lapped
around the edges of the main house, stopping just short of
sloshing in.

Kiem was playing on the veranda behind the house, pretending to be the captain of a ship at sea, when he heard the song—
a strange song, like a march:

> The Viet Minh troops are marching on
> With one unified goal, to save the country.
> Their footsteps echo on the long road. . . .

Intrigued, he waded out to a tall tree and climbed up into its
branches. From there he could see a sampan with three or four
men riding in it, waving an unfamiliar flag. He knew that the
Vietnamese emperor's flag was yellow and that the Japanese
flag had a red sun on a white field. But this flag was red with a

yellow star. One of the men was shouting through a megaphone: "Atten-tion! Attention! Tomorrow at noon, there will be an important assembly in the marketplace."

Kiem climbed down from the tree and splashed back to the house to tell his mother what he had seen. "Oh, yes," she said, "the Viet Minh, most likely." *So she had heard of them!*

The following afternoon all of Phu Tai turned out for the meeting, despite the floodwaters. Overnight a rickety wooden dais had risen out of the muddy ground of the marketplace. The villagers gazed at the strangers sitting up there, as if they had dropped down out of the sky.

It was shocking to see young men like that in positions of power, and the words that came out of their mouths were just as outlandish as their appearance. They claimed that the Japanese had surrendered to the Allies and that the Vietnamese emperor had abdicated in favor of *their* leader, Mr. Ho Chi Minh. They said that they were members of the "Vietnam Independence League"—"Viet Minh" for short—who had been fighting to free their homeland from the yoke of foreign oppres-sion, both French and Japanese. From now on, they said, they would be running the affairs of Phu Tai.

"What a bunch of great guys!" was the unanimous reaction—even from the village chief and assistant chief, who had just lost their jobs. In a matter of minutes and without question the villagers of Phu Tai shifted their allegiance to the strangers. Humming the Viet Minh anthem, Kiem went home and made a red and yellow flag for his toy boat.

A few weeks later Mr. Sach called his younger children back to Hanoi to resume their studies. It was the autumn of 1945, and Kiem was twelve years old. Independence was in the air like a cold snap, making everyone feel more alive.

On posters, in public speeches, in newspapers, and on the radio, the Viet Minh were urging everyone to turn their gold over to Ho Chi Minh so that he could buy guns for their self-defense. "Husbands, convince your wives!" they ordered. "Youngsters, convince your parents!"

"Mr. Ho Chi Minh needs my help!" Kiem marveled. The idea that young people could contribute to society was new to him and thrilling. He paraded in the streets with the rest of the children, singing: "Wom-an, why are you wearing that gold when your country needs that gold? You should be ashamed of wearing that gold. . . ." Women ripped off their earrings, necklaces, bracelets, brooches, and rings as Kiem and his friends marched by. Men came rushing out of their houses to hand over gold coins. "What's this?" Kiem asked the boy next to him of a hard, lumpish object someone had pressed into the palm of his hand.

"A gold tooth, dummy."

"Yecch!" said Kiem.

Back at home, even glamorous Aunt Dam was flashing bare fingers and earlobes. But she didn't seem happy about it.

"A thousand pounds of gold!" bragged Uncle Tich. "A pretty good catch for a week's fishing, eh?"

"When I catch a fish, I like to watch and see whose stomach it ends up in," said Mr. Sach.

"Eh, Elder Brother? What did you say?" asked Uncle Tich.

"Nothing important, Younger Brother," said Kiem's father.

Everybody seemed to have a niche in a Viet Minh support group: children, teenagers, young men, old men, housewives. Kiem joined the Auxiliary Youth Group and marched up and down the streets of Hanoi, banging a drum. All three of his big brothers signed on with the Civil Defense organization. Nam became a medic. Lam puffed out a uniform with his muscles. Tri accepted a commission as a company commander.

Kiem didn't think much of it when one of his aunts appeared at the back door hidden behind a black French hat-veil. He heard muffled weeping noises, then the sounds of his father rummaging in the dining room curio cabinet. Kiem knew that his father kept a secret stash of piastres there, hidden inside a Chinese vase. He heard more murmuring and sniffling noises from his auntie, and soothing tones from his father, and the squeak of the back door opening and closing.

Months went by before Kiem learned that his aunt's husband, Kiem's mother's brother, had been dragged off and shot by the Viet Minh. "He was a big-time landlord," explained Nam. "A capitalist, buddy-buddy with the French."

Kiem decided that his uncle must have done something very, very bad, something that Nam didn't know about or didn't dare tell him about. Why else would those great guys, the Viet Minh, kill him?

Now that World War II was over, though, the French weren't about to let their profitable colony get away so easily. When, under the terms of the postwar Potsdam Agreement, the British Army arrived in South Vietnam to disarm the Japanese, they let hundreds of French prisoners out of jail and gave them the weapons they'd confiscated from the Japanese. The French ex-prisoners began rioting and looting and shooting Asians on sight, so the Viet Minh struck back by killing more than a hundred Europeans in Saigon. Trying to restore order, the British declared martial law in the South. The next thing everybody knew, the French were back in power down there.

The Japanese in North Vietnam had been disarmed by the hungry, shabby Chinese Army. And that's where all the confiscated gold had gone, as a bribe to secure Chinese favoritism for Ho Chi Minh and his political party.

Kiem followed the developments in the Hanoi newspapers, amazed to find current events suddenly as exciting as an American Western. For awhile there seemed to be hope that France might let Vietnam join the French Union as an independent state. But then Ho Chi Minh broke off negotiations.

"The French pushed him too far," said Uncle Tich. "It was either walk away from the bargaining table, or lose face."

"Perhaps," said Mr. Sach. "Or perhaps one can buy more time to arm one's troops by pretending to negotiate."

"You don't trust Ho Chi Minh, do you, Elder Brother? You see, I walk with wooden clogs in your belly."

Mr. Sach smiled at the old folk proverb. "How could I distrust a true Vietnamese nationalist?" he asked.

"Yes, but some say that Ho Chi Minh is a communist in nationalist's clothing. They say that he left Vietnam as a young man and spent nearly thirty years wandering abroad. They say that he trained as a cadre in Moscow and was jailed as a communist agent in China, that he founded the Indochina Communist Party in Hong Kong. They say he never came home to help the Vietnamese nationalists in their struggle against the French, but waited until the plum was ripe for plucking by the communists."

"Do they say all that?" asked Mr. Sach. "Really, they should be more careful. The Kitchen God reports all household conversations straight to heaven."

"War!" crowed Lam, walking with a rolling swagger. "Just you wait and see."

Mr. Sach could also smell war in the air. He decided to pull the younger children out of school and send them back to the countryside. Just for a little while, just until the political situation stabilized. Kiem was heartbroken. He was willing to fight the French in the streets with a sharpened stick if necessary. But he didn't dare cross his father.

Back in boring old Phu Tai, Kiem joined the Village Self-Defense Group. What a joke! Not a single gun among them: only knives, sticks, crossbows, and slingshots—for the children. The other members were kids like Thinh and Frenchy or old men Kiem had known all his life. How he longed to be old enough to join a real military unit, like his brothers.

One morning in late November, Kiem was gathering rocks for sling-shot practice when he heard far-off rumbling sounds. More ominous than thunder, the sounds seemed to be coming from the direction of Haiphong. They continued all day, becoming part of the normal back-ground noise of the village: bird-song, cricket-song, wind-song, rum-bling. Toward evening there was one tremendous *boom*. When the sun slipped below the horizon, an eerie red glow painted the sky.

By morning the road running from Haiphong past Phu Tai was a river of refugees. Some pedaled bicycles or tugged rickshas. Most had carrying-poles bending their shoulders or children's arms gripping their necks.

"French gunships fired on Haiphong," they reported. "Many thou-sands were killed!"

"What was the big boom?"

"The ammunition dump exploding."

"Ah," the villagers said.

That was how the war with the French began. A few weeks later, French soldiers captured the railroad station near Phu Tai. By day they marched into the countryside to hurl mortar at nearby villages. By night they retreated to the safety of their outpost.

One day they ventured as far as the footbridge across the river from Phu Tai, shelling it for three or four hours. Afterward, when the smoke had cleared enough for the villagers to count their dead, a cousin of Kiem's lay among them, half-submerged under the waters of his rice field. Everyone hoped that he had died from his wounds and not by drowning, as the ghost of a drowned person could lure other family members to drown in a puddle or a bowl of soup.

"I wish I could reach your father," Kiem's mother fretted. Of course there was no more mail delivery between Hanoi and Phu Tai, since the French controlled the main road and the railroad line. Stay in Phu Tai or flee with the children? She would have to make the decision on her own.

Growing up in a wealthy family had not dulled Mrs. Sach's survival instincts. Her family liked to tell how once, when she was a teenager riding horseback in the countryside, her horse's reins had snapped and he'd gone bolting away with her. The future Mrs. Sach had yanked on his mane to stop him, jumped down, stripped to her underwear, unhooked her bra, and tied it to the horse's bridle in place of reins. Then she'd put her clothes back on and walked the horse home.

"Flee," those instincts told her now. So, like a mother cat carrying her kittens in her teeth, she set about finding a safer nest for her children. First she sold off her rice reserves and a few valuables. Then, under a sliver of moon, she buried coins, jewelry, and Chinese porcelain in the backyard. When that was done, she gathered all seven children—four of her own and three of Aunt Dam's—and moved them three kilometers farther from the French outpost. They crowded into the home of a family friend, sleeping and dressing in a small space behind a hanging curtain.

Kiem did his best to help his mother with the younger children, but he longed to be part of the action. At night he lay awake imagining the adventures of his three older brothers back home. Nam would be splinting the arm of a famous Viet Minh general. Lam's muscles would be carrying a beautiful Vietnamese girl from the wreckage of a bombed building. And Tri would be leading his men into battle and running one, two, three, four Frenchmen through the gut with his bayonet. . . .

One morning Kiem's mother sent him to the marketplace of their new village to buy rice and a bit of dried shrimp. Who should be there but Mr. Mien, the commander of the district troop, ordering provisions for his men? He was husky and squat, and his voice boomed above the squawking of chickens and the tinkling of women's laughter. Everybody knew he'd been a sergeant in the French District Troop before the liberation. Kiem crept closer to get a good look at him.

Suddenly the barrel-shaped officer turned and roared at Kiem: "You! You there!"

"Me, sir?" asked Kiem.

"Aren't you the boy from Hanoi?" asked Mr. Mien.

"Yes, sir," said Kiem. He knew he must be dreaming.

"I need a brave boy about your age to scout for the District Troop. How about it?"

"Oh, yes, sir," he said. "If my mother agrees to it, sir," he suddenly remembered.

"Run home and ask your mother for permission, Son; then report back here to me."

For once it was a good thing Mrs. Sach couldn't contact her husband, because, loving her country and hating the French with all of her heart, she said yes right away. Kiem's father would never have allowed it.

That night Kiem bedded down on the floor of the village pagoda with the sixty other members of the troop. "I'm a grown man, a soldier, a member of the crack District Troop!" he kept marveling to himself. He was so puffed up with pride that he could hardly fall asleep.

"Pssst," the youngest of the troop's three female members hissed in his direction. *Oh, no! What did she want, a kiss?* This was war! He had no time for such foolishness. "Pssst," she insisted.

"What?" Kiem finally snapped.

"Would you be a good boy and sleep between us and the men?" she asked.

What an insult! But he got up and changed his position. Sleep arrived soon after.

In the morning they jogged around the yard in formation: "Hut, hut, hut!" Kiem noticed that each man was plucking lice off the man in front of him. His own skin was beginning to crawl—or was that his imagination?

After the run he washed up as best he could and started to put on his shirt. The oldest of the three women, the one they called "Big Sister," stopped him. "Not yet, dear," she said; "watch." She turned the shirt inside out and spread it flat. Kiem could see reddish-brown specks swarming in the seams. She took a heavy-bottomed glass bottle and positioned it expertly above a lice cluster. Then she lowered the heel of the bottle, pushing and twisting it up and down the shirt-seam, crunching and crushing the tiny bodies. She shook out the shirt, eyed it appraisingly, wiggled a loose button, then handed it back to Kiem.

"Bring me that shirt later on tonight, before bedtime, and I'll sew the button back on tight for you."

"Thanks, Big Sister," he said, a little embarrassed at having acquired a mother in the military.

After breakfast they camouflaged themselves with leaves and branches and marched, marched, marched until the sun had passed the midpoint of the sky. They rested for awhile and broke out dinner rations. Then they marched, marched, marched back to the base. There Mr. Sang—who, as the political commissar attached to their troop, ranked even higher than Mr. Mien—gave them a lesson on the life of the Chinese general Lan Buu. Kiem wasn't sure what Chinese history had to do with fighting the French, but he did his best to pay attention.

That evening in the village square Mr. Mien addressed the townspeople. "Citizens!" he boomed. "Today we engineered another successful enemy ambush! One Frenchman was killed and many wounded, with not a single casualty on our side!" The villagers applauded.

What? Had Kiem missed something? An incident taking place at the head or tail of the marching line? No, the news would have hopped from one soldier to another quicker than lice. Then how come nobody else looked surprised by Mr. Mien's announcement?

The two younger women pulled out stringed instruments and began to play patriotic folk songs. The villagers sang along. When everybody was in the desired sentimental mood, the women passed a hat around, and Mr. Mien thanked the crowd for their donations of food, cash, and supplies.

After a few weeks of marching, marching, marching and studying Russian and Chinese history with the troop, Kiem was singled out for a solo mission. Mr. Sau Dau, the Viet Minh explosives expert, had recently joined them; he'd be teaching them to blow up the French troop transport train. Kiem's assignment was to make his way to the railroad station near Phu Tai and learn what he could about French troop movements.

It was late in the morning when Kiem arrived at the depot. He hid himself in some bushes where he could watch the front door. Pretty soon a group of Frenchmen emerged, talking in their language to a Vietnamese, a collaborator. Kiem made sure to memorize the traitor's face. He could have touched the men's boots, they were that close—but they couldn't see him. To Kiem's surprise he could understand their conversation. They were talking about marching south two kilometers and attacking a hamlet. *Good.* If he knew which way they were going, he could go by a different route and catch up with them.

Giving them ten minutes of lead time, he set off on their trail. As he neared the hamlet, he heard shooting, screaming, and cheering. He froze in his tracks for about twenty minutes, then crept out to see what had happened.

He saw blood on the ground and a lifeless form. It might have been a dog or a pig: he didn't dare get close enough to check. He turned around and ran back to headquarters.

It was most probably a pig, he told Mr. Mien. But that evening in the village square Mr. Mien told a hushed crowd that the enemy had slaughtered two innocent civilians! He even furnished names for the victims.

It was thrilling to hear himself described as a hero—but Kiem knew in his heart that it wasn't true. He wished he could talk to his father for just one hour. His father would know the right thing to do.

After the sing-along Mr. Mien took Kiem aside and made a show out of giving him something—his own gun. It was a big pistol, a .45, with a little secret: when you fired a bullet, the shell didn't automatically eject; you had to pry it out of the chamber with a chopstick before you could fire again.

"You know that, and I know that," Mr. Mien confided, "but the French will never know that, eh, Kiem?"

"No, sir," he agreed. Chopstick-assisted or not, the gun was his treasure.

But it was much too heavy for a thirteen-year-old boy to carry. Kiem struggled with it for a day or two until he hit upon the solution, borrowed from a Pancho Villa movie he had seen in Hanoi. With Big Sister's help, he rigged up a chest holster from an old leather belt. It was not only practical; it was somewhat dashing! Pretty soon other members of the troop began wearing their guns the same way. Kiem began to understand that other men might follow his example, even though he was still a child.

The first time the troop tried to blow up a French train, things didn't go exactly as planned. They couldn't find a ditch close enough to their target, so they had to knot a second length of telephone wire to the piece attached to their land mine. That done, they crouched down in the muddy ditch and waited as the soldier selected for the job gave the wire a mighty tug and jumped into the ditch with them. Nothing happened.

That night a very wary scout retraced the length of the wire and discovered that it had snapped. He reinforced it. The next morning, they climbed back into the ditch.

"Don't blow up the first few cars," Mr. Sau Dau cautioned the triggerman. "The middle cars are the ones loaded with soldiers. OK now, line it up along the sight brushes. Get ready now. . . . Now!"

There was one tremendous *boom*, and the earth shook under Kiem's knees as bits of dirt and rock rained down on him. Poking his head up out of the ditch, he saw the train rise in the air and hang there for a moment, as if it were steaming to heaven. Then it buckled and collapsed.

Seconds later the French began raking the troop's position with machine-gun fire. Kiem and his fellows all jumped up and ran like crazy back to headquarters. One man fled in such a hurry that he dropped his gun. *Finders keepers*, thought Kiem, scooping it up. But he knew the man. Their families were friendly, and he had a pretty younger sister. So Kiem gave it back to him when nobody was looking. It would have been hard for the man to live down the shame of losing it.

Kiem and his troop blew up two or three more trains after that, getting better at it every time. But they knew it was only a matter of time before the French got sick of their harassment and struck back. Kiem was the first one to spot the *canot*, or French advance boat, steaming straight for their position, looking just like the ones he used to watch on the Red River in Hanoi. As he stared at it, transfixed, a black German shepherd stared back at him from between two mounted machine guns. Kiem broke from the dog's red glare and ran to warn Mr. Mien.

Knowing that his men were outgunned and outnumbered, Mr. Mien gave orders to retreat. The troop melted into the brushwood flanking the riverbank just as an observation plane bore down on them and the first burst of machine-gun fire came sizzling across the water. As the men slashed their way upstream, French troops and gunboats attacked the innocent villagers left behind. But all sixty members of Kiem's troop escaped unharmed.

After that operation they were summoned to regional headquarters for an awards ceremony. About a thousand Viet Minh were there, including some celebrities. Spread out on banquet tables were all the food, cigarettes, and ammunition anyone could ever want. Kiem was stunned by the many titles and layers of organization. He began to understand that he was part of a vast machine.

One night not long after the regional assembly, the troop was out slogging in the rain far from their headquarters, and Kiem began to feel rubbery-legged and faint. For some reason he began to fantasize about a piece of boiled chicken. The longer they marched, the bigger and juicier it grew. He imagined dipping it into *nuoc mam*, fermented fish sauce. He would alternate bites of it with mouthfuls of rice.

By the time they reached their destination, Kiem was shivering and delirious. It was late, and the rest of the troop was too tired and wet to cook a meal. But Big Sister brought Kiem some soup and felt his forehead. Then she told Mr. Mien that, like it or not, she was taking Kiem home to his mother in the morning. He was too sick to walk, and they couldn't very well carry him.

Kiem didn't notice much about the journey home, except for the chicken leg dancing in and out of the trees. He heard his mother burst out wailing when she saw him, because he was so skinny and covered with lice. But then he sank back into a long dream.

He had a case of malaria that kept him bedridden for a month. All of his hair fell out from the high fever. When he finally started walking and eating again, his mother said there was no way he was going back to the troop, and that was final. She confiscated his gun. So it was back to civilian life for the thirteen-year-old explosives expert—at least, for a while.

CHAPTER 4

Viet Nam Warns That War Will Be Long
Moutet Says in Paris That All Possible Aid Will Be Given to Army
to Crush Rising

New York Times, 18 January 1947

As the shadow of new hair growth began to darken Kiem's head, the French began closing in on his family's new position. "We're going to have to move again," his mother fretted. "But first I'll need to make one more trip back to Phu Tai, to retrieve the last of our cash and valuables. If you're feeling strong enough by the new moon night, you can come with me."

All week the moon was a lump of soap bobbing and shrinking in the wash pond of the sky. When the last sliver of soap had dissolved, Kiem and his mother steered their sampan across the Big River, straining their ears above the noise of frogs for the sound of a patrol boat engine.

They reached the other side and moored in darkness. By then their eyes had adjusted enough to the lack of light for them to make out the dim shapes of things. But there were no dim hut-shapes to be seen where the first hamlet of their village used to stand.

"Burned, all burned," said Kiem's mother. "Dirty white devils."

Sliding one foot in front of the other, they made their way across the open field that had connected the four hamlets of their village. Kiem went first, with his mother following a few steps behind.

All of a sudden a shape reared up out of the darkness and sprang toward him. "Mother!" Kiem hissed. "Back!" The attacker's weight hit Kiem full in the chest, knocking him over backwards. He could taste blood inside his mouth. He shoved his hand into his pocket and came up with his slingshot just as the thing lunged again and struck. And licked his face.

"Lu Lu," he whispered. "How are you, girl? How's my good girl?" Lu Lu was the fluffy yellow mutt they'd had to leave behind when they fled Phu Tai. The younger children were still crying themselves to sleep over her, and it hurt Kiem now to feel the bones under her too-large coat. Without asking his mother's permission, he unwrapped his dinner for her.

Kiem, his mother, and Lu Lu made their way up the path to their farm. Charred stubble flanked the path—all that was left of the bamboo thickets. The brick wall and lookout tower were still standing although the wooden gate was missing, like a tooth knocked out of a smile.

Madame Thin's hut had vanished, and Kiem's grandfather's house was just a roofless shell, open to the stars and rain. But the brick-and-tile house seemed to be intact. Kiem's mother paused to light a candle, shielding it with one hand as they stepped through its carved front door and into the ancestors' shrine room. Candlelight danced off the surface of the mirrored charm Mrs. Sach had tied to a crossbeam just before moving out, to keep demons from entering. But demons had entered, regardless. Unable to burn the house, the French had shot up its walls and ceilings. As Kiem and his mother crept along, their feet crunched over fragments of broken pottery.

But there were still a few things buried in the yard: coins, statues, vases. Mrs. Sach paced off the locations, and Kiem dug in the muddy earth with his bare hands. Most of the buried treasure would be sold for quick cash; the rest would go to their host family as "goodwill gifts" in lieu of rent money.

Quickly, because it was starting to get light, they hurried back to their sampan. Lu Lu whimpered softly as they untied the rope and climbed in. Kiem knew better than to ask his mother if they could take her with them. He tried not to look at her as the boat caught the current and pulled sharply away from shore.

Mrs. Sach pooled the profits from that night's expedition with some money of her uncle's, and together they bought a sampan big enough for sixteen people: Kiem, his mother, his six little brothers and sisters, his mother's parents, his mother's uncle and his wife, and the uncle's daughter and her family. Their plan was to travel north on the Big River until they reached a village north of Hanoi where one of their relatives lived. They would cut a wide swath around Hanoi to the west, since it was now back under French control.

It was to be no pleasure cruise. The sun beat down, and the rain leaked through the flimsy canvas awning. Kiem's grandfather had just suffered a stroke. So, counting Kiem, there were only three able men among them to pole when the river was shallow, row when it was deep, and drag the boat by a rope along the shore when the current was strong. On the third day, a pair of blunt-nosed American Hellcats came screaming down out of the clouds at them, stitching the surface of the river with machine-gun fire, and the family had to jump out of their boat and crouch neck-deep in reeds and muck until the strafing was over—everybody but Grand-father, who was too sick to be moved. Miraculously, the boat didn't get punctured anywhere below the waterline, though it was riddled with bullet holes everywhere else.

They set off again, traveling for a few days, tying up for a few days, fighting the river's will. One afternoon as Kiem was sitting on the river-bank trying to teach the smaller children a school lesson, a sampan came drifting toward them carrying a lone Viet Minh in a Boy Scout hat. Something about the angle of that hat disturbed Kiem, although he didn't know why.

The boat passed them, skimming along, about to thread the arch beneath a wooden footbridge. Kiem kept staring at the hat. "Hey!" he began to yell. "You there! Soldier! Come back!"

It was his big brother Nam, sent by their father to search for them. Mrs. Sach took one look at him and began to cry all of the tears she'd been holding back since losing her farm and watching her father's health deteriorate and shielding her children from machine-gun fire and worry-ing about her three oldest sons in the Viet Minh. She cried so loudly that they could hardly hear Nam explaining that their father and Aunt Dam were well, having fled Hanoi and found shelter with a friend of Mr. Sach's in the countryside. Nam was going to have to rejoin his unit, but he promised to help them row, pole, and drag the boat to their destina-tion first.

When they reached the third district to the north, the weather turned cool and rainy. The ground was so slick that Kiem tripped and went sprawling in the center of the village square. To save face, lying there in the mud, he said, "Hey, that was fun! Just like skating!"

"Skating?" asked a young man wearing a soldier's hat over brown civil-ian clothes, as if he were traveling undercover. "Are you from the city? Boys from around here don't know anything about skating."

"Yes, sir. I'm from Hanoi," admitted Kiem.

The man told Kiem he was from Hai Duong, a city midway between Hanoi and Haiphong. Kiem told him that his brother Lam had been in the forestry service there before joining the provincial troop.

"Mr. Lam?" asked the stranger. "Not Mr. Lam with the big muscles?" The man was on his way to join Lam's unit at that very moment—and he offered to let Kiem's family sail behind him the rest of the way there.

They sailed for one day and one night, then tied up their boats. Kiem and his family stayed behind while the man went into the woods alone, since the unit's location was secret. When Lam came striding out of the woods behind their benefactor, the first thing everybody noticed was the yellow star on his hat. He was an officer now, just like Tri: a squadron commander! Mrs. Sach began to cry all over again. She insisted that Lam take the food they'd brought with them for the rest of their journey.

At the last minute, just as he was getting ready to go back to his men, Lam told them the bad news: he'd heard a rumor that Tri had been wounded in the Battle of Cau Bang City. Lam had been pressing travelers from that region for more details but without much luck. Mrs. Sach stopped crying, an indulgence she could no longer afford with the work that had to be done: there was still one son left to find.

Back at the sampan, Mrs. Sach convened a family conference. Her father's condition was worse; he needed to rest in one place for a week or two. Nam and Kiem would go north to find Tri and their father while the rest of them waited here.

Mrs. Sach had just discovered a fresh source of cash. Hoping to entice people to stay in the war-torn countryside rather than flee to the French-controlled cities, the Viet Minh had set up a loan program. If you could furnish proof that you owned a house or a rice field, you could borrow money against it. Mrs. Sach had borrowed the maximum. Measuring out a handful of coins, she gave half to Nam to carry and sewed the rest into a secret compartment in Kiem's pocket—whether to be safe from his own hands or from a robber's, Kiem wasn't sure.

Carrying a knapsack, canteen, and slingshot, coins jingling in his pocket, Kiem set off behind his big brother. Learning by word of mouth which areas were dangerous and which safe, they squeezed past thousands of other refugees clogging the rutted country roads. It was strange to see women wearing white "city" pants in the countryside, even when the white pants were mud-stained or cropped short for freedom of movement.

It took them almost a week to reach the village where their father and Aunt Dam were staying. They arrived tired and hungry. Looking forward to a good meal and a long sleep, they made their way to the house of their father's friend Mr. Khach and knocked on the door. "Hello," said Nam when the door opened. "We're here to see our father, Mr. Sach."

Mr. Khach's faint smile disappeared. "You must have the wrong person. I don't know any Sach," he said.

"Your old friend," prompted Nam. "The one who was staying here last month, when I stopped by. . . ."

"Get out of here!" he hissed. "I don't know anything about that man."

"But. . . ."

"Out! Out! Get out!"

That night Kiem and Nam bedded down under the overhanging roof of the village temple, debating their next move. The next morning Kiem stayed behind while Nam went to knock on Mr. Khach's door again. Nam wasn't gone long. When he came back, his eyes were red from weeping.

"He's dead, isn't he?" asked Kiem.

"No, not dead," said Nam. "Worse than dead."

"Worse than dead? What do you mean?" asked Kiem. "Tell me the truth, Big Brother, or I'll . . . I'll punch you in the nose. I swear I will." He balled his right hand into a fist and waited.

"He's gone back to Hanoi. To the French side," Nam added—as if Kiem wouldn't know what "Hanoi" meant by now.

"No!" shouted Kiem. *It was impossible. Mr. Khach was a stinking liar!* But it would certainly explain Mr. Khach's puzzling behavior. If the Viet Minh were to learn he'd been sheltering a traitor. . . .

Walking dejectedly now, they set out to find Tri. They thought it would be easy to catch up to his unit, since it had a crack reputation. But though everyone had heard of it, nobody seemed to know where it was now.

In every middling-sized village Kiem and Nam came to, the civil temple in the center of the square, next to the Buddhist pagoda, had been turned into a "hospital" for wounded soldiers. The injured lay on benches or the blood-slickened floor, moaning softly to themselves. Nam did what he could to help them, although he couldn't find medicine or bandages anywhere. There didn't seem to be any real doctors or nurses around.

"Anyone here named Tri?" Kiem and Nam would call out hopefully upon entering, and usually they'd get a chorus of three or four voices saying "That's me!" "Tri here!" It was a common name. But they couldn't find their Tri.

Finally somebody directed them to an officers' hospital across the river. "Anyone here named Tri?" they called out again. They talked to two or three Tris without any luck. "Let's go," said Nam, just as an arm thrust straight up from a cot and a voice rasped "Tri?"

One eye socket had been scooped out like an eggshell, and one leg was missing just below the knee. Kiem could hardly bear to look at him. Still, he knew that the man was one of the lucky ones because his family was standing around him, washing blood and pus out of his bandages.

"I was with Tri at the Battle of Cao Bang City," the man said. "We were winning, on account of Tri. Captured the ammunition dump. But we didn't count on those damned Frogs committing suicide—blowing the whole thing up in our faces. Not even any bodies. Only me."

Not Tri, Kiem thought. There must have been some mistake. *Not Tri, not Tri, not Tri* went the rhythm of his feet all the way back to the sampan.

Mrs. Sach had already dreamed the bad news about Tri. Looking at their faces, she confirmed it. But they still had to break the news about her husband's defection—with Aunt Dam, which made it worse. There was no work for their father in the countryside, argued Nam. What use is a civil engineer in a rice field? How else could he support his family? Farm labor would have killed him, agreed Kiem; his health was too delicate. They managed to convince themselves—but not their mother.

With Grandfather doing a little bit better, they decided to press on. Wrestling the Big River for a few more weeks, they finally made it to their cousin's farm. It was a big farm with a comfortable house, but Kiem couldn't relax just yet. Uncle Tich had just died in a nearby village, leaving four daughters but no sons, and Nam had to return to his unit. Kiem would have to attend the funeral and perform the duties of the eldest son.

It was just a small ceremony. There was no pig killing, nor even a chicken killing. But the mourners put on white rags and leaf sandals, out of respect for Tich the Nationalist. They whispered among themselves that Mr. Tich had died of dashed hopes, having joined the local Viet Minh only to be used and deceived by them. *Gossips*, thought Kiem. *What do they know about anything?* He walked in front of the coffin and made motions as if to halt its progress. He knew what to do, and he did it well.

Back on the farm he led a sad but peaceful existence with his family for a few months. Then the French began closing in on them again.

One morning the family woke up to a commotion of gunfire and barking dogs. Grabbing the smaller children, they ran to the village pagoda and crowded inside. A lot of other people seemed to have had the same idea. They were just beginning to catch their breath when a tall, thin figure entered the semidarkness, a rifle or bayonet pointing ahead of him. They all went diving under the wooden seating platforms. The man began to feel his way along the wall with one hand, but he must have crunched Hanh's foot in the darkness, because she let out a shriek.

"Come out before I shoot!" he shouted in French. Immediately there were sounds of heads thumping on wood and people scrambling to their feet. Mrs. Sach grabbed hold of her daughter's wrist and began begging for mercy in the only language she knew. The Frenchman kept having to look away, to scan the room for trouble, and Mrs. Sach used the opportunity to pinch the little ones and make them cry. Hanh was fifteen years old and very pretty. Her mother was now hurting her, gripping her wrist tightly, and Hanh wished she'd let go. Hanh didn't realize how lucky she was that the Frenchman was an officer and not a common man.

When he saw that there were no adult males among them, the Frenchman relaxed. He unwrapped a chocolate bar and broke it into pieces, smiling and motioning for them to put out their hands. In between their mother's furtive pinches, the children began to smile back at him. He rummaged around in his pockets and pulled out a handful of peppermints.

"Parles-tu français?" he asked.

"Non!" said Kiem without thinking. *How could he have been so careless?* The next thing he knew, he'd been pressed into service to translate back and forth between the French and a group of young Vietnamese males they'd managed to round up—Viet Minh suspects. Finally, after two or three hours of it, the young men were loaded into a truck and carted away. The officer who'd stepped on Hanh's foot patted Kiem on the shoulder and asked whether his family would like a ride to Hanoi in the morning. Kiem wasn't sure. "Well, meet us here in the morning if you decide to go," said the Frenchman.

"No!" said Mrs. Sach when Kiem relayed the Frenchman's offer. "No way!" She still had two sons fighting for the cause. She was not going over to the French side, no matter what her husband had done. Then reality began to set in. Her father's condition was getting worse—and there seemed to be no safe haven for her children anywhere in the countryside. So she backed down. "But don't tell anyone we're doing this," she told Kiem. "We must save face. We'll simply disappear."

As promised, the Frenchmen returned with a truck the following morning. They drove Kiem's family to an overnight screening camp, then picked them up the next day and delivered them to Hanoi. All the way there, Kiem's grandfather kept bragging about his brave freedom-fighter grandsons. It was a good thing the French couldn't understand his stroke-slurred Vietnamese.

The family reunion in Hanoi was bittersweet. The smaller children clung to their father, who, for once, was too overcome with emotion to speak. Aunt Dam kept wiping back tears and circling her children's arms with a thumb and finger to see if they'd lost weight. Nobody mentioned Tri, although the Hanoi townhouse swirled with memories of him. And Kiem's mother did not seem at all happy to see her husband. But now there was no more Phu Tai for her to escape to.

FIRE

All things are on fire; the eye is on fire, forms are on fire, eye-consciousness is on fire; the impressions received by the eye are on fire, and whatever sensation originates in the impressions received by the eye is likewise on fire. And with what are these things on fire? With the fires of lust, anger, and illusion, with these are they on fire, and so with the other senses and so with the mind.

Buddha, *The Fire Sermon*

CHAPTER 5

Vietnamese Heads Army

Command of Indo-China Force Given to Gen. Nguyen Van Hinh

New York Times, 17 April 1952

Kiem's father had thought of almost everything when he de-signed the plans for his two-story, gray-painted town house in Hanoi: high ceilings for coolness, wiring and sockets for elec-tric lights, a side passage to the privy—everything but equal bedroom accommodations for two wives. Kiem's mother found it just too humiliating to have to sleep on a cot in the children's quarters while her sister shared Mr. Sach's bed upstairs. With-out saying anything to anyone, she went searching for a room to rent and, when she found one over a garage near the covered market, moved herself and her four youngest children into it.

Summer vacation was almost over by then, so she tried to enroll the children in school. But because of the war she didn't have their transcripts, and the school officials were insistent—particularly in the case of Kiem, who had passed the exam for his primary school diploma. Hanh had earned her diploma too, but her Catholic girls' school was not as fussy about demand-ing proof.

Three years before, when he was twelve, Kiem had dressed in his best clothes and traveled to the parish school of Bat Nao along with a hundred other jittery candidates, many of them adults competing for a civil-service position or promotion. Each candidate had brought five or ten family members along, all jabbering loudly or calling out questions to the soldiers sta-tioned at the school-yard barricades while food vendors pushed through the crowd or chanted their jingles from bright-ly colored tents. It was more like a party than a serious exam that could make or break one's career.

The daylong test had begun with math questions: rice-field measurement, rice-paddy water flow, that sort of thing—not too hard. Then science. Then an essay on an ancient Vietnamese proverb. During the lunch break a grownup candidate who'd been sitting next to Kiem during the morning tests introduced himself as the assistant chief of Que Phuong village. He said he'd heard that Kiem came from Hanoi and was very good at French; he himself had no talent for it, but he needed his diploma to apply for the chief's job when he retired next year. Then he pulled out a one-piastre bill. "If you let me copy your dictation, I'll be eternally grateful to you and your family," he whispered. There was no thought of refusing him: the man was Kiem's elder, and children were supposed to help their elders. With the bill rustling in his pocket, Kiem made sure that his writing-hand didn't block the page from view. The afternoon hours brought the dreaded French *dictation* and *rédaction* but with a nice surprise: the young Frenchwoman who read the dictation had the sweetest voice Kiem had ever heard—and she was pretty, too.

That night, instead of finding a bed in a shop or private home, Kiem had paced the main road past the school, staring at the lit-up windows where silhouetted teachers sat grading examination books by lantern-light. In the morning, even after hearing his name called—"Do Kiem, pass with honors"—he'd stormed the bulletin board with everybody else to check the posted list. Those who had heard their names called wanted to be sure they weren't dreaming, while those who had heard nothing were still hoping for a miracle. Kiem saw that his friend the assistant chief had also passed, although without special distinction.

It was not the kind of thing a boy would want to go through again if he could help it.

"We'll see what your father can do," said Mrs. Sach.

Mr. Sach had no luck with the local school officials, either. "Well then," he said, "it's time to turn misfortune into fortune. We'll try the Lycée Albert Sarraut." This was Hanoi's private French high school, one of only three in the entire country. The sons and daughters of the French colonials went there, along with the crème de la crème of Vietnamese society. Kiem felt sure they'd turn away a dummy like him, who couldn't even get admitted to a Vietnamese high school. But to his surprise they let him in. Mrs. Sach was not at all pleased. Neither was Kiem, who knew right away that he was in over his head. He could read French almost as well as the other students, even after being out of school for almost two years, but he could barely understand his teachers' spoken instructions. They talked so fast, with funny accents. In the past his French-language instructors had always been Vietnamese.

Just a few weeks into the semester Kiem was placed on academic probation, then demoted one grade. Aghast at the thought of having to tell his father, he marched into the principal's office and asked to be given one month to catch up with the others.

The young, red-bearded Frenchman seemed amused by Kiem's presumption. "But if you haven't caught up with your grade by then, then what? You'll be too late to catch up with the grade below."

"Then kick me out!" said Kiem. "I'd rather be kicked out than demoted any day."

The principal gave him one more month and wished him luck. "Next time, though, make an appointment before you barge in," he said.

That night Kiem broke down and told his father everything. "Don't worry," said Mr. Sach, "your book-knowledge of French is fine. We just need to give your ears more practice. From now on, you and I will speak French to each other for a half-hour every evening. And I'd recommend that you make friends with some of the French boys."

The next morning Kiem struck up a conversation with Paul-Eugène Auborgh. Paul-Eugène was the second-worst student in French class—he could understand French but not spell it. The two of them closed a deal: if Paul-Eugène would write out the *dictation* and let Kiem copy it, Kiem would recopy it with correct spelling and let Paul-Eugène peek.

It worked. Both of their grades improved—although not by the means that Mr. Sach had had in mind.

Beginning to feel more confident, Kiem tried out for the Ping-Pong and swim teams, then the drama club. Without benefit of bribery, he made five or six more French friends. After school they played soccer together or rode their bikes to the Botanical Gardens. On weekends they went to the cinema or lounged around the giant banyan tree outside the Fine Arts Museum, flirting with French girls their age. Kiem's Vietnamese friends looked down on that sort of thing: romance was for later, after a young man had finished his education and provided for his parents in their old age.

The two nicest French boys were Georges and Michel Mougenel, the husky sons of Kiem's mathematics teacher. She was his favorite teacher, too. One day after class Madame Mougenel invited him to have dinner with the family. Kiem said he'd have to ask his father's permission.

"Very good," said Mr. Sach. "Of course you will go."

"What should I expect, Father? What sort of foods will we eat?"

Mr. Sach got up and walked to the wall and very carefully straightened the frame of his engineering diploma. It was two meters long by a half-meter wide, lettered with red-and-black Chinese characters. The emperor's seal was as big around as a man's head. "I can't tell you, Son," he said quietly; "I've never been to a French home." At that time Mr. Sach had been working for the French government for over twenty-five years.

The following weekend Kiem eyed the confusion of glasses, plates, and utensils at his place setting and began to shake. A Vietnamese maid was ladling smelly soup into his bowl and calling him *Monsieur,* even though she was old enough to be his mother. He wanted to run right out the door.

"The Vietnamese people don't eat onions, do they?" asked Madame Mougenel. "Not *bulb* onions, at any rate. It occurred to me at the last moment that you might not like the soup. If so, please don't feel you have to force it down to be polite."

Kiem took a swallow and relaxed. The soup was delicious. He was about to say so, when Monsieur Mougenel cut in. "Don't humor the boy! If one person in a group eats onions, the rest must eat them in self-defense. The same goes for garlic."

Georges and Michel giggled, and even Kiem risked a smile. *The table setting is so formal, but the conversation so casual!* Kiem thought. Mealtime in a Vietnamese home was just the opposite: people served themselves from a few bowls set down on a bare table, but no one would dare crack a joke.

Kiem helped himself to roast beef with gravy, baked potatoes, green beans, sliced-tomato salad, and apple tart. He washed it all down with several glasses of watered red wine. *No wonder Georges and Michel are so husky,* he thought, not realizing until much later that Madame Mougenel had planned a special menu in his honor.

After dinner Monsieur Mougenel, an archaeologist, showed Kiem some of his Southeast Asian artifacts. "Your people can trace their written history back to 208 B.C.," he told Kiem. "You make the nations of Europe look like Johnny-come-latelies." Kiem blushed.

Most of the teachers at the Lycée Albert Sarraut were like the Mougenels: young and enthusiastic, with liberal ideas. They weren't afraid of being called *indigènophiles,* lovers of the natives, though to most French colonials it was the worst possible slur. Kiem's friends teased him about being their *chou-chou,* or "favorite." And it was true. He guessed it was

because he always volunteered to clap the erasers and wash the blackboard. He loved the blackboard: its inky color, its slippery feel, its pow-
dery smell, and even its high-pitched squeak. He didn't understand that
every good teacher's greatest joy is to watch the petals of a young mind
unfolding, like a lotus pushing through mud, water, and wind to reach
the light.

Kiem's teachers urged him to question them—to question even the
words printed in books! They steered him to the writings of Voltaire,
Rousseau, and Victor Hugo; and he devoured their ideas. His mind traveled to the bottom of the sea with Jules Verne and to the North Pole with
Jack London, read in French translation. *Liberté, égalité, fraternité:* the
very words made his insides tingle like a glass of wine.

"But why not us, Father?" he asked at home. "Why do the French glo-
rify their own revolution but keep us a colony against our will?"

"Because our time hasn't come yet," said Mr. Sach. "For two thousand
years we've been a vertical society, looking up to the father, the teacher,
the king. If we try to change things overnight, we'll court disaster."

"But this is 1949, Father! The British have given up Burma and India,
and America the Philippines. The Dutch are about to free Indonesia. . . ."

"It is not time," said Mr. Sach with finality. And Kiem's Eastern mind
deferred to him, while his Western mind itched to continue the argu-
ment.

It was all very confusing to Kiem, the issue of the French. He adored
his teachers. But why were their countrymen trying to kill his brothers?
How could the French governor-general, sitting in the front row of
Hanoi's National Theater, leap to his feet to applaud Kiem's performance in a school play, while a French MP on a motorbike had thought
nothing of kicking him in the rear end with muddy brown boots, only
because Kiem had bumped into his motorbike on a bicycle while watching a column of French soldiers drill in the street? It hadn't been anything *intentional*, and Kiem had apologized in good French.

Kiem could never quite forget that the war with the French was raging
just beyond the city limits. Now and then—especially on cool, dry days
during the winter months—he could hear the boom and echo of the can-
nons. But mostly the war made itself known through absences, not pres-
ences.

There had been no word from Nam or Lam. Mr. Sach explained that
they shouldn't expect to hear until the war was over, because messages
were just too risky on both sides.

There would be no word from Tri, not ever again: not unless Kiem's French Christian friends were right about heaven and Judgment Day.

And it felt strange to be exiled from Phu Tai. In dreams Kiem could still hear its background of cricket-song: loud and warlike at daybreak, soft and pleading at midday mating time. But he could no more go there than he could fly to the moon. Travelers from that area said that the village lay in ruins and that no one had dared move back.

He couldn't go *anywhere*, for crying out loud! His big brothers had been able to roam a hundred kilometers in every direction—even south of the city, to the cemeteries and the leper colony—but all he could do was pedal his bike to Tram Mountain, on picnics chaperoned by his teachers. He wished he could visit the far northern village Lam had bragged about, the one whose guardian spirit had been a prostitute in her early life. Once a year, on the anniversary of her death, Lam had confided to him, the village girls would dress up in costume and act out the story of her life. On that day alone, they would not take offense at a stranger's advances!

But the war dragged on and on, fueled by developments in other parts of Asia. In 1949 Mao Tse-tung's Communist Army defeated Chiang Kai-shek's Nationalist Army in China. Chiang Kai-shek's forces fled to the island of Taiwan, where they set up a government in exile. In 1950 the North Korean Communists invaded South Korea. The United States sent troops to back up the South, while Red China backed up the North. All of a sudden, the governments of Russia, China, and the United States began to pay a lot more attention to the "little colonial war" going on in Vietnam. All three of the major powers stepped up their military aid: the United States siding with the French, and the Chinese and Russians with the Viet Minh.

"Victory Near at Hand!" proclaimed the French-controlled newspapers of Hanoi. "Pacification Program Working." "Defending the Independence of Vietnam."

"Thousands of French Killed," countered the propaganda leaflets distributed by pro-Viet Minh students at the University of Hanoi. "French Outposts Overrun." "Help Comes from China."

Kiem knew from whispered conversations with Georges, Michel, and Paul-Eugène that the war was losing its popularity back in Paris. It was costing too much money and too many lives, with no promise of victory. Dreaming that they could one day turn the whole thing over to Vietnamese loyalists, the French chartered a Vietnamese National Army and passed a law drafting young Vietnamese males into it. Then they chartered a tiny Vietnamese Navy and gave it a few French patrol craft and minesweepers that had already been obsolete in World War II. The new policy was called *jaunissement*, the "yellowing" of the French forces in Vietnam.

One evening in late 1952 or early 1953 Aunt Dam's son Tuan came knocking on the door. By then Mrs. Sach had scraped together some money and managed to buy a little house of her own, so she and the children were no longer crammed into one room over a garage. "Father says to come at once," Tuan panted. "There's a visitor."

"Who is it?" she asked.

"An ugly soldier" was all Tuan could get out.

Many years had passed, but Kiem recognized the shelflike lower lip at once, jutting out over the collar of Thinh's French Partisan Army uniform. The Partisans were not draftees but volunteers. People called them *Viet Gian*, or "bad Viets."

"I had to make a living somehow," Thinh apologized. "It's hard to find a job, with the war on." The lower lip trembled as he told them that Madame Thin had been killed in the war. Mrs. Sach, who had bristled at the sight of Thinh's uniform, softened at the news about his mother and helped Aunt Dam bring out food for him.

"One has to choose a side," Mr. Sach assured him. "One can't stay neutral and expect to survive."

"But what about the draft? How can I fight my own brothers?" Kiem asked his father as the date of his high-school graduation grew near. Mr. Sach had a temporary solution: sending Kiem back to the Lycée Albert Sarraut for a second high-school diploma that fall. He'd have to take military training during the year, but at least he wouldn't have to shoot anybody.

Meanwhile, in the spring of 1953, Kiem passed the examination for his first degree with honors, and his relatives showered him with lucky red envelopes full of cash. It was time to celebrate! He'd been invited to stay with a classmate in a villa by the beach in Do Son, and his father had said he could go.

Kiem and three friends caught the dawn train from Hanoi to Haiphong, a ten-hour trip. In Haiphong, a rust-colored port city, they hired a car and driver. Soon the oily industrial fumes of Haiphong gave way to a crisp ocean breeze. Their car turned onto the sandy peninsula that was Do Son, then braked in front of a white villa crowned with purple bougainvillea vines. "We'll be sharing it with another family, but they're nice folks," Kiem's friend told the others. "Wait'll you see their two daughters!" He clutched at his heart, and they laughed.

After stashing their bags in the villa, the boys spent the rest of the afternoon swimming and lying in the sun. They bought a sack of live crabs and roasted them on the beach after the sun had gone down in streaks of pink and lavender. One of them passed a pack of cigarettes around, and Kiem took one and smoked it manfully, but when he tossed the lit end on the sand and its red eye rolled over and over, Kiem's head felt like it was rolling, too. That night he toppled onto his sitting-room cot with his muscles aching and his lungs caked with smoke and salt.

The next morning he woke up early and thought about a swim before breakfast. One of his friends had had the same idea; he was already dozing by the water's edge, a palm-leaf hat shading his eyes. Kiem decided to let him sleep. As he stood knee-deep in the glittering surf, gazing back toward the villa, he caught sight of an angel gliding down the path to the beach. She was wearing a loose white robe that rippled in the early-morning breeze, and the sun at her back was casting a halo around her.

As she came closer, Kiem could see that she had the smooth, oval face of a Japanese princess. Yes, and her hair was piled up on her head and pinned with chopsticks in the Japanese fashion. But what would a Japanese princess be doing in Do Son?

At the edge of the water she paused and stuck out one tiny foot. She was now so close to Kiem that he could see that her nose and mouth were Vietnamese. No question about it! As he stood there gazing helplessly, she flashed a smile in his direction. What could he do to save face, bare-chested in the waters of the Gulf of Tonkin? Nothing but dive underwater and stay there until his breath ran out.

When he came back up, sputtering for air, he saw that the creature was gliding away from him. He ran to his sleeping friend and shook him awake. "That girl!" he pointed. "Do you know her?"

"Yeah, sure," he said. "That's Le Thi Thom. Her family's sharing our villa."

Great! thought Kiem. He'd get to see her every day! *Shit!* he thought next. He was sleeping in the sitting room. If she saw him in his pajamas, he'd die.

"She's a little beauty, isn't she?" asked Kiem's friend. "But she's only fifteen."

"Is she engaged?"

"No way! She's still in high school, and the mother is big on education. One son is studying in France, and the older girl, Huong, is about to join him there."

"They must be rich," said Kiem.

"They've worked hard for their money," said his friend. "It's a sad story, really. In 1946, the mother and her children traveled north from Annam to visit her parents. You can guess what happened next. The war broke out, and they got stuck. After seven years they still don't know if the father is dead or alive. The war has separated many families like that. Ours are lucky."

Kiem thought of Nam, Lam, and Tri, but he said nothing.

"The mother had to support them somehow, so she started her own contracting business. Can you imagine that?" continued the friend. "They say she has twenty men working for her. She's remarried now, to another contractor—a former business rival."

That evening Kiem's friends built a campfire on the beach, and the warmth and light drew the Le family. Le Thi Thom sat down so close to Kiem that he could smell the coconut oil in her hair. *Fragrant* was all he could think: the meaning of the word "Thom."

Kiem's friends had been singing folk songs to Kiem's harmonica, and now the Le family joined in. Kiem discovered that Thom had a high, pure, silvery singing voice—like a temple bell pealing in a noisy village square. Everybody kept urging her to sing a solo, but she said she was shy with so many people around. Then Kiem asked her, blowing the first few notes on his harmonica, and she changed her mind.

That night Kiem lay awake for hours, staring at the moon through the sitting-room window. Had she sat down next to him by accident or on purpose? It must have been by accident. And why had she favored *his* request over her mother's and stepfather's? He must have asked her to sing at precisely the right moment, after the group had worn down her resistance.

But she had sung every time Kiem had asked, and not once for the others! Could she like him? Could it be possible?

She liked my harmonica playing, that's all, he corrected himself. *She thinks my teeth are silver. She thinks my smile is rectangular and as wide as two hands.*
. . .

At some point during the night he must have fallen asleep, because the sun was in his eyes when he felt something kicking his cot. He opened his eyes to that exquisite oval face.

"Come on, lazybones," she said. "Let's hunt for shells. You can check and see if they have those icky, slimy things inside before I touch them."

Kiem didn't find many shells that morning. He was too distracted by the sight of Thom's tiny footprints chaining the sand as if someone had made a doll's legs walk across the beach to amuse a child. That afternoon, that evening, and for the next two weeks, they could think of nothing but each other. If Thom's mother and stepfather noticed what was going on, they did nothing to stop it.

Before Kiem knew it, his vacation time was up, and he and Thom were promising to write to each other every day. Riding the train to Hanoi, he felt in his pocket for the keepsake she had given him: a silver knife engraved with the German words *Fergidch Meine Nitch*, "forget me not." He was twenty years old. He had fallen in love with Le Thi Thom and the sea, the sea and Le Thi Thom, and his future had been sealed by fate.

CHAPTER 6

French, Reds Sign Indochina Truce
Communists to Get Northern Vietnam, 12 Million People

Pacific Stars & Stripes, 21 July 1954

Over the next few months, like a shower of plum-blossom petals, pink envelopes scented with French cologne began descending on the little stucco house in Hanoi's Old Quarter. Back to Haiphong floated pale green envelopes the color of dragonfly wings. Mrs. Sach couldn't help but notice. Was her son about to throw away college and a profession for a cheap seductress? Well, she would see about that! Intercepting a pink envelope, she copied down its return address. Then she caught the dawn train to Haiphong and hired a ricksha to Mrs. Le's house.

Mrs. Sach knocked on the door and introduced herself, and Mrs. Le invited her in for tea: not plain chrysanthemum tea but special "dustbuster" tea, to clear the grit from her journey. Soon the two women were laughing and chatting like sisters. They gave their blessings to a long, happy marriage and many healthy children—provided, of course, that Kiem and Thom finished their educations first. When it was time for Mrs. Sach to catch her train, Mrs. Le called to her husband to take a picture of the two of them with his new camera. In the back of the car on the way to the train station they held hands and promised to keep their meeting secret.

The Year of the Snake, 1953, gave way to the Year of the Horse, 1954. And with Kiem's second high-school senior year drawing to a close, it was time for him to start worrying about the draft again.

"Think about civil engineering school," said Mr. Sach. "It would keep you out of the draft for the time being and keep you out of a combat corps once you're an engineer."

"With all due respect, Father," said Kiem, "I don't think I'm the kind of person who could sit behind a desk all day."

"Sit behind a desk!" snorted Mr. Sach. "Believe me, young man, a civil engineer has to wear out many, many pairs of boots before he gets a chance to sit behind a desk!"

How could Kiem explain to his father that his head was full of books and films about the sea—that he was drunk on the words of Jules Verne and Jack London, that when he closed his eyes he was a sea captain threading a cutter through blue-green icebergs dotted with penguins and polar bears. . . ?

"Father," he tried, "have you ever heard of the French Naval Academy?"

"L'Ecole Navale de France," said Mr. Sach, "the most famous naval officers' academy in the world, in Brest, France. Of course I've heard of it. What makes you ask?"

"Well, sir, my teachers say they're recruiting Vietnamese students this year to train as officers for our new navy."

"But, surely, you can't be thinking . . . ," said Mr. Sach. "The men on my side of the family have always been scholars. My father, his father, his father before him. A scholar commands everyone's respect, but a military man. . . . A soldier works with his body, like a farmer, but a scholar works with his mind."

"Perhaps you're thinking of the army, sir," said Kiem. "The navy is different, sir. They don't take anybody without a high-school diploma. And surely you know that our country has a long, distinguished naval tradition going all the way back to the tenth century, when Ngo Quyen, the 'Sea Lord,' sank the whole Chinese fleet by making them sail over stakes he'd planted at high tide. . . ." Even as the words began tumbling from his mouth, he was shocked to find himself challenging his father's authority. Had his French instructors put their Christian devil into him?

Mr. Sach stared at his son until the defiance had disappeared from his eyes. "I'm getting close to retirement age, and I'm not in the best of health," he said. "Pretty soon you'll be the one supporting the family. A civil engineer makes good money—enough to put your younger brothers and sisters through school." Aunt Dam had just given birth to a little boy, her fourth child, and she was still a young woman. There could be more.

"Yes, Father," said Kiem numbly, "whatever you wish." But the Western half of his mind kept dreaming, plotting, and rebelling.

The night before his civil-engineering entrance exam, Kiem hatched his plan. He had shot up in height during the previous year, with no weight gain to match—he was as skinny as a chopstick. Suppose he were to flunk the physical fitness portion of the test: who would be suspicious? The next day he did his worst on the broad jump and hundred-meter dash. But when he came close to flunking the long distance run without trying, he put on a burst of speed and managed to pass it. His strategy worked: his application was rejected, despite his high score on the academic exam. Best of all, he didn't think his father suspected a thing.

"Very well," sighed Mr. Sach, "apply to the French Naval Academy. You'll get an excellent education there, and you'll be safe from the fighting for the next three years. Plus, our navy will pay you a small stipend to go there. All in all, you could do worse."

Not all the pink envelopes in the world, not even his mother's superstitious chatter, could burst Kiem's bubble now. "Oh, but the navy is a bad career for someone born under the element metal!" wailed Mrs. Sach. "A metal sword grows stronger in fire, more precious in the earth, but it gets rusted in water. . . ."

Kiem didn't listen. He shut out all thoughts of his two brothers fighting on the opposing side, his mother weeping for him in Hanoi, his future bride getting tired of waiting in Haiphong.

While Kiem was imagining how he'd look in Vietnamese Navy dress whites, Viet Minh general Vo Nguyen Giap was busy massing tens of thousands of troops around the French-held valley town of Dien Bien Phu, near the Laotian border. Giap's forces choked off the French supply lines, ringing their noose tighter and tighter as the French got thinner and weaker and monsoon rains beat down on their encampment. The French appealed to U.S. president Eisenhower and British prime minister Churchill for help, but it was not forthcoming. On 12 March 1954 Giap's army of fifty thousand men attacked French general Navarre's eleven or twelve thousand with everything in its arsenal. In early May, as Kiem was preparing to take the written exam for the French Naval Academy in Hanoi, Giap's men overran the last of the weakened French forces—and the Viet Minh won the war.

Kiem was thrilled that his country had finally gained its independence, but he couldn't help worrying that the French defeat might ruin his future plans. Mr. Sach said not to fear: no matter what happened at the postwar negotiating conference, the French would still want to help shape a young navy just starting out. They were human, and that was human nature.

Mr. Sach seemed to be right. In June fifty Vietnamese boys gathered in

Saigon to take the oral and physical examinations for the French Naval Academy. Twelve of them passed, including Kiem. He barely had time to savor the fast pace of life in the South—jumping into the basket of a motorized *cyclo* and careening through the streets of Saigon with the wind ruffling his hair—before he had to sign the papers and return home. He had thirty days' leave to get his affairs in order before he sailed to France.

He sent Thom a telegram telling her the date and time he'd be stopping in Haiphong en route to Hanoi by train. She was there at the station to greet him, sixteen years old and even more beautiful than the year before, with her silky black hair falling straight down her back. He couldn't help noticing that her figure had blossomed under her silk *ao dai*, but he made no move to touch her, not even to hold her hand. That would have been disrespectful.

"I'll wait for you," she said. "I love you, Kiem."

He wanted to tell her that he loved her too, but he couldn't get the words out. "We'll write to each other," he said. "It's only three years."

When the train whistle blew, Thom started to cry. Kiem couldn't believe that he, a mere student, was the cause of it. "Maybe you'll visit Huong and your brother in Paris," he said. "We might see each other sooner than we think."

He waved to her out the window as his train pulled away, but she just stood on the platform with her teary face in her hands.

Back in Hanoi, Kiem's mother was inconsolable. "How can I be sure you'll come back? If you come back, I promise you, you can marry the woman of your choice," she sobbed.

"You don't have to bribe me, Mother," he said laughing. "I'll be back in three years, no matter what." Still, it was a relief to find out that she wasn't planning to betroth him to somebody else while he was away. Even in Hanoi, among the children of the middle class, most marriages were still being arranged by the parents.

Kiem gave his butterfly collection to Hanh, his clothes and bicycle to Frenchy, and his art supplies to Trung, keeping only the silver pocketknife for himself. His little half-brothers and sister followed him around the house in a pack, as if they could keep him from leaving by watching him all the time.

"I'll be back," he assured them.

Kiem's father showed almost no emotion. He said that Kiem had mastered all of the lessons he had to teach him and it was now time for Kiem to venture into the world on his own, bringing great honor to the family, even though he would travel far from the graves of his ancestors.

"But I'll be back!" said Kiem. "It's only three years, Father, not a lifetime!"

"You have made me a fortunate man," said Mr. Sach. "Because now, whatever happens in the future, I'll have at least one son on the winning side."

Father always expects the worst to happen, thought Kiem: *sending us to Phu Tai during the war, betting on the French to win. But he isn't always right—even though he thinks he is.*

Kiem was in Nha Trang, waiting for the next ship out, when the terms of the postwar agreement were announced. Vietnam was to be cut in half along its seventeenth parallel. The French would have to leave the North, and the Viet Minh the South. For a period of three hundred days, Vietnamese people would be allowed to move north or south, as they chose; then the borders would slam shut. Two years from now, free elections would be held to reunite the country.

The North or the South: which would Mr. Sach choose? Kiem's last telegram to the family was full of unvoiced questions: I AM WELL BUT MISS EVERYBODY STOP YOUR SON KIEM. In September he set sail for France on board the *Louis Pasteur,* a French troop-transport ship.

One would like to paint a picture of the young officer-to-be standing smartly on the upper deck, his eyes trained on the horizon. But in truth Kiem was doubled over the rail most of the time, seasick—and the greasy lamb they served for almost every meal didn't help matters much. Pride helped a little, though: he trained himself to hold his sickness down until at least one French sailor had gone to the rail ahead of him; then two; then three. . . .

Since Kiem and his companions weren't even cadets yet in the eyes of the navy, they'd been assigned berths on the lowest deck. Two decks above them rode some Vietnamese petty officers being sent to Toulon for training. According to custom the men in fourth class had to clean the decks of those above them, toilets and all. Kiem did it for one day and then rebelled.

"No way," he told his group leader. "Not me. I'm not going to clean a petty officer's toilet."

"I'll have you thrown in the ship's brig if you don't!" the man threatened. "Show up here next morning with a scrub brush in your hand. Or else!"

The next morning, instead of reporting to the second deck, Kiem went straight up to the captain's cabin. "Please understand, sir," he explained, "the twelve of us are going to be among the first commissioned officers of the Vietnamese Navy, and here you are asking us to scrub the toilets of our own petty officers. Three years from now, when we return home, how will we command them? They'll never respect us."

"I see your point," the captain said, "but I can't go against regulations." He frowned.

"Aha!" he said, smiling at his own cleverness. "I could move you boys to the upper deck! Of course, you wouldn't have rooms to speak of—but you'd have the hanging lifeboats for shelter."

"That would suit us just fine, sir," said Kiem.

Kiem and his classmates thought it was fun to be camping out on the upper deck, even though the sun and wind turned them as red as firecrackers. The fresh air helped settle their stomachs, and the other passengers got so used to seeing the twelve young men around all the time that they smiled when they saw them and stopped to chat and learned their names. Many of the other passengers were soldiers in the French Foreign Legion being shipped back to France now that the war was over. One of them, a roly-poly giant of a man with a thick German accent, attached himself to Kiem. "You'll have to come visit me in Düsseldorf on your Christmas vacation. I'll introduce you to my sister: a big girl, like me. . . ." Kiem was flattered that an older man, a well-traveled European, would take an interest in someone like him. But one night the German had too much to drink and told Kiem the story of his life. When he reached the part about joining the SS under Hitler, he broke down and cried. Kiem was confused. How could such a kind man have such a shameful past, and how could a grown man lose control of his emotions in front of a youth? There was clearly much to learn about life in the world beyond Vietnam.

After three weeks at sea the *Louis Pasteur* docked at Marseilles. Kiem and his eleven companions caught a train to Brest and spilled into a crowd of red-nosed, red-cheeked people with mustaches—men and women alike—speaking in a rough dialect the Asian visitors couldn't understand.

A hulking French petty officer was there to greet them at the Brest station. "Poor fellows," he said after counting their heads, "you don't know what you're in for, do you?"

He explained that the Naval Academy was actually across the bay from the city of Brest, in the village of Lanveoc-Poulmic, a short boat-ride away. They all piled into the bottom of a motor launch with their luggage and huddled together under a cold, drizzling evening sky. A lighthouse beam raked across the boat, illuminating their frightened faces. They could hear the moaning of a foghorn and the distant clang-clang-clanging of a bell-buoy.

"Over there is the Isle of Ouessant," said the petty officer, gesturing seaward. "You can't see it tonight because of the fog, but believe me, the rocks around it are littered with ships' bones—and it's on nights like this that the big ships go down. When the drowned bodies wash ashore, the islanders bury them like their own, with wooden crosses, even if they're English. . . ."

Kiem began feeling seasick again. *Why didn't I listen to my father?* he asked himself. *I could be sleeping in a nice warm dorm at civil engineering school, with solid ground below me. . . .*

Over the days and weeks to come, things didn't get much better. Life at the French Naval Academy was *nothing* like Kiem's dream of blue-green icebergs and polar bears. When the bugle blew at five o'clock in the morning, Kiem would leap out of his hammock—meant to simulate the rocking motion of the sea—and into his gym clothes. He and the rest of the first-year class would rush downstairs and out the door for their morning run through the Breton countryside.

Huffing up and down the sheep-flecked hills, past church spires and stone ruins and thatched-roof cottages with geraniums nodding in their window boxes, always straggling far behind the French cadets, Kiem and the other Vietnamese were the funniest thing the women of Breton had ever seen. Dressed in starched white caps and black dresses, enormously fat, they'd lean over their fences and wait—laughing and wiping their mustache spit on their aprons as the Asians came wheezing by.

By the time the twelve young men crossed the finish line, there'd be no more hot water left. Sometimes they'd be so late they'd have to skip even the cold shower and hop right into their uniforms.

After the run came the sunrise flag-raising ceremony, followed by inspection. If Kiem's shoes weren't shining, his belt buckle gleaming, his pants perfectly creased, he'd lose his weekend pass to Brest. Not that it mattered: the residents of Brest all seemed to be retired naval officers with nothing better to do than spy on cadets. Smoke a cigarette or hold a girl's hand in public, and the old salts would be burning up the phone lines to the school officials. Kiem would just as soon stick around the school on weekends, practicing the ten-kilometer run on his own.

Breakfast was delicious: simple French country fare with lots of butter, cheese, eggs, potatoes, beans, and lard. From seven until noon, the naval cadets had their academic classes: military history, international diplomacy, logic, philosophy, and French classical culture. Kiem was surprised to find the curriculum so old-fashioned. Even though an A-bomb had been dropped on Japan nine years before, and Wernher von Braun had invented the V-2 rocket in Germany, his science courses revolved around the winds, tides, stars, and currents. Instead of antisubmarine warfare, the focus of study was famous naval battles of the seventeenth through nineteenth centuries. "Tradition!" chirped the instructors. "Tradition, tradition, tradition! Your fathers, your grandfathers, your great-great-grandfathers learned it in just this way."

It was true that the four hundred French cadets all seemed to be the sons and grandsons and great-grandsons of former graduates. Many of them had "De" in their names, the mark of the French aristocracy. Many came from the leading families of Breton, the wild Celtic region around Brest where men were said to be moody and daring and given to strong drink. Not all of the French cadets were snobs: some were just bullies, and some just conservative and opinionated.

At noon they would break for lunch: more butter, eggs, cheese, potatoes, beans, and lard, with sardines or salty mutton or horse meat and a quarter-liter of red wine to wash it all down. On the first day, Kiem drank all of his wine at lunch, then nearly fell overboard during afternoon rowing practice. After that, he learned to barter his wine ration for extra fruit.

In the afternoons they would row, sail, march, or drill. Kiem dreaded having to march in his thick gabardine uniform, lugging a heavy rifle and a knapsack full of sand, in boots that were several sizes too big for his blistered Vietnamese feet. But crew practice was even worse. The oars were as thick as a man's leg and twice as heavy. When everybody was pulling together, ten men to a boat, the Vietnamese cadets could blend in with the others. But when they passed another boat and had to give a synchronized salute with their oars up in the air, the game was over: a lone oar waving all by itself, like an insect's antenna, was a sure sign of a Vietnamese cadet on the other end.

They were graceful at ballroom dancing, though—where being small was an advantage. Once a week they took waltz and fox-trot lessons from an elderly Frenchwoman who carried a wooden cane, rapping time with it while they pranced around the school gymnasium or bashing them with it if they leaned too close to one of her young female assistants. Duchesses, princesses, and countesses were said to flock to the Naval Academy's annual ball, held in Paris in the spring—and it wouldn't do to stomp on their toes. This part of the cadets' training was every bit as serious as military science.

Dinner brought more hearty peasant fare and more red wine, followed by long hours of studying into the night. At last, lights out and a moth-like sleep in their cocoon-like hammocks.

Sleep was not always restful, however. Sometimes the instructors would rouse the cadets and make them grab their sextants and slide rules, then drag them outside to calculate their position by the stars, to five or six decimal places. "Tradition! That's the way your fathers and grandfathers and great-great-grandfathers learned navigation," the instructors would explain. *What about modern instruments?* Kiem would think but never dare to ask.

Or the upperclassmen might wake them for a "military drill"—a favorite form of hazing, like making them stand on one leg and smoke two cigars at once. One rainy night, Kiem and some classmates were awakened, blindfolded, and herded into a truck. They were driven around for at least an hour, with so many turns they lost track of their direction. Then the upperclassmen barked, "Out! Out!" The truck squealed away, leaving Kiem and his fellows on the roadside. Two hours later, their pajamas soaking wet and their bare feet blistered, they trudged onto the school's parade ground, only to see their hammocks and blankets dangling from trees and bushes in the rain. And it was almost time to begin the morning run.

One afternoon at mail call, Kiem was handed a familiar pink envelope, his first communication from Vietnam. He inhaled its faint perfume, then tore it open.

"Surprise! My family has moved south," Thom had written. Her family was now living in Saigon, and she herself was a boarding student at the Lycée Yersin in Da Lat. Along with Kiem's Lycée Albert Sarraut, it was one of only three French high schools in the country—in fact it was the best of the three. "Da Lat is so beautiful, with mountains and waterfalls and parrots and every color of orchid you can imagine. Newlyweds like to come here for their honeymoons. . . ." Kiem had a sudden vision of Thom being kissed in a romantic setting by the top scholar of the Lycée Yersin. He tossed the letter aside.

Although he was too proud to tell Thom that he hated France and the

Naval Academy, he wrote her a letter whose tone, he hoped, would con-
vey the seriousness of his situation. Back came another silly schoolgirl's
note.

"Guess what? I've been elected 'Miss Yersin'! Now everybody wants to
be my friend. I go to lots of parties and dances. I'm drinking coffee
now—not tea. It's much more sophisticated. Is Brest far from Paris?
Have you seen the Eiffel Tower and the can-can dancers yet?"

"Frivolous girl! Scatterbrain!" he yelled, hurling the pink envelope at
the wall.

He wrote another solemn letter and got another airy one back. "Cheer
up!" Thom wrote. "You sound so glum! You ought to go to Paris for a
weekend. You could buy me some cologne while you're there. It's getting
hard to find here, with the French leaving in droves. Even some of my
teachers have left—not the hard graders, though, damn it!"

Kiem didn't bother to reply. But one weekend, on a whim, he took the
train to Paris and looked up Thom's sister Huong. She took him to the
Louvre and then to an outdoor café, where they sipped green crème de
menthe on ice and talked politics for hours.

City of angels! Everywhere fountains were gurgling, chestnut trees
blooming, lovers embracing. Kiem bought some perfume in a midnight-
blue bottle and mailed it to Thom without a note.

"Come back two weeks from now," urged Huong. "There's going to be
a Vietnamese youth camp in Versailles. You'd enjoy it. You really need to
meet more people."

Kiem had no intention of going, but two weekends later he found himself alone in a roomful of empty hammocks. On an impulse, he bought a
round-trip train ticket to Versailles.

The first night of youth camp was fun. They roasted hot dogs and sang
folk songs from home. It felt good to Kiem to see so many Vietnamese
faces around him; for once, he didn't feel like a freak. But his happiness
faded on the second day as he was watching a documentary film about
the Battle of Dien Bien Phu: "the noble victory of the People's Army
over the capitalist oppressors," the camp counselors called it. They split
up the campers into small groups for "discussions" that turned out to be
boring lectures on Marxist political theory. Kiem's instincts told him to
get out of there. Without saying anything to Huong, he sneaked out
under the tent and escaped through the woods.

Not long after that, he received a letter from his father. It was stained
and faded with age, having been mailed from North Vietnam to South

Vietnam right around the time that Kiem was shipping out to France. Somebody at the base in Nha Trang must have known enough to forward it to Brest. *Like a letter from the grave*, thought Kiem, running a finger over his father's elegant, artistic script—because, now that the country was split, there was no more mail from North Vietnam to France.

He slit it open with his silver knife. "Dear Son," Mr. Sach had written, "I am writing to let you know that we'll be staying here in the North. I'm too old now to endure the hardships of life as a refugee. Here in Hanoi I have my house and my professional reputation. In the South I would have nothing. So I must be practical about this choice and hope that those in power will leave me alone to die in peace. But I have to caution you against trying to come back here any time soon. Your association with France. . . ." The rest of the words were covered by censor's ink—even the line that must have read "Your Father."

At least they could have spared Kiem that closing bond of kinship. He put his head in his hands and sat that way for a long, long time.

Then suddenly someone was saying in a lively voice, "Hey! Don't you know who I am? I'm your new 'father'!" Kiem recognized the rising tones of the North Vietnamese accent and looked up. It was Dinh Tuong, from the class ahead of him.

Midshipman Tuong was short, smart, cocky, quick with a joke, and very popular with both the French and Vietnamese cadets. "Didn't anybody tell you?" Tuong continued; "after the hazing period is over, each firstie gets assigned a 'father' to show him the ropes of the school."

"Nobody told me," Kiem said.

All around the school now, one could pick out the father-son pairs: the father with a gold stripe on his cap and a trim-fitting uniform, and the son with a plain cap and baggy pants, waddling like a duck because of his sore muscles. Kiem could hardly believe his good fortune. In a matter of weeks Tuong taught him how to study more efficiently, how to act at dances and receptions, and even how to use his body's flexibility at sports to make up for the slightness of his build. Tuong even treated him to restaurant dinners in Brest—above and beyond a "father's" duty, which got people's attention. The French cadets began to pass Kiem in the halls with nods of respect. In physical education he moved up from Group D, the lowest, to Group B.

That summer Kiem's class sailed to Norway, Sweden, Finland, and Denmark on board a small fleet of minesweepers. One sun-dazzled afternoon, his ship dropped anchor in a Norwegian fjord, and a fellow sailor handed him a pair of binoculars. There on the side of a snow-capped mountain, frolicking in a meadow full of wildflowers, was a band of nudists!

In Copenhagen a newspaper reporter came on board looking for a story—and Kiem happened to be the first Vietnamese he'd ever met. The next day Kiem's face beamed out from the front page of the paper, over an article on Copenhagen's "adopt a sailor" hospitality program. And a line of young women had formed at the dock, all waving the newspaper and clambering to adopt him! Kiem was supposed to be on watch that weekend, but the captain let him off when the daughter of Copenhagen's mayor showed up to claim him. She was eighteen, pretty, and full of fire. Her name was Annette.

"I think that all of the races should intermarry and have children, until the whole world is all one color. Don't you agree?" she asked.

"Why not?" said Kiem.

The mayor's house was as big as a castle, except that it was made of wood and painted cheerful tulip-colors of red, yellow, and blue. After dinner Annette attacked a piano while her father peppered Kiem with questions. The mayor had never heard of Vietnam—he still called it "Indochina"—but he acted as if it were the most fascinating subject in the world.

Later that night Annette drove Kiem back to the docks in her father's car. When he thanked her again for her family's hospitality, she leaned over and squeezed him so hard that he could feel the pressure of her bosom against his chest. His face felt hot. He had not yet held hands with Thom, his girlfriend of two years—and here he was, locked chest-to-chest with a stranger.

"I'll write," Annette promised. "I'll come visit you in France."

He tried not to look guilty.

The first time Kiem took his turn commanding the ship that summer, he felt seasick and full of fear, but the French cadets snapped to his orders and carried them out *d'un seul élan*. He could see it was not that way with everybody, and he felt good about it. He discovered that there was nothing he loved so much on earth as facing nature alone on the bridge of a ship. Slashing winds, treacherous currents, numbing sleet, colossal waves: *even when nature is trying to destroy you*, he said to himself, *she always elevates your thoughts.* Maybe his choice of a naval career hadn't been so wrongheaded after all.

CHAPTER 7

South Vietnam Gets Status of Republic

New York Times, 27 October 1955

"Who is this Diem of yours anyway?" asked Thom's sister Huong. She and her Marxist boyfriend were scowling at Kiem from across the iron web of a café table.

"What do you mean?" Kiem asked.

"Now that he's the president of South Vietnam, he's the boss of your stupid navy."

"Well, he seems all right to me," said Kiem. "Well-educated. Patriotic."

"He's a kook," said Huong. "No wife, at his age."

"Hey," said Kiem, "I'm not a Catholic either, but you have to respect their beliefs. President Diem studied for the priesthood. They say he took a vow of chastity in the monastery."

"Yeah, so he studied for the priesthood," said the Marxist boyfriend, "and he lived with his mother in Hué for ten years, with no job. So how does that qualify him to lead the South?"

"For a thousand years, our rulers have come from the mandarin scholar class. Now suddenly you want Western-style politicians? At least Ngo Dinh Diem stayed in Vietnam during the French occupation, working secretly for independence. Your Ho Chi Minh left the country when he was twenty-one and didn't come back till he was fifty. And what was he doing all that time? Organizing for the world communist party! Some nationalist! *Opportunist* is more like it," said Kiem.

At that, Huong sat up straight and rattled the ice in her glass.

"At any rate," said the Marxist, "it looks like your man Diem is going to call off the July 1956 elections. He's no dummy. He knows he'd lose in a popular vote. And the Americans aren't going to push him. He lived over there for awhile and has powerful friends in their Congress—Catholics, like him."

Kiem fell silent. The Marxist was right. Kiem's own father had warned that Vietnamese society could not change from "vertical" to "horizontal" overnight. But change had come despite Kiem's father's warnings, despite his country's lack of preparation for it. And now what were they supposed to do? If an election were held tomorrow, most people would vote the way their local strongmen ordered them to. All of the North's votes would go to Ho Chi Minh, and enough of the South's—coerced by threats and propaganda—to swing the election to him. That wasn't the way democracy was supposed to work.

"Education has to come before self-governance," Mr. Sach had insisted. "Civic responsibility is not an instinct. It has to be taught." But how? That would take years, and they didn't have years—only months.

"Anyhow," said Huong, sucking up the last of her Coca-Cola through a straw, "*nobody* takes that Diem of yours seriously, and you know it."

Now that he was a second-year midshipman, Kiem was able to spend most of his free weekends in Paris, arguing politics with Huong and her friends. School had become a breeze: the hazing was over, his courses were easier, and his pay had tripled. He felt sorry for the four Vietnamese in his class who had flunked out or been sent home with tuberculosis before they could reap the rewards from their year of suffering. Why, the French cadets even called them *Vietnamiens* now, with the proper suffix for a civilized people—*Parisiens, Alsaciens, Algeriens*—and not *Annamites*, a slur implying that they were less than human.

If only Thom weren't being quite so distant. He had mailed her a few terse postcards but had heard nothing back. Meanwhile, Annette was flooding him with passionate letters vowing to marry him, bear his children, and follow him back to Vietnam. The mayor had written to Kiem as well, saying that he would welcome him as a son into his family.

And if only the rumors from home weren't quite so unsettling. Over tables littered with cups and saucers and crumpled packs of Gauloises, the Vietnamese expatriates of Paris were whispering that Ho Chi Minh *se conduit comme un fou.* He was executing thousands of Northerners with ties to the old French regime: *tens* of thousands, said some. Was Kiem's father among them, for the crime of planning bridges? His mother, for the crime of owning land?

Meanwhile, down South, Diem was cozying up to the Americans and getting rid of the last traces of French influence. He had to, Kiem knew, in order to demonstrate a break with the colonial past. For the Vietnamese Navy, that meant replacing the last few Frenchmen still in command positions and taking over control of the Naval Training Center in Nha Trang. But Kiem wished Diem hadn't ordered the burning of the navy's French-style insignia. The Paris newspapers had made the situation worse by publishing a front-page photograph of Vietnamese officers tossing their hats into a bonfire.

The school officials and the French cadets had been too polite to mention the photograph, but some of the petty officers had made nasty remarks just loud enough for Kiem and the other Vietnamese to hear. A few months later the Vietnamese cadets had received their new American-style insignia in the mail from Saigon.

As the end of his second year of course work approached, Kiem could hardly contain his excitement about the final phase of his training: the practical year at sea. "I'm counting the days till the *Jeanne d'Arc* arrives in Copenhagen," wrote Annette. "By the way, it's all right with Father if the children are raised Buddhists." From Thom, there was nothing. *To hell with her!* thought Kiem. *Let her kiss those brainy Lycée Yersin boys! What do I care?*

But the dream year was not to be. Kiem and his seven remaining Vietnamese classmates were summoned into the office of the French Naval Academy's commandant. "I'm so sorry, so very, very sorry," began the commandant, leaning across his desk to face them. Because of the political situation, he explained, they were being expelled and flown home to Saigon. It was no reflection on their conduct: they had performed admirably. In fact, if they would serve for a year in the South Vietnamese Navy, the French Naval Academy would count it as fulfillment of their practical year and would mail them their diplomas—"because the navy is really one big international family, even though our political leaders sometimes have their differences." The commandant went on: "You have a *young* navy, a young but *growing* navy. Her ships may seem small to you after ours, but you've been well prepared for anything."

Expelled to the South? Impossible. Kiem's mother, father, brothers, and sisters were still in Hanoi. But the French-trained, French-equipped navy belonged to the South, and his fate was with the navy now. What had he been thinking when he sailed to Brest? That the two halves of his country would somehow glue themselves together like the halves of a mended plate while he was gone? No, the truth was that he hadn't been thinking at all. And now he was in a bind. He wished he could talk to

Tuong, a fellow Northerner, about it. But Tuong was off on his own practical year at sea, having a ball and not yet informed about the news.

I could flee to Denmark, thought Kiem, trudging back to his sleeping quarters. *I could marry Annette and get citizenship there. Surely the mayor would help me find a job.* He tried to picture himself in front of the tulip mansion with a pretty European wife and a row of sallow-skinned children. But slowly his father's words began to seep into his consciousness: "A man of honor will always uphold his duty to his country, his community, and his family. He will always put himself last."

Kiem let out a sigh so great that it extinguished the spark of life in each of his imaginary children, like a row of candles being blown out. "All right," he told his father, "I'll honor my commitment to the navy. I won't run."

He stuffed a few possessions into a duffel bag. One by one, his French friends came to pay their respects. Some of them kissed him on both cheeks. Some just crossed their arms in front of their chests and stared at the floor. "Shit, shit, shit," they said, or "Rotten luck, pal."

The school had made arrangements to put them on a military flight. Sitting on an airport bench with his duffel bag propped against one knee, Kiem had just enough time to compose a note to Annette: "I'm sorry to have to tell you that I won't be visiting Copenhagen this summer as we had planned. I have had to return home quite suddenly. Although you have offered to follow me there, my conscience won't let me accept." *For more reasons than one,* thought Kiem, pausing with his pen over the page. He resumed writing: "Life in Vietnam would be tough for you. I would be away at sea much of the time, and you would miss your family and your piano. You deserve to marry a fine Danish gentleman like your father. I will always remember you with affection. . . ." He gave it to one of the guards who'd accompanied them there to post.

Kiem's plane had to make a refueling stop in Karachi, where they learned they'd be grounded till the following day. They decided to get off and check into a hotel for the night. It had been years since Kiem had felt the Oriental heat on his skin, in his lungs. He could hardly sleep: he felt as if it were strangling him. Finally he threw off his mosquito netting, yanked a cord to turn on the light, and sat with his legs dangling over the side of the bed. He watched as a gecko darted across the ceiling, in and out of the shadows cast by the flickering, generator-powered light fixture. It was so primitive. So much like home.

Night had fallen again when they arrived at sleepy Tan Son Nhut airport. Kiem was expecting some sort of receiving party from the navy, but the only persons waiting there to greet them were the Southern students' family members. "Come home with us!" they urged Kiem and the other Northerners, and all but Kiem accepted. *There must have been some delay,* he was thinking. *The naval party would be arriving any minute, and it wouldn't be polite to have everyone gone.* One, two, three hours crept by. Kiem stood there like a toy-shop soldier, clutching the hilt of his sword.

At last he spied a familiar figure bearing down on him. "Mr. Kiem!" she cried. "It's me, Miss Ly, your sister Hanh's friend! I work for the army now, as a stenographer. I read your name in the wire-service report. I knew it was you!"

Then the news had been official—the navy had known they were coming was all Kiem could think. Grateful for the chance to save face, he followed Miss Ly home. She lived with her parents in a tiny apartment with buckets placed around to catch the rain from the leaking roof. There wasn't any mosquito netting, either; he scratched at his bites all night until they bled. But he was grateful for the human companionship.

The next morning he and his classmates reported to Saigon Naval Headquarters. You'd have thought they were trying to rob the place, judging by the frosty reception they received. It didn't take long for them to figure out what was going on. Now that relations between France and South Vietnam had soured, their French connection was clinging to them like a bad smell.

Lt. Comdr. Le Quang My, naval deputy to the chief of staff, armed forces, and commander in chief of the Vietnamese Navy, strode into the room where the expelled midshipmen were waiting. They saluted. He looked them over for thirty or forty seconds, then pointed the stem of his pipe at Kiem. "Vous," he said.

Me, what? thought Kiem. But the top officer was now looking at his flashy wristwatch and hurrying out the door.

Ensign Kiem had just been officially assigned as gunnery officer on board the navy's flagship: the *Van Kiep* (HQ-02)—the ex–French *Intrepide* of Indochinese service. A World War II–era "submarine chaser," the gracefully aging craft still carried an impressive array of weapons, including one 3-inch and one 40-mm gun and four 20-mm guns. Unofficially, however, HQ-02's gunnery officer seemed to be assigned as Lieutenant Commander My's lackey. From what he could gather, his job responsibilities were to (1) stand up tall, (2) appear to be well-bred, (3) speak French to Lieutenant Commander My, and (4) speak English to visiting Americans. He felt as if he had wandered into the cast of a stage play about the navy, without having read the script beforehand. Lieutenant Commander My didn't seem to know what was going on, either, but he was very good at bluffing.

Night after night Kiem lay awake in his bunk in bachelor's quarters, wondering *Who am I? What am I doing here? What ties me to these people? Why can't I contact my family? North or South—what damn difference does it make?* He wanted to talk to his father. He wanted to know if his mother had moved back to Phu Tai, if Frenchy and Trung were growing up all right, if Hanh had married the ex-landlord's son, and if Nam and Lam had come home after the war. He realized that he'd either have to put all this out of his mind or go crazy. Nothing was real anymore; nothing was what it seemed. His late-night thoughts began to drift to the pistol lying on the bedside table in a jangle of keys and coins.

He was grateful when a real, live combat mission cropped up as a distraction. The Binh Xuyen, an organized crime ring with ties to the French, had been driven out of Saigon by Diem's armed forces the previous year. The navy had been instrumental in destroying their leadership in the Battle of Rung Sat. But there were still pockets of resistance hiding out in the giant mangrove swamp that sprawled between Saigon and the South China Sea. The battle plan called for a frontal attack on a broad access beach as a diversion while four assault units modeled on the famous French naval *dinassauts* of the Indochinese War pushed deep inside the swamp, circling the area and blocking all escape routes. Fifty patrol gunboats, four command monitors, and four platoons of marines would be involved in the operation.

HQ-02 led the task force with Lieutenant Commander My and his assistant, Maj. Hung Le of the Vietnamese Marines, on the open bridge one foggy morning. The men aboard ship were tingling with excitement—and Ensign Kiem was no exception. As the force moved into position, he took advantage of the last few minutes to give instructions to his gun turret crews. He had asked Lieutenant Commander My to let him test the ship's entire firepower. It was going to be a full-scale rust-out exercise for the new navy.

The first blasts of the 3-inch gun seemed to wake up all of nature. In all directions birds were wheeling and screeching as the deafening roar subsided and a string of echoes rippled the foggy morning air.

"Five hundred meters short of target. Two hundred meters to the left," came a report from a forward monitor, crackling eerily over the PRC-10.

The correction was quickly made. "Right on target!" announced the monitor.

"Très bien," said Lieutenant Commander My, taking the pipe out of his mouth. "Feu à volonté."

Salvo after salvo, the 3-inch gun roared, punctuated by the clinking sound of spent shells hitting the deck. One of Kiem's earplugs fell out, but he barely noticed. The smell of gunpowder in his nostrils was like blood to a hunting dog.

As HQ-02 neared the beach, Kiem asked permission to have her turned around so that he could fire her 40-mm turret. The rapid cadence of the antiaircraft gun added a sense of urgency to the situation. Contact-explosion ammunition tore into mangroves like giant clippers, sending trunks, branches, and sparks sky-high as the crew directed the gun in a side-to-side sweeping movement along the beach. Soon they were close enough for the 20-mm antiaircraft cannon, the 12.7-mm machine gun, and even the 7.2-mm submachine gun on the bridge to join in the final cacophony—so loud that, when the time came, Lieutenant Commander My had to yell his cease-fire order several times before they all stopped shooting.

Now Kiem was ordered to the bridge to serve as communications officer, not because they didn't have one but because Lieutenant Commander My wanted his rapid French orders translated into Vietnamese. It might have been the way the commander had learned things from his own French instructors, or he might have just been trying to impress Major Hung. Kiem hoped it was the former.

"Assault units 1, 2, 3, 4. Report position and progress. Over."

"Unit 1 reports. In position. Prepare to insert troops. Over."

"Unit 2 in position. LCM ramp door not operated. Landing delayed. Over."

"Unit 3 is about to land troops. Over."

"Unit 4 is saturating the landing beach. Over."

"Très bien," said Lieutenant Commander My. "Ensign Kiem, tell Unit 2 I don't want any delay. Beach the LCM and let her men jump overboard. Tell them to watch out for crocodiles, though."

All of a sudden the PRC-10 crackled excitedly: "Unit 2 reports landing party backing out."

"Pourquoi? Nom de Dieu!" fumed My.

"Bees! Swarms of bees are attacking our men! Two marines need medevac. Request permission to shift landing five hundred meters downstream. Over."

"Permission granted. Nom de Dieu! Weren't those idiots prepared for Rung Sat: bees, crocodiles, sticky mud? Major Hung," said My, turning to the marine leader, "your men need better training to operate with the navy."

"Aye, aye, sir," said Hung in a low voice.

Word had spread quickly up and down the ship about the marines' being routed by bees and not the Binh Xuyen, and the sailors were all enjoying the joke. But when the first casualties were carried on board, nobody thought it was funny anymore. The men's faces were puffed up like balloons, so that Major Hung couldn't even tell who they were, and one of them was having a seizure. They were quickly evacuated to Vung Tau for medical attention.

Then came the good news: a cache of several hundred gasoline drums had been discovered, followed by a second cache of hundred-piastre bills stuffed into gunnysacks. The bills were so new they must have come straight from the printing presses of the National Bank.

"Unit 3 reports. A sampan with two men carrying a white flag is approaching us. Over."

"Très bien. Treat them well. Interrogate them for the search operation; then send them over here."

As it turned out, those two men and four others hiding in a water-filled hole belonged to a logistic group of the Binh Xuyen that had been separated from the main force since the defeat the previous year. They were the last of the gang, and they were fed up with running and hiding from the navy.

Lieutenant Commander My ordered champagne for dinner that night in the officers' mess and double rations for the ship's crew. He was in such a good mood that Kiem dared to ask him the question that had been bothering him all day: "Sir, what would have happened if the Binh Xuyen had poured their gasoline on the river and ignited it?"

My put down his fork for a minute and looked attentively at his young gunnery officer. "Merde alors! They would have burned us alive, that's what, with a strong ebb tide and a south wind like today. Too bad for them they didn't draft you instead of that old fool Ho Huu Tuong!" They all knew the name of the Binh Xuyen's famous advisor.

The next day HQ-02 and the task force docked with great fanfare at the Admiral's Pier in front of Saigon Naval Headquarters. Government and military officials, civilians, students, news reporters, and the Navy Band were all there to greet them. After the obligatory press conference in the officers' mess, Kiem stood at the ship's rail watching sailors in white pour down the street for some well-deserved time off, and he felt a new and stirring sense of kinship with them.

But things were bound to quiet down again, and soon the empty feeling returned. One day while on a routine training exercise with another ship, Kiem ran into his former "father" from the French Naval Academy. He and Lieutenant Tuong greeted each other warmly. "I need to talk to you," the older man whispered.

"Come have dinner with me on my ship, then," said Kiem.

"Privately," hissed Tuong. "Tonight, on the beach at Con Son Island. Eight o'clock sharp. Don't mention it to anyone else."

So that's what Kiem was doing shivering on the cold, wet sand of Con Son Island in the dark, slapping sand fleas from his ankles. The two of them swapped news of their former classmates: the Southerners were doing so-so; the Northerners going nowhere.

"Friend," said Tuong, "you know I trust you more than anyone else down here." Then he confessed that he and another classmate were making plans to sneak back to the North. "It's a good plan. I don't see how it can fail," he said. "I'm asking you to join us."

Kiem sat stunned. "No," he said finally. "There's no going back for me."

Tuong tried to argue with him. "Are you satisfied with your present situation?"

"No," Kiem had to tell him.

"What's your future here in the South?"

"Not much," Kiem answered honestly.

"You see—I'm thinking about getting married to a girl down here," Kiem said suddenly. The news surprised him even more than it did Tuong.

"Married!" said his friend. "Married! Well, that's different. Congratulations! Imagine, a 'son' getting married before his 'father'! In the army, maybe—but not the navy!" The two of them laughed over that. They talked a little while longer, and Kiem wished him luck. Then they returned to their separate ships.

Kiem was able to confirm that Tuong and an accomplice made it back safely to the North, because he heard their voices over Radio Hanoi for a few months afterward. Then the broadcasts stopped. Kiem feared that they might have outlived their usefulness to Ho Chi Minh. After all, who could trust a defector? If he'd betray his own side, why not yours?

After that, it was time to find Thom. He made a few inquiries and tracked the family down to a shabby rental house grown over with moss stains and banana plants. He stared at it for a long time, surprised to see that the contracting business must have been slow. Finally he decided to wait until the next long holiday weekend, when Thom would be home from school.

One month later he knocked on the front door. Mrs. Le seemed delighted to see him, inviting him in and bringing out a dish of candied lotus seed. Kiem told her about visiting Huong in Paris, leaving out the details of the Marxist youth camp and Huong's revolutionary boyfriend. "I miss my little girl so much," she said. "I beg her to come home, but she won't hear of it. But you must miss your own family," she said, shooting him a pitying look. Not knowing what to say, Kiem sat there twirling his officer's hat in his hands.

"I have something to show you," she announced. She disappeared into a back room and came out holding a black-and-white photograph, which she placed in his hands. It was a snapshot of two tiny, middle-aged Vietnamese women standing side by side. They might have been sisters, except that one had had her teeth dyed black in countryside fashion, while the other was wearing a pearl necklace. They were smiling at the camera as if enjoying a good joke together.

"How can this be?" he asked. "You've never met my mother. Is it some sort of trick?"

"Your mother is a resourceful woman," said Mrs. Le. "One day she took the train to Haiphong and knocked on my door. Oh, we had a good laugh together, once we had introduced ourselves! She's a fine woman, your mother. Keep it. It's yours," she said of the photograph. Kiem slipped it into the pocket where he kept the silver knife.

They heard a door slam and the *thunk* of books being dumped on a table. Thom stuck her head into the sitting room, saw Kiem, and froze.

"I'm glad to see you are well," she said coldly.

"And I to see you," he said. He wished she weren't looking quite so beautiful. It made him feel as dumb as a sheep in her presence. The hair around her face was all wavy, and her mouth was a perfect red flower.

"I'll get us some tea," said Mrs. Le. "Oh!" she exclaimed. "We're all out of tea. I'll have to go to the market."

"We had plenty of tea this morning," said Thom.

"No, no," said Mrs. Le, "we drank it all up."

"I'll go, Mother," said Thom.

"No, dear. I'll have to go myself; those merchants would overcharge a young girl like you," she said, backing out the door.

Suddenly they were alone, except for Mrs. Le's mother, lying in her sickbed in another part of the house. Thom folded her arms and scowled at Kiem. "So," she said, "how's your Danish sweetheart?"

"Who told you about her?" he asked.

"Huong. Who else?"

"Huong? I never said a *word* about Annette to Huong."

"You didn't have to. Your classmates read her idiotic letters with lipstick kisses on them. They told Huong everything."

"There was nothing to tell," he said. "We met once in Copenhagen, and then she wrote to me. She chased me, to tell you the truth."

"Well," she said, "I suppose that Huong has told you about the pharmacist."

"What pharmacist?" Kiem asked.

"The one who sent me the candy you're eating," she said.

He spat it out.

"Are you jealous?" she asked.

"Jealous? Of course I'm not jealous!"

"Then why are you so red in the face?" she asked.

"Because . . . because I'm disappointed in you, that's why," he said. "A pharmacist! Science is for sissies. A real man studies *math*, not science."

"Pharmacists make a lot of money," she said.

"Money?" he asked. "Is that what you care about now, *Miss Yersin?* What about integrity?"

"Why shouldn't I enjoy life, now that the war is over?" she asked. "I'm only eighteen—not old and serious like you. Other men send me flowers and candy. They write poems about me. What do I get from you? Nothing but postcards! Heartaches! Tears!"

"Here, then," he said. "Take it back." He fished in his pocket for the silver forget-me-not knife. "Give it to your sissy pharmacist."

He thought he saw her face soften for an instant. "Do you still carry it with you, then?" she asked.

"Why not? It's useful. A sailor needs a knife to cut ropes and things," he said.

"I see," she said coldly.

"I guess I'll be going, then," he said. He turned and stalked out of the room so fast that he nearly collided with Mrs. Le, who was on her way in with a tea tray.

"Did you have a nice visit?" she asked.

"Mmf," he said.

"You drive her crazy, you know," Mrs. Le whispered. "The other boys chase her, but you're aloof. She has to chase you."

He made another grunting noise, which he hoped would pass for human speech.

"Come back soon," said Mrs. Le. "Your mother would be so happy! She gave her blessing to the match, you know."

Later, when his temper had cooled, he reasoned, *Who am I to dishonor my mother by ignoring her wishes for my future?* Perhaps, for his mother's sake, he would go back one more time, in his white dress uniform, with his harmonica in his pocket—but not with flowers! *No, flowers would be a definite loss of face.*

So Kiem started "courting" Thom again. He learned that her new life in the South had not been easy. Her family had lived in a resettlement camp; then, released at last, they'd run through all of their money. A contractor has to know people in order to get jobs, but here in the South, Mrs. Le and her husband knew nobody. Blaming each other for their unhappiness, they had quarreled and separated. Thom had been homesick. She had missed her old school, her old friends, her boyfriend, her favorite sister away in Paris.

Of course she had told Kiem none of this in her letters. If there was anyone on earth as proud and stubborn as himself, he slowly realized, it was Le Thi Thom. They were a perfect match.

CHAPTER 8

Diem Lauds U.S. Aid in Talk to Congress

New York Times, 10 May 1957

Like all actors and gamblers, Le Quang My had a dream: that
one day the navy would be as rich and powerful as the army—
or at least the air force. The conditions seemed right. Vietnam
was a long and narrow country, edged by seacoast all the way.
And with bad roads or no roads, jungly or swampy terrain, and
monsoon-season flooding, the only reliable way to get around
inside the country was by boat—not only on the main rivers
but on the tens of thousands of small canals.

In those days, President Diem was always traveling around
the South—checking up on local officials or trying to drum up
popular support for the future election. It didn't take much for
My to figure out that whichever branch of the military had the
president's body would also have his pockets and his ear.
Besides the fact that the army had few roads to roll on and the
air force had few places to land, President Diem was known to
be claustrophobic inside cars and terrified of flying. So, flush
with his victory over the Binh Xuyen and newly promoted to
the rank of captain, My arranged to have HQ-02 refurbished
into a VIP ship for Diem and his entourage. He appointed himself its captain and made Ensign Kiem its navigation officer.

Kiem would never forget the first time President Diem came
on board—not because Diem was so special but because he was
so shockingly ordinary. A brass band was tooting as the president approached the gangway. Kiem and the other junior officers were scurrying about in their white dress uniforms. Flags
were waving, and the ship was bristling with guns. Along came
a short, plump man stuffed into a white Western suit. He was

moving in twitchy bursts of energy, like a flea. And he was obviously frightened out of his wits to be walking a few feet of gangway above the choppy Mekong River.

As soon as he had crossed to safety, he started fumbling in his pocket for a cigarette. Captain My and an army general both reached to light it at the same time. Kiem noticed that they were using the pronoun *con* with Diem—the form of "I" or "me" used only in conversation with one's father. It was disgusting to Kiem: *toi* was the correct term, not *con*. A man has only one father.

That night the claustrophobic Diem came out on the bridge to get some fresh air, and Captain My played the opportunity for all it was worth. "Ensign Kiem, shoot me that star," he said in French, pointing to Venus.

"Excuse me, sir? Shoot that star, sir?" Kiem wasn't sure he had heard correctly. They used the sextant when they were out in the middle of the ocean. At the moment they were midway between the banks of the Mekong River, cruising slowly downstream. He could have pinpointed their position by simply looking at the riverbank.

"Mais oui," said Captain My. "Shoot me that star and fix me the position of our ship."

"Aye, aye, sir," said Kiem. He seized the sextant and began measuring the height and azimuth of the planets. "Position, sir," he said, and gave the readout.

"How accurate is that, Ensign?" Captain My shot back.

"To within meters, sir," said Kiem. He was telling the truth.

The president smiled approvingly and tossed a cigarette over the rail. Sadly it was neither the last nor the worst time Kiem would see Diem duped by those around him.

Toward the end of 1957, Kiem's second year in the South, Captain My was sent to the United States for training. Kiem was promoted to lieutenant junior grade and given command of HQ-537, an LCU with a crew of about a dozen. The following year he was reassigned as commanding officer of HQ-331, one of five LSILs transferred from the United States through France in 1956. Forty-eight meters long, with a speed of 14.4 knots, and built to carry two hundred infantry, the landing ship packed one 3-inch, one 40-mm, and two 20-mm guns, plus machine guns and mortars. Five officers besides Kiem and forty-nine enlisted men kept her guns oiled and her diesel engines running. Along with the new commission, Kiem was given orders to renovate HQ-331 for the president. He had the mess enlarged to seat Diem's entourage, and—on a hunch—an easy chair mounted on a platform installed on the bridge so that Diem could sit and talk to Kiem while he was working.

Half the night, every night, the president sat in that chair firing technical questions at Kiem. How did the depth finder work? How fast was the current? How much power did the generator put out? Diem was quick to grasp even the most complex technical theories, but he never let fresh information interfere with his opinions. As soon as he encountered something new, he would make up his mind about it—and that was that. He stubbed out one cigarette after another as he spoke, already itching to light the next before he'd smoked a centimeter of the first.

He spoke abruptly, and Kiem did not always understand his meaning. Sometimes Kiem would rephrase the question, just to make sure. The president's hangers-on were not always so polite. Kiem had seen them spill out of meetings and ask each other what the hell the boss had meant while Diem was still within earshot. When he was angry with them, Diem would turn red and blurt out two or three words. Then he'd go hide in his cabin, ashamed.

Was Diem beginning to trust him? Kiem couldn't be sure, but it seemed so. One day they sailed past a pretty village full of chubby children waving from well-tended gardens. "What a *charming* village!" said Diem. "What province does it belong to?"

He had posed the question to Kiem, but the province chief on the other side of him cut in: "It's *my* village," he said, using the cloying pronoun *con*.

Diem turned squarely to Kiem: "Is that so, Captain?" he asked. Kiem told him the name of the village and explained that it belonged to a province whose border they'd crossed half an hour before.

"So!" said Diem, repeating its name. "And you, Colonel—answer me only when you know!"

Another time, Kiem had to dock the ship in front of the Cao Lanh province government building at low tide. The wooden pier was ridiculously small, and the ebb-tide current strong. Knowing Diem's fear of the gangway, Kiem explained that it might be rough maneuvering alongside the pier. He drew a sketch of the current, the ship, and the dock to illustrate.

Their landing efforts failed, just as Kiem had predicted. As the long gangway was being rolled out, one of the accompanying generals remarked that the landing had not been very professional. "What do you know about technical matters, General?" Diem snapped. He plucked the officer's pen out of his pocket and drew him a sketch of the current, the ship, and the dock.

Of all the times Kiem saw the president fooled by his aides, one stood out above the others. The presidential ship had docked at a remote village, and Diem—who usually hated making conversation—had been seized by the idea that this would be the perfect place to grow mangoes. Taking the province chief aside, Diem lectured him for an hour about the fine points of mango farming. The province chief was no dummy. He said he'd put in a crop at once, making sure that the soil's pH and nitrate levels were exactly as Diem had specified.

A year or so later, when HQ-331 happened to bring them close to the same village, Diem asked Kiem how the new mango crop was doing. Kiem radioed ahead to the province chief to let him know that the president was coming, and the response on the other end was sheer terror. Of course, there were no mangoes.

But when they docked by the side of the village, they could see rows and rows of mango trees studded with ripening yellow-red fruit. A strong piney scent filled Kiem's nostrils, and all at once he understood its source: the mango trees had been cut down from somewhere else and stuck in freshly dug holes in the ground. Diem got off the ship and paraded up and down the too-neat rows, clutching a mango in one hand and a cigarette in the other. It was sickening to watch, and there was no way for Kiem to tell the president the truth without causing him to lose face.

Nobody could have fooled Madame Nhu like that. The wife of Diem's brother Ngo Dinh Nhu, she was by far the smartest person in Diem's entourage. In fact she had graduated from the Lycée Albert Sarraut seven or eight years ahead of Kiem. But she came from a high-ranking mandarin family, used to giving orders and ignoring the consequences, and she was selfish and spoiled.

Unfortunately for Kiem, Madame Nhu was the bachelor president's hostess for parties on the VIP ship. Kiem would never forget the first time *she'd* come on board, either. Late one afternoon she'd rung Captain My to book HQ-02 for a sunset pleasure cruise, leaving only two or three hours for Kiem and the rest of the crew to buy flowers, hire musicians, shop for food, and prepare a banquet. Somehow, by five o'clock everything had been in place: champagne chilling, candles flickering. But there was no sign of the Dragon Lady. Six o'clock came and went, then seven, eight, nine, and ten. Ice cubes melted. Candles guttered. Dinner scorched.

It was almost eleven o'clock when she came wobbling up the ramp in high-heeled shoes, followed by half a dozen drunken foreign "dignitaries." Captain My and Kiem were waiting at the top to greet her, prepared to be civil if it killed them. Stepping onto the deck, Madame Nhu paused and looked dramatically around her. Then she raised a long, crimson fingernail and shook it in Captain My's face. "Such a *small* boat," she hissed. "Turn up the lights! It's dark as a cave in here."

Not many famous beauties over the age of thirty would have insisted on having every light on the ship blazing during party cruises—but Madame Nhu was one-of-a-kind. When Kiem took command of HQ-331, the lights became one of his biggest headaches because visibility would drop to zero and the Saigon River was always heavily trafficked at night.

One such night, as Kiem was craning forward in his bridge seat with his headset draped around his shoulders, calling back and forth to the signalman he'd posted on the bow as a lookout, he heard the crackle of the ship's intercom: "Bridge, this is the executive officer. Madame Nhu requests the captain to come down and join her in a toast."

Kiem switched his mike to individual contact, making sure that only his XO could hear what he had to say: "XO, screw her toast. You go stand in for me. Tell her I can't get away from the conning station right now."

"Aye, aye, sir," said the XO, acknowledging the order with a barely suppressed giggle.

"Lookout to bridge!" That was his signalman, Chief Ban: "We have a cluster of sampans straight ahead about a hundred fifty meters."

"Stop both engines. Starboard backward one." Kiem paused for a few seconds. "Lookout, are we cleared?"

"Not quite, sir. Another sampan is coming from port side, low to the water." *Carrying a full load of contraband, no doubt,* thought Kiem: black-market cigarettes or liquor.

"Recommend we stay put," continued the lookout, "or we could swamp it."

Just then, Kiem heard a commotion on the stairway leading to the bridge: shrieks of laughter and the high-pitched voice of Madame Nhu, getting louder and louder. And he'd thought he was safe from her up here.

"Good evening, Madame Advisor," he said as she planted herself a few feet away from him. "I hope you and your guests are enjoying the pleasure cruise."

"Pleasure cruise?" she asked. *"Pleasure cruise,* Captain?" Her perfume filled his lungs like gasoline fumes. "I beg your pardon, Captain, but this is a high-level national affair. We're about to drink a toast to the Colombo Plan, and I've asked you to come down and join us."

"I'm sorry, Madame Advisor, but there are too many small sampans out on the river tonight. I'd like to join you in your toast, but I can't leave the bridge and risk a collision—particularly with so many VIPs on board."

"What sampans? Where are they? I don't see any," she barked.

"That's just the problem, Madame. With so many lights on, I'm having a hard time seeing them myself."

"Then why don't you post a man on the—what do you call it?" she asked.

"Bow," said Kiem. "That's just what we're doing, Madame. If—"

"Look out!" yelled Chief Ban.

"Stop the engines! Right full rudder! Both engines backward, full!" Kiem shouted. The ship lurched to the right, throwing everybody off balance. With a loud shriek, the First Lady grabbed hold of Kiem's arm. Her fingernails hurt him like cat claws. In the sudden hush that followed, he could hear the sampan's occupants cursing.

"Catch them!" she shrieked. "Throw them in jail, Captain! How dare they cut off the president's ship like that!"

"By the time I turned this ship around, Madame, they'd be hiding in one of a thousand canals," said Kiem.

"Then next time, just run right over them!"

"Yes, Madame," he said. He thought he could hear coughing and titters coming from the direction of Chief Ban.

She turned to her companion and began to speak in fluent English: "Let's get out of this boring hole. Let's go down where the *lights* are." Then she swept off, leaving behind traces of her perfume and faint smiles of complicity on the faces of Kiem's sailors.

When not being used by the president, HQ-331 was usually escorting a "pacification" mission somewhere in the Mekong Delta. The purpose of those missions was to publicize government programs in remote areas—and, of course, to boost public support for Diem's presidency. Kiem's ship would carry the drama troupe and public information specialists; the second ship would be a "floating hospital," with doctors, dentists, and nurses. The two ships would beach in front of the village pagoda or marketplace, then announce their arrival over one ship's public-address system. Within minutes, villagers would begin lining up for free medical attention. And they would wait all day, if necessary, to get their wounds dressed, their rashes salved, their bones splinted, their stomachaches soothed with medicine wrapped up to take home in unreadable government leaflets, their children's rotten teeth pulled. Sometimes, when the sun had gone down, Kiem would have to tell those still waiting in line to come back the next day.

After dark, the members of the entertainment team would rig their stage lights to the generator of Kiem's ship. First a man in a Ho Chi Minh mask and long, bushy foxtail would come out on stage. That would get a big laugh. The Ho-fox would chase imaginary chickens around while trying to hide his foxtail between his legs. When everyone had laughed themselves silly, the Ho-fox would exit with a chicken tucked under each arm.

The next skit would be more serious: a bunch of communists coming into a village, telling the people lies, forcing the children into their ranks, and shooting the old people. Then the army would burst in to battle the communists and save the villagers, with lots of sword fighting and firecracker sound effects to make the children in the audience happy.

Then came the best part, the *cai luong* singers. The first two lines of each lyric would be sung in a flat tone, but on the third, the punch line, the singer would have to descend in tone. When the lyric itself contained a pun about falling or dropping, the audience would go wild: "My darling, since you left me, my life is so unhappy; I'm going to have to *flatten* the man whose fault it was. . . ."

When the last musical notes had died away and the grunting of bullfrogs could be heard once again, and the audience members would be sitting there spellbound by the sweet-sour happy-sadness of their lives, the members of the educational team would take the stage. They would lecture about programs like "The Farmer Plows His Own Rice Field," where every family could get a free plot of land; or "Countryside Banking," where they could borrow money to buy seed, fertilizer, and tools—even heavy machinery.

Finding himself with time on his hands when his ship was docked, Kiem would stroll around and mingle with the villagers. Babies would point to his hat and giggle. Old men would call to him to sit beneath a shade tree and drink coconut juice with them. And everyone, hearing his curious Northern accent, would make him repeat whole sentences while they called to their friends to come hear the funny high-pitched tones.

In the North, where the soil was poor and survival was a constant struggle, people believed that Southerners were greedy and lazy; but really, Kiem discovered, they were just fun-loving and hospitable. Even in the poorer parts of the delta they always tried to give half of their mango or banana crop to the ships. Once Kiem docked next to a wedding party, and the bride and groom's families invited the whole crew to the pig roast.

"Tell me, Captain," a village elder asked him once, "why does this government want to give us something for nothing? A man's relative or neighbor might give him a gift, but never the *government!*"

"Not the old government," said Kiem, "but this is a new kind of government." He tried to explain as best he could. Then he posed his own question to the old man: "Why do you trust *me*, a stranger in your village, but not your own government?"

"Because you are the captain of a big ship that I can see with my own eyes!" said the old man, as if the answer should have been obvious. "The government is far away in Saigon. I've never seen it."

If that's what a village wise man was thinking, what were the less-educated people thinking? At times like that, Kiem's hopes for the new republic would waver. Most of the time, though, he felt proud to be associated with Diem's programs. He was sure he'd made the right decision by staying in the South.

It was the last week of February 1958, and Kiem's ship was a day's journey from Saigon, when one of his men brought him an urgent telegraph message: GRANDMOTHER VERY ILL STOP PLEASE COME HOME AT ONCE STOP SINCERELY MRS. LE.

There was no mistaking the real intent of Thom's mother's message: "If you want to marry my daughter any earlier than three years from now, you have exactly twenty-four hours in which to act." When a close relative such as a parent or grandparent died in a Vietnamese family, it meant three years of mourning for the rest of the family. Weddings and other celebrations were absolutely forbidden. But three years was a long time for a healthy young couple to wait, so Vietnamese society had come up with a face-saving way out. The family could pretend that the dead one was just sick while they arranged a "rushy-rushy" wedding ceremony.

So Kiem had a big decision to make—but really it was no decision at all. There were plenty of sensible reasons for marrying Thom, aside from the fact that he was crazy about her. She was his only human tie to the South, and marriage would link him to a family, a community, and a country once again. It would also show the navy he was serious about his commitment.

But what about Thom? he worried as a motor launch ferried him to shore. Would she be willing to drop out of school to get married? That was the rule at the lycées because married students had secrets that the school officials didn't want them passing on. And suppose she *were* willing to get married: would she be willing to marry *him?* Mrs. Le was modern enough to let her daughter choose for herself, and Thom had many followers. She might pick the pharmacist or somebody else with a more secure future.

Trusting that Mrs. Le knew her daughter's mind better than he did, Kiem booked a commercial flight to Saigon, then arranged to borrow a Western suit from a friend at Saigon Naval Headquarters. Just before sundown on the same day he'd received the telegram, he knocked on Thom's front door.

Thom let him in. She herself had arrived home just minutes before, and her face was as pale as white jade. "All right," she said before he'd had a chance to say hello, "I'll marry you, under two conditions. One: you won't stop me from going back to school."

"But they'll expel you as soon as they find out," said Kiem.

"How are they going to find out? Da Lat's a long way away."

"Well, I won't stop you," said Kiem. "What's the other condition?"

She scowled. "You still haven't told me you love me."

Kiem's face reddened.

"Well?" she said.

He looked down at his feet.

"All the other fellows say it. You're the only one who doesn't," she said.

Kiem cleared his throat and coughed, but nothing happened. First his father, then the French Naval Academy had trained him too well against revealing any sign of weakness. He could no more admit his vulnerability to Thom than he could surrender his ship to an enemy.

"I'm sorry," he said. "I'll be a good husband to you. I'll always protect you."

"I know you will," she said, letting out a long sigh. "That's why I've picked you over the others."

In the next few hours Kiem managed to get in touch with his mother's sister and her husband: Mr. and Mrs. Bich, his only relatives in the South. They would have to fulfill the obligations of the groom's parents, including paying for everything. Forty minutes after he called, they came rushing over with a hastily assembled tray of rice wine, flowers, and fruit, which they placed on the Le family's ancestral altar. After being formally introduced to Mrs. Le, they asked her for her daughter's hand in marriage. Thom—who had slipped into the room, carrying a tea tray for the traditional "showing of the face"—began to cry. And Mrs. Le said yes.

Normally an astrologer would have fixed the date and time of the wedding, but they had no choice: the ceremony would have to take place at noon the following day. Grandmother was indeed quite "ill": she was as stiff as a little bird that had dropped down out of the sky. Mrs. Le advised the Bichs that she'd need fifteen gift-baskets for her wedding guests, with a can of tea and loaf of cake in each. The Bichs got off easy: if it hadn't been for Grandmother, there would have been hundreds of guests and baskets piled high with champagne and choice betel nuts.

The Bichs rushed off to pack the baskets and deliver them on foot with the wedding announcements. Thom set to work sewing her wedding dress from a bolt of yellow satin Huong had sent from Paris the year before; her mother had been hoarding it for just such an occasion. Mrs. Le began polishing the altar brass and borrowing extra chairs from the neighbors. And Kiem returned to bachelor's quarters for his last night on earth as a bachelor.

Betel nuts were swarming in his brain: the ones that used to grow on his mother's farm in Phu Tai, as big as a man's fist, with fifty to a hundred big round betels to a head. Nuts like that were too fancy for everyday consumption. Whenever a matchmaker in Phu Tai or a neighboring village closed a deal for a wedding, the groom's family and servants would rush to Kiem's mother's farm, with carrying-poles slung on their shoulders, to buy them all up.

Betel nuts and weddings, weddings and betel nuts: there was a reason why the two went together. Once upon a time in Vietnam, two brothers had fallen in love with the same pure woman. When she'd married the older brother, the younger one had set out for the jungle, not wanting to ruin their happiness. He walked for many days until he came to a river so deep and wide that he couldn't cross it. There he sank down on the ground in exhaustion, crying for his two lost loves. He died during the night, and his soul grew up in the shape of an areca palm.

But the older brother had gone to look for him, with his bride's consent. When he reached the river's edge, he felt strangely pulled to the palm tree growing there. He sat down underneath its umbrella and began to cry for his lost younger brother. That night he too died of exhaustion and a broken heart, and his soul was transformed into a limestone rock. Worried at not hearing from her husband, the faithful wife set out to look for him. When she came to the river's edge, she sat down on the limestone rock and leaned her back against the palm tree and cried for her husband and his brother, her friend. She died there during the night, and her soul became the betel vine that twists around the rock and the tree and binds the two together.

Every day in Vietnam, when people rolled slices of betel nut and fragments of tree bark inside a leaf smeared with lime paste and placed it in their mouths to chew, they were honoring the memory of those three faithful lovers. Of course sailors on a boat at night, sitting around smoking, might also joke about somebody getting his betel wrapped up in a nice, tight leaf. . . .

Late in the morning of 28 February 1958, dressed in his borrowed Western suit, Kiem walked to the Le house holding a box of betel nuts: nothing like those of Phu Tai, but the best the Saigon markets had to offer. His two best men, former classmates at the French Naval Academy, preceded him, one of them carrying Thom's gold ring on a tray. Behind him came Mr. Bich, waving a black umbrella for shade. It was hot outside, but it was not yet the rainy season and the dry heat felt pleasant.

About two dozen people were waiting at the Le house, and the groom's party accounted for eight of them: Mr. and Mrs. Bich, two of their children, Kiem's two best men, Kiem himself, and Miss Ly, his airport greeter, who seemed to have a talent for nosing out secret events. Mrs. Le's estranged second husband was also there, looking miserable. And because of Grandmother, nobody else dared to laugh or smile, either.

Precisely at noon, a door opened and Thom glided in, wearing a sheer white tunic floating over a long yellow satin gown. *Like a cloud passing in front of the sun,* thought Kiem. She'd pinned up her hair under a dark blue turban, and her hands clutched a nosegay of lemon-colored flowers. It was just the way she'd walked into his heart five years before, with the sun at her back and her beach robe fluttering in the wind on the beach at Do Son.

Mrs. Le and her ex-husband and Mr. and Mrs. Bich exchanged ritual greetings. *Our daughter will become your daughter,* said Thom's parents; *we have raised her in the traditional way, according to the family's good name. We welcome your daughter to our family,* said Mr. and Mrs. Bich; *we can see that she will be a fine support for our son.* And so forth. They opened a few bottles of champagne at the end, but the mood was somber. A normal wedding would have gone on for two or three days with music, dancing, and three or four pigs. But for this one, the guests didn't stay long. And when the last visitor had left, Mrs. Le began to wail for her dead mother.

Grandmother's funeral took place the next day, in front of the same altar. Kiem and Thom put on ragged white mourning clothes and staggered behind the coffin on its way to the graveyard. After the burial they changed clothes and caught a train to Vung Tau, a seaside resort a few hours from Saigon. They spent one perfect day and night together, and then it was time to go back to their old lives. The last thing they did before leaving Saigon was to go sign the marriage book in city hall.

At the end of the spring semester Thom came home from school sick, and it soon became obvious that she would not be going back in the fall: she could hide a marriage from the school officials, but not a pregnancy. If she blamed Kiem for ruining her dream of a Lycée Yersin diploma, she didn't let it show. They were wildly in love with each other and miserable when Kiem's boat trips split them up for even one night—even if Thom had to guess Kiem's feelings from his actions and not his words. It seemed to Kiem that Diem's lackeys were always rousing him out of bed at three o'clock in the morning, shouting that the president had a whim to go somewhere, so hurry up and get the ship ready! Then Kiem would have to get the word out to his scattered crew, who'd scramble to meet up with the ship at points downstream—rowing out to it, if necessary. And scavenging a week's worth of food for the ship in the middle of the night, before the market stalls had even opened, was quite a challenge.

"Cast the nose guard! Cast the back guard! All engines ahead one-third. Rudder amid ship! Signal officer, report to headquarters. Ship leaving harbor: special mission. . . ."

Luckily Kiem was at home the night that Thom went into labor, a month too soon. He borrowed a jeep and rushed her to a military hospital, where the doctors decided to hold her overnight for observation. He dragged a spare cot into her room and slept beside her in his uniform. The next day she went into labor again, this time in earnest. An aide strapped her to a gurney and wheeled her away, and Kiem began to panic. How could a child-sized woman give birth to a child? Never more than an occasional smoker, he smoked himself dizzy in the hall. Finally a nurse stuck her head out. "It's a boy, small but healthy," she said. "Give us about ten minutes, and then you can come in."

While Kiem stood outside waiting, one of his junior officers came rushing down the hall. "Orders to go, sir," he announced; "the president is waiting." Kiem ticked off a list of instructions and promised to join the ship in an hour. Then he went in to see them.

The boy was just a little wormy, red-faced thing, but the more Kiem looked at him, the more he gave way to a strange new emotion: a great wave of it, like a storm-surge washing from one side of a ship to the other. This boy would assure that Kiem was buried properly and that his family name lived on. He would say *con* to Kiem without hesitation. Kiem turned from the boy to Thom's pale, exhausted face. He wanted to tell her how much he loved her and their child, but all he could do was squeeze her tiny hand. She squeezed his big hand back.

Then Mrs. Le came sweeping in to see her first grandchild, and Kiem had to excuse himself. "Presidential business," he explained. "You take good care of her, Mrs. Le. I'll be back by the end of the week." He almost forgot to tell them the name he had chosen for the boy: "Khai," which means "elation," "great joy."

EARTH

The earth before us is but a handful of soil; but when regarded
in its breadth and thickness, it sustains mountains like the
Hwa and the Yo, without feeling their weight, and contains the
rivers and the seas, without their leaking away.

Confucius, *The Doctrine of the Mean*

CHAPTER 9

Reds Push Drive in South Vietnam
Pressure Shifts from Laos to Neighbor State—Acts of Violence
Increase

New York Times, 2 May 1960

In the spring of 1959 Ho Chi Minh authorized the use of force to overthrow the South's government. Construction work began on the "Ho Chi Minh Trail," a north-to-south supply route running through the neighboring country of Laos, and several thousand communist cadres were dispatched to the South. The "Viet Cong," or Southern communists, began stalking and assassinating minor Southern "officials" from schoolteachers to village and district chiefs. Kiem's ship continued to shuttle Diem and the pacification team between cities and the larger villages, where it was still safe; but they stopped visiting the less-populated regions of the delta, where the guerrillas were gaining control. The navy's mission began to shift from pacification to war and specifically to stopping the infiltration of arms and supplies to the guerrillas by sea.

Under President Harry Truman, the United States had set up a small Military Assistance Advisory Group for "Indochina" in 1950, which had been replaced by a new advisory organization after the French lost the war. Now, with the Northern communists shifting to warlike tactics, U.S. president Dwight Eisenhower decided to send several hundred more advisors into Vietnam. Most of the advisors were targeted for the Army of the Republic of Vietnam (ARVN), since the Vietnamese Navy, with only 3,600 men, didn't have much pull in Saigon, let alone in Washington. So it came as a surprise to Kiem to hear that his ship was getting one of these advisors—probably for the reason that he carried the president around, he guessed. *Co van:* even in a polite language like Vietnamese, the term for "advisor" was irritating—because nobody, not even a saint, likes to be on the receiving end of "advice."

Already there was a story going around about one of the new *co van* reviewing troops with an ARVN colonel. The American, oblivious to protocol, had gone barging ahead down the line. Spotting a glob of grease inside the barrel of an M1 Garand rifle, he had scooped it out with his finger and then turned to wave it in the colonel's face. But the colonel was already taking a step forward, right into the loaded finger. Cold black goo smeared his cheek, and the only thing he could do to regain his men's respect was slap the advisor's face and walk away.

Hoping that their experience would be different, Kiem and his crew planned a "welcome aboard" ceremony for Lt. Wayne Valin, USN: a big, heavy, slow fellow with a pained expression on his face. Afterward Kiem sat down with him in the officers' mess to discuss his responsibilities. Lieutenant Valin had no idea what those responsibilities were, and neither did Kiem. "I'm here to help," the American kept saying. He didn't know any Vietnamese, and Kiem's English—memorized from textbooks during his years at the French Naval Academy—was his fourth language behind Vietnamese, French, and Chinese.

Over the next few weeks it became obvious that Lieutenant Valin was miserable about his assignment to Vietnam. The native food gave him diarrhea. The heat made him break out in flowery pink splotches. The humidity watered a fungus that grew in his body's crevices. The rainy season only worsened his melancholy disposition. "Too much earth in his makeup!" Kiem's sailors agreed privately.

Eventually the new advisor settled into a routine. In the mornings he'd get up, plod to the officers' mess, drink a cup of coffee, plod to the head, then plod around until he found Kiem. He'd ask Kiem what the Plan of the Day was, then plod around the ship for a few more hours, writing things down in a notebook. At first he tried taking Kiem's men aside to ask questions, but those who could speak English kept pretending that they didn't understand, and he soon gave up. By early afternoon he'd get bored and plod to his bunk to sleep. Once, Kiem woke him up from a nap to meet President Diem, but the advisor grumbled about having his sleep disturbed. After that, no matter who came on board, Kiem just let him snore.

Then Kiem got called down to Saigon Naval Headquarters to go over his advisor's first monthly report. "No inspection lineup first thing in the morning," recited Kiem's commanding officer, sliding his reading glasses down his nose.

"Of course not, sir. That would be a standard practice on the big ships my advisor is used to, but for us it's just a waste of time."

"No prebreakfast clampdown or wash-down," the CO continued.

"Insufficient fresh water, sir. There's scarcely enough for my men to drink and wash with. If we could get the parts to fix the evaporator . . . they've been on order for six months now, sir."

"Captain's orders not being typed or posted."

"What? But I don't have a secretary—and our typewriter's keys are always jammed. It only takes me a few minutes to give my officers their orders in person, and they prefer it that way. They've said so."

"Torn and frayed uniforms. One junior officer spotted wearing civilian clothes at sea."

"You know yourself, sir, that a man gets only two uniforms when he enters the navy, and then one replacement uniform per year, if he turns the worn one in. So if a man gets seasick on the newer uniform, and the worn one is stinky with fish, and it hasn't rained for weeks so there's been no chance to wring them out in fresh water, what with the evaporator on the blink. . . ."

"Canvas awnings mildewed. Life-ring float lights inoperative. Exhaust vents rusted. . . ."

Disgraced and helpless to defend himself, Kiem was reminded of a similar experience earlier that year. The U.S. Navy had invited his ship and crew to Subic Bay for training: quite an honor, even though not many other VNN ships could have made it all the way to the Philippines without getting towed. Kiem and his men had worked on the engine for weeks and had even given HQ-331 a fresh coat of paint. The weeklong voyage across the South China Sea had been rough, with the ship tilting forty-five degrees to starboard, then forty-five degrees to port. They'd had to seal all the doors and hatches as if she were a submarine. But when they'd arrived in port, the Americans hadn't even let them tie up to the pier! They'd been quarantined while teams of U.S. petty officers inspected them for "sanitation"—meaning rats—and ultimately pronounced them "unfit for training."

Unfit for training? After they'd made it all the way there? But there'd been nothing to do but turn around and sail home through waves of shame.

Lieutenant Valin's next advisory report was just as negative as the first.

Kiem stopped acting friendly toward the lieutenant. And Kiem's men began picking up on the change. Little things belonging to Lieutenant Valin began to disappear: a pack of cigarettes, a ballpoint pen, his socks, his magazine. . . . Kiem went back and forth between reprimanding his men for the harassment and secretly enjoying the American's annoyance.

Then the hated notebook disappeared. And, for once, Lieutenant Valin showed some animation. "Your men know where it is," he accused Kiem. "They're all laughing at me behind my back. Don't think I can't see it on their faces."

"Look," Kiem said, "my men hate that notebook. I hate that notebook, too. Why don't we try things *without* the notebook for awhile instead of ripping up the ship trying to find it? Here's what I propose: before you bring a problem to headquarters, bring it to *me*, and let me try to resolve it at this level. If I can't fix it, then go ahead and put it in your report."

"All right," said Valin dispassionately; then he plodded off to his bunk for a nap.

Over the next few months Kiem and his advisor managed to carve out a halfway decent working relationship. Then Lieutenant Valin's one-year advisory tour ended, and he was sent back to the United States. Lt. Jack Quimby, USN, arrived to take his place.

Quimby *never* seemed to sleep: it might have kept him from catching a crew member in the act of breaking a rule. "Captain Kiem, the men are smoking in a nonsmoking area!" "Captain Kiem, the cook isn't washing his hands after using the lavatory!" "Captain Kiem, the men are throwing things into the toilets!" The toilet violations, in particular, made Kiem mad enough to spit. First of all, Quimby had no idea how many of Kiem's sailors had never even *seen* a flush-toilet before joining the navy. In the countryside, people just squatted over a hole in the ground. A square of tissue was something precious to those boys, suitable for a verse of poetry, not for tossing into a latrine. And secondly, such matters were below the dignity of the ship's captain. Whoever was supposed to be teaching his crew the fine points of personal hygiene, Kiem knew that it wasn't himself.

Now here came Quimby, his face pink with exertion, grabbing Kiem on the arm right in front of his shocked men: "Captain Kiem! The ship's toilets are all jammed up again. The men aren't using the proper grade of tissue. Those diaphragm valves are very delicate. Rough paper. . . ."

That was it. Kiem had had enough. He could see that his men were beginning to lose respect for him, to smirk behind their hands. "That's enough!" he snapped. "I am the captain of this ship. Don't talk to me about toilets or hand washing. That is not the captain's concern. You insult me."

"I'm sorry, Captain. I didn't realize. . . . I thought. . . . You see, it's just that nobody else around here speaks English."

"No," said Kiem, "because this is Vietnam, where we speak Vietnamese. And another thing," he said, lowering his voice so that only the American could hear, "don't you *ever* undermine my authority in front of my men. No more pushing in the door to my cabin without knocking. No more poking me on the shoulder or sticking your finger in my face."

"I had no idea, Captain," Quimby apologized.

"I have a suggestion to make," Kiem continued. "Why don't you start keeping a notebook? Then when you spot a problem, instead of interrupting me right away, you could write it down. Once a day, at a prearranged time, the two of us could sit down behind closed doors and go over your notes."

To think that Kiem would have voluntarily revived the hated notebook! But it helped keep the peace between himself and Lieutenant Quimby until Quimby's one-year tour was up. Then, just as Kiem was wondering what new advisory surprise the U.S. Navy was going to spring on him next, he got unexpected orders from Saigon Naval Headquarters: he and three other officers were going to be sent to the Naval Postgraduate School in Monterey, California, for a year of training. Was it a coincidence that three out of four of them were French Naval Academy graduates? Evidently somebody wanted to slap a coat of American paint over their French paint.

Kiem, Thom, and Khai said their hurried good-byes at Tan Son Nhut Air Base—Thom standing a little apart from the other navy wives, who resented her good looks and outsider's accent, and Khai pointing and laughing at the planes. "Promise you'll write to me!" "Stay healthy, now." "Watch out for those Chicago gangsters!" "Take good care of our son." "What if your checks are late? What if I have to borrow money?" "You'll do fine. It's only a year, after all." Then Kiem and his classmates were boarding their commercial jet, fastening their seat belts, lifting off, and watching their country's network of marsh, bays, swamps, canals, and rivers disappear under layers of clouds.

They flew to Clark Air Force Base in the Philippines, then to Travis Air Force Base in San Francisco. One bus took them to Fort Mason to pick up their checks, and a second to Monterey to check into their dormitory—a beautiful old hotel with high ceilings and crystal chandeliers in the lobby. Their American group leaders warned them not to miss the "get acquainted" party being held for their class later that night.

At the appointed hour, Kiem and his friends looked around the dormitory lounge and counted at least ten other foreigners besides themselves: a Turk, a Thai, a Filipino, a South American, and half a dozen western Europeans. Everybody, even the other foreigners, seemed to be talking very fast in American slang, over rock-and-roll music blaring from a hi-fi. Despite their high scores on their navy's English-language proficiency test, the four of them couldn't understand a word. Still, they smiled and nodded when they were spoken to, not wanting to offend.

Everybody else was drinking highballs, including the two pretty wives of the senior American officers assigned as group leaders to help them feel at home. Kiem and his friends accepted drinks but just held onto them and let the ice cubes melt. Although they might sip a glass of rice wine back home, they didn't trust strong American whiskey. They were afraid they might get drunk and lose face in front of the others.

One of the wives was trying to get the new students to dance to the music. Several of the Americans danced with her, and then the South American took a turn, snapping his fingers and singing along with the record. Laughing and out of breath, she wiggled across the room to where Kiem was standing. "Ready, Freddy?" she asked. She was wearing a dress with a deep "V" neckline, and her bosoms were popping out like balloons. It was rude to look but even ruder to look away, so Kiem looked.

The commander's wife saved him. "I don't think he knows how to jitterbug, honey," she told the other woman. "Come on with me and I'll fix you up with some chips and dip," she said to Kiem. Full of gratitude, he followed her across the lounge.

Over the next few hours, one of the American students vomited into a wastebasket, and the officer married to the happy woman in the low-cut dress had to fetch her coat and button her into it, over her protests. Kiem and his friends stayed to the end of the party, not wanting to offend. Climbing the stairs to their rooms—where the radiators would soon be hissing like snakes and startling them awake all night—the four of them let out sighs and yawns. "How can they enjoy this type of party?" one of them asked. And they all shook their heads.

Classes in navigation, strategy, ordnance, and other core subjects began later that week. Learning that they could take one or two electives as well, Kiem signed up for public speaking and international relations.

"He thinks he's Winston Churchill," one of his friends joked.

"No, Abe Lincoln. He's tall, and we're fighting a civil war."

Teasing aside, the others were grateful to Kiem for going first in line at the school cafeteria, which was run by Filipinos. At first the only food he knew how to order for everybody was eggs.

"Eggs!" he'd announce with what he hoped was an air of authority, holding up four fingers.

The Filipinos always smiled and winked at them because they were Asian. "How do you want them cooked?" they'd ask. "Over easy?"

Whatever style they suggested, Kiem would agree to. In no time he had eggs mastered: "over easy," "sunny-side up," "poached," "scrambled," "hard-boiled," "soft-boiled," and "omelets." Then he moved on to hamburgers.

But Kiem was still intimidated in the classroom—for awhile, at least. At the French Naval Academy, their lectures had dragged on for two hours or more. Here, however, the emphasis was on practical application, not theory, and the bell rang to end class after only fifty minutes. Often in France an instructor would enjoy taunting them with his superior knowledge. But here, when an instructor didn't know the answer to a student's question, he or she admitted it. Kiem and his three cohorts did poorly on tests at first because they kept searching for a trap or a hidden meaning in the questions. But after a few weeks they caught on: in America you were expected to understand the basic technique, not to be a genius. They started sticking up their hands like the others to ask questions or to contribute to the class discussion.

In the afternoons they liked to play tennis, and in the early evenings they watched TV in the dormitory lounge. When a soccer match came on, the Americans would get up and leave and the four of them would move closer to the screen. At the start of a talk show, they'd leave the room to study and the Americans would take their places. But they never missed an episode of *Gunsmoke* or *Bonanza*, not even if they had a test the next day. And they followed the TV coverage of the 1960 presidential election. They knew that Senator John Kennedy was a Roman Catholic and a friend of President Diem's, and they rejoiced when he won. They felt sure he was talking about Southeast Asia when he said in his inaugural address that he would "pay any price, bear any burden, meet any hardship, support any friend, oppose any foe, to assure the survival and the success of liberty."

On weekends they stayed in the suburbs with a host family, rising early with the children to watch cartoons on TV. That's where they *really* learned English, because the children spoke slowly and delighted in explaining obvious things to them. Sunday afternoons they'd all pile into the back of the family's station wagon for a long drive along the coast, or to a redwood forest, or to San Francisco's Chinatown. Dropping in on two of their countrymen who taught English at the Presidio Army language school, they could catch up on political gossip from home. In early November, they learned, rebel paratroopers had attacked Diem's presidential palace in an attempted coup, and the acting head of the navy had sent his marines in to run them off. Certainly, now, the navy's stock would be on the rise!

On warm weekend evenings, their host family would barbecue in the yard while the children twirled hula hoops or raced bicycles down the street. When the stars came out, everybody would squint and look for Sputnik overhead, and Kiem would feel a surge of homesickness mixed with peace and contentment.

On a weekend outing to an American toy store, Kiem spotted a red plastic car big enough for Khai to ride in. It even had a working horn that went *ah-oo-ga* like the magical cars that had come to his grandfather's funeral in Phu Tai. "If you can mail it to Vietnam, I'll buy it," he told a flustered salesclerk before even asking how much it was going to cost him: half a week's pay.

But how could he show Thom how much he missed her? If he bought her a costly present, she'd just scold him for wasting money, and when he sat with pen over paper, a gulf opened up between his words and his emotions. "Your husband, Kiem," he signed his letters home, while Thom's to him were all signed "Love." Fortunately the months passed by quickly—for Thom, too. "Your son is growing up fast," she wrote. "You'd hardly recognize him, he's so tall now. . . ."

At the end of the academic year, all four Vietnamese students graduated near the top of their class—not because they were smarter than anyone else but because they'd studied every night while their classmates were relaxing with beers. Before going home, though, they still had to travel to San Diego for eight weeks of technical training.

The Americans in their fire-fighting class all seemed to be six feet tall or over, with hands as big as gingko leaves. They had no problems grasping the thick fire hose. But the Vietnamese were shorter and smaller-boned, and their hands couldn't get a grip on it. One time a hose jumped right out of Hoang Co Minh's arms and whipsawed across the floor, spraying everybody and everything in sight until the instructor managed to shut off the water source. "Oh boy!" the instructor laughed. "That was a good one!" Minh stalked out of the room—because, he explained to the others later, the instructor had called him "boy." Minh was the only one of them who hadn't studied in France—and the only one who never quite adjusted to America, complaining all year long about its weak "blond" cigarettes, its dry and tasteless rice, its ugly Hollywood starlets with monkey hair on their arms. By then, the rest of them were so homesick that they didn't even bother to explain "Oh boy!" to him.

CHAPTER 10

U.S. to Help Saigon Fight Reds with More Experts and Planes

New York Times, 17 November 1961

Upon his return to Vietnam in 1961, Kiem was assigned as an instructor at the Midshipmen's School of the Naval Training Center in Nha Trang. Opened by the French in August of 1952—five months after the Vietnamese Navy was established—the Vietnamese Naval Academy had graduated its first class of officers six months later. Kiem and the other French Naval Academy graduates tended to look down on those early classes of "homegrown" officers, joking that they were still "learning by doing": heave the rudder to the left and see what happens, heave the rudder to the right and see what happens.
. . .

Class Eight had been the first to be trained by Vietnamese instructors, after the French were kicked out of the Naval Training Center and the country. As of the fall of 1961, Class Eleven would be entering the Midshipmen's School; the year after that, the class size was scheduled to double from fifty to a hundred cadets, and the length of the training program would be condensed from two years to eighteen months. The United States had agreed to support Vietnamese Armed Forces expansion with cash, equipment, and training; and the Vietnamese Navy was slated to grow from its current level of 3,600 men, not counting the marines, to an authorized ceiling of 5,712.

His first morning in Nha Trang, Kiem rose at five-fifteen, planning to join the cadets on their morning run. A cool, salty breeze whistling through the pine trees made him feel like a cadet himself as he stepped toward the parade ground. The breeze ruffled the gaudy red flowers of the *phoung vi*, "tail of the

peacock," trees—named for their showiness, he supposed, because a peacock's tail has no red—and released the heavy, sweet perfume of plumeria
blossoms. Oh, it was good to be alive, good to be twenty-eight years old
and in the navy, good to be married to his high-school sweetheart with a
son to carry on the family name! He waited by the flagpole. And waited.
At a quarter to six he strode over to the midshipmen's quarters.

They were all still snoring and sighing in their bunks, looking—with
their black eyelashes spidering their soft faces—not much older than
three-year-old Khai. Spoiled by their mothers, he realized: their heads
full of book-knowledge and not much else. He doubted whether any of
them had traveled more than a hundred kilometers from home, dated a
girl, or played a competitive team sport. Well, he'd see about that.

"Hey," he said, shaking the arm of the boy in the end bunk. "It's ten
minutes to six. Why aren't you up?"

The boy jackknifed to a sitting position. As he moved, something tum-
bled out from under his bedding: a package wrapped in dry green
banana-husks. Kiem picked it up and sniffed: sticky rice cakes, giving off
whiffs of pork fat and sugary mashed beans.

"We're supposed to get up with the bugle, sir," the boy explained. "But
the petty officer comes so late. . . ."

"What petty officer?" asked Kiem.

"The one who supervises our morning run, sir. He comes to get us so
late that we've taken to sleeping in till he gets here."

"What about the rest of the officers?" Kiem asked.

"What officers, sir?"

"Don't the others meet you at the flagpole first thing in the morning?"

"Oh, no, sir. The officers don't show up till seven, when breakfast is
served."

"Class?" asked Kiem.

"Beg your pardon, sir?"

"What class are you in, Midshipman?" Kiem asked him.

"Oh, Ten, sir. Class Ten."

Kiem let out a long sigh. Class Ten was entering their second year;
their bad habits had had a whole year to crystallize.

By now the other boys had begun scrambling out of their bunks, and
the petty officer, looking like a stick-whipped buffalo, had slunk in unan-
nounced.

"There's a good reason why we insist upon punctuality in the navy,"
Kiem told the cadet who'd been caught sleeping. "It may not be obvious

to you now, when you're in school, but remember that you're being trained for a life at sea. An officer on a ship has to report to the bridge a few minutes before the start of his watch. He can't very well pull a blanket over his head and wait for a friend to wake him up."

"Another thing," he continued, "I like sticky rice cakes, too, but I would never smuggle them into my cabin on a long sea voyage. Not just because it's against the rules but because it makes the other men envious, and sailors on a small ship have to get along like brothers. Understand?"

"Yes, sir," the boy nodded, handing over the squarish bundle.

Kiem caught the eye of the guilty-looking petty officer and gestured toward a neat bunk still made up from the day before. "Is one of the boys sick?" he asked.

"No, my lieutenant. The boy's father is a Khanh Hoa Province official. From time to time we let him sleep out with his family."

"No more," sighed Kiem.

The next morning, Kiem was dressed and parked in his jeep by the flagpole when the five-thirty bugle blew. The only way to teach a hard-headed youth anything, he had decided, was by his own example. From that day forward, he ran the ten-kilometer run with his students—a little out of shape at first but pretty soon back to his old Brest form. Several of the other young officer-instructors who had trained in France or the United States started showing up for the morning run as well. Like Kiem, they were determined to turn Classes Ten and Eleven into first-rate naval officers. If they could do it by working their tails off—without a whole lot of support from the governments in Saigon and Washington—they were going to try.

Long after the school's secretarial pool had gone home for the evening, Kiem and the other young instructors would still be translating their personal copies of French and American textbooks into Vietnamese, banging out ditto stencils on manual typewriters, cranking out warm-to-the-touch pages on the base's only mimeograph machine. Finding an error in an original French text made the long hours worth it.

"Look!" one would call to the others across the clatter of typewriter keys. "The French assume open-sea conditions for weather forecasting, but when your ships stick close to the coastline, like ours, you have to take regional geography into account. I'll have to rewrite the whole passage. . . ."

"This whole French chapter on data gathering is obsolete. . . ."

"According to the French, the only two variables in a ship-handling equation are wind speed and water current. But what if you have a second engine—or direct-thrust propulsion instead of reducing-clutch? A ship's going to respond differently under different conditions. . . ."

Whenever they started to nod off over their typewriters, one of them could always get a laugh by retelling the story of Lieutenant Hung—a Brest graduate and fellow instructor so indifferent to worldly things that he rode a bicycle back and forth to class instead of a jeep or a Vespa. One afternoon a fat army general had been spotted chasing Lieutenant Hung's bike across campus. Examination scores had just been posted, and the general's son had flunked a big test. The general jogged; the lieutenant pedaled; the general jogged; the lieutenant pedaled; the general jogged; then, finally, the exasperated lieutenant braked with his feet and fished his wallet out of his pocket. "If you want money, I'll give you my money!" he shouted. "But not . . . one . . . point!"

Six hundred boys signed up to take the entrance examination for the one hundred slots in Class Twelve. Suddenly it seemed that everyone wanted his or her son to be a naval officer, not just because the navy was safer than the army, with rumors of a mandatory draft in the future, but because the navy was acquiring a reputation as an elite, international organization. The school's administrators were proud of never having to bend their academic standards under political pressure—although they couldn't always control the Saigon doctors who administered the physical portion of the exams. Now and then the school got a little "minnow" who was nowhere near being tall enough to peer through the sight glass of an American-built ship. But if he could survive the grueling physical regimen, he was welcome to stay.

A few months after his arrival Kiem was promoted from instructor to commandant of the Midshipmen's School. Along with the promotion came a U.S. advisor, Lieutenant Commander Jensen, a graduate of the U.S. Naval Academy at Annapolis and the first of Kiem's advisors to outrank him. "He doesn't even look like an officer," Kiem grumbled at first. "Too short. Too bald." But the short, bald Jensen carried himself with dignity, Kiem had to admit, and he seemed to have an inside track with the U.S. Navy's procurement department. Not only did he manage to get up-to-date textbooks for the entire school, but he also procured an English-language laboratory with twenty acoustical booths and a lanky civilian English instructor from the United States.

Whenever a U.S. ship was in the area, Jensen would signal it and talk the captain into dropping anchor in Nha Trang for a day or two. He'd coax the American officers into visiting classes, then nudge them into letting the whole school tour the ship. "See how the American sailors specialize in different jobs and do everything by procedure—even rust picking," Kiem would point out to his students. It was so different from the attitude of the French and Vietnamese navies, where men prided themselves on knowing how to do every job on the ship without asking for help. "Have them show you the steps of the procedure. Don't be shy," Kiem urged his students.

Jensen also helped place their second-year students on U.S. ships for practical training. After cruising to Hong Kong or Singapore for several months, they often stopped by to thank Kiem for their training in the English-language lab. It had helped them save face when communicating with Americans, they always said.

Kiem got to make a long sea voyage himself in March of 1962. He was invited to tour the Philippine Naval Academy, taking three *Bluebird*-class coastal minesweepers and forty-nine cadets with him. It was embarrassing at first because the commandant of the Philippine school had five stripes to Kiem's three. Diem sure didn't like to promote anybody: there'd been three lieutenants on board Kiem's last ship, including Kiem—and he'd been the captain! But when Kiem saw how inferior to his own the Philippine training program was, he relaxed. Their program was just built around ROTC.

Back in Nha Trang, Kiem instituted a weekly two-hour "commandant's talk." His focus was on the "intangibles" of leadership: self-discipline, self-respect, integrity. No one is *born* sophisticated, he would tell his cadets: if someone is willing to learn how to command respect from others, then he can learn. "Every one of you has the potential to equal or excel any naval officer anywhere in the world," he promised. He warned them that they would meet up with negative influences once they were on their own and that they would have to be strong in order to resist. "Model yourselves on the great naval leaders of world history and not on the army and air force generals you'll see around you," he advised them.

He tried to focus his attention on Class Ten, knowing that if he succeeded, the class behind them would fall in line. Motivation was an uncertain science: the cadets studied communism in their psychological warfare classes, but no young officer was going to risk his life for a decentralized economy or for a two-party political system. Yet he'd give up his life for his superior officers if they earned his respect.

Sometimes in his weekly lectures Kiem liked to set up a tricky situation—a battle at sea or on the river—and then ask his students how they'd react. What if the enemy shot from this side of the river? What if the enemy shot from the other side? He peppered the boys with questions, trying to instill the habit of always thinking one step ahead. Quick reaction, even *wrong* reaction, was important: once a man was reacting, he was moving in a positive direction and not just sitting there in panic and indecision.

But cadets also had to be taught how to socialize, so part of Kiem's work was play. Throughout the school year he and Thom hosted open-house teas for the public, where the boys could practice their etiquette and small talk. In the spring the Naval Academy put on a graduation arts show and ball that drew hundreds of outside guests, including the president—who looked right through Kiem as though he'd never seen him before—and dozens of ambassadors, attachés, and bodyguards. Nha Trang families were proud to send their daughters to that ball, and every year a couple of dozen romances bloomed beneath the red and blue and purple spotlights blinking in time to the music—courtesy of a talented technician on the staff of the class-A school.

Thom was the happiest he'd ever seen her. She liked having Kiem on shore duty, coming home to their flat in officers' quarters every night. And the sugary beaches, turquoise waters, and purple mountains of Nha Trang were like the backdrop of a fairy tale. There may well have been fairies in Nha Trang at one time: certainly the names of places like "Fairy Stream," "Fairy Grotto," and the "Fairies' Chessboard" rock formation would suggest it. Kiem and Thom's second son, Hao Kiet, was born during their stay there. And even with the war heating up in the Mekong Delta, their lives together seemed enchanted for almost two years.

CHAPTER 11

Monk Suicide by Fire in Anti-Diem Protest

New York Times, 11 June 1963

In 1963 Kiem was given command of the ship every VNN captain wanted: the *Van Don* (HQ-06), a submarine chaser like his old ship HQ-02 but a later and faster model. As the ex–USS *Anacortes*, she'd been mothballed after brief service in World War II, then turned over to Vietnam in 1960—almost as good as new. Her shallow draft of 3.2 meters made her agile near shore, and her cruising speed was an impressive 19 knots. Her firepower consisted of one 3-inch and one 40-mm gun and four 20-mm guns, plus a 60-mm mortar, twin depth charges, and two "mousetrap" ramp launchers. She was so fat with ammunition that her ballast tanks couldn't hold enough fresh water when they put out to sea.

When not out on coastal patrol, she docked directly across from naval headquarters on the Saigon River, pointing her big guns at potential attackers of the five-story building or the presidential palace down the block. Late in the day, when Saigon families came down to the docks to take in the breeze and the river view and watch Kiem's sailors lining up for their evening shipboard inspection, the possibility of violence always seemed remote. But there had been two failed coup attempts in the past two years.

The Vietnamese Navy had nearly doubled in size during Kiem's two years in Nha Trang, to just under six thousand officers and men. That meant that naval housing in the Saigon area was scarce. Kiem and Thom had to put their names on a waiting list for space in officers' quarters. In the meantime Kiem managed to find a small civilian rental house near Vien

Hoa Dao, the Buddhist Institute for the Propagation of the Faith, at a price they could afford.

But the house was no bargain, as he learned the first time he came home from work and found the street that ran past the Buddhist Institute blocked by a police barricade. Beyond the barricade he could see only streaks of color and light: orange monks' robes, red-on-white-lettered placards, popping flashbulbs. Fumbling for his ID cards, he hopped down out of his jeep and pushed his way through the crowd. "Lieutenant Do Kiem, VNN," he told a pair of policemen. Even with his military ID, it wasn't easy talking his way through.

Other afternoons he wasn't as lucky: he had to abandon the jeep and pick his way home through a maze of back alleyways. He'd walk in late to find Thom rocking baby Kiet with one hand and, with the other, smoothing the wet washcloth she'd draped on his face to shield him from the tear gas. Once or twice she'd even failed to meet Kiem's eyes, making him feel as if the house and the demonstrations were all his fault.

What a mess, the whole Buddhist situation! Kiem himself had been raised a Buddhist. And while he could honestly say that no one in the navy had ever asked him his religion—he'd been discriminated against for being a *Northerner*, yes, but hardly for being a Buddhist—he knew that in some spheres it could be a political handicap. Yet his instincts told him that the communists were exploiting the situation, stirring it up to make it seem worse. Something that had happened to him recently had seemed to confirm those suspicions.

Just after coming home from work one evening, and before changing out of his navy uniform, he'd climbed up on the roof to fix a loose shingle. As soon as he'd stood up straight, two men in the yard next door had taken off running and jumping fences until they'd disappeared into the fringes of Cholon. Asking around the neighborhood, Kiem was told that the two men had rented the place next door just a few days before. Nobody seemed to know them, and they didn't come back after that, so he tried to put them out of his mind.

A week or two later, waiting behind a police barricade to get into his lousy neighborhood, Kiem caught sight of a familiar face among the demonstrators. Although the head was shaved and the neck swathed in monk's robes, the face clearly belonged to the same person who had glanced up at him in fear when he had been standing on the roof. Slowly, deliberately, Kiem searched the faces of the others until his eyes came to rest on the man's associate.

The thought of communist agitators wearing holy robes—no, he didn't want to believe it. The idea made him sick to his stomach. But he knew that the opportunity was there. Anybody could walk in off the street, shave his head, and become a Buddhist monk the same day. He didn't have to train for years as a Catholic priest did. He didn't even need to know how to read and write.

In August of 1963, when paramilitary forces reporting to Madame Nhu's husband attacked the Buddhist pagodas, beating many monks and arresting over a thousand others, Kiem's lingering sympathies for the Diem government dried up like the weather in December. Diem himself wasn't ordering the violence, but because of his detachment from reality and his reliance on unreliable family members to govern for him, he was allowing the violence to take place. The old folk-saying was right: *Ai o trong chan, moi biet chan co ran*—"One who sleeps in a blanket should know it has lice."

By then Diem's popularity had sunk so low, even with his top military leaders, that he had to send a two-star army general, Ton That Dinh, to plead his case before them. Several hundred army, navy, air force, and marine officers, including Kiem, gathered in a Nha Trang auditorium to await Dinh's speech. They weren't expecting much. General Dinh was a crude, uneducated man who had come up through the ranks. He liked to call himself Diem's "adopted son."

"Sonny" was more than an hour late for the afternoon meeting, and as soon as he opened his mouth, everyone in the auditorium could tell that he was drunk. "There's no such thing as motherfucking repression of the Buddhists!" he shouted. "It's all a bunch of motherfucking lies!" Well, at least the meeting was livelier than the boring *To Cong* (tearing down the communists) meetings they were now forced to sit through every Friday afternoon for three or four hours—Ngo Dinh Nhu's crazy idea, borrowed from the communists themselves.

"Were you motherfucking convinced?" an old friend of Kiem's from the French Naval Academy asked on the way out.

"Not on your motherfucking life!" Kiem told him.

Then the friend confided that he was hoping for a coup because he'd lost his faith in the Diem government. Kiem told him he was disgusted with the government, too, but he was trying to keep his priorities straight: first, defeat the communists; then, clean up the government. Besides, whom did they have to replace Diem with? The alternative might be even worse.

"You're right," sighed Kiem's friend. "Motherfucking right, goddamn it."

Shortly after noon on 1 November 1963, Kiem was sitting in the officers' mess of his ship, eating a simple lunch of rice and fish. Suddenly one of his guards came rushing in, wild-eyed and out of breath. "Captain, some units are taking over headquarters," he managed to get out.

Kiem hurried to the bridge. *Motherfucker!* It looked as if ARVN troops were holding naval headquarters at gunpoint. "Sound the alarm to man battle stations," he ordered. As the alarm blasted and men in white scurried to their stations, the ship's gunners quickly lined up the rebel soldiers through their sights. Then, crack! Somebody, not on Kiem's ship, had fired the first shot. "Hold fire," he commanded, first ringing up naval headquarters, then Fleet Command. Neither one answered. He asked his men where Lieutenant Peterson, his current U.S. advisor, was, but nobody had seen him since that morning. That was odd. "Pete" Peterson seldom left the ship without telling Kiem where he was going.

Kiem looked downriver and saw that the other ships were leaving their piers, retreating to the buoy line in the middle of the river, out of reach of the ground forces. Kiem gave the orders to do the same, and the *Van Don*'s twin 280-bhp diesel engines started up with a burst of power that kicked her away from the dock.

Only then did he give the command to release firepower—and not the big guns, either, but only the machine and submachine guns. "Aim high—at the roofs and treetops," he added hastily, conscious that he was shooting at his own people and that his guns could kill. With a deafening roar the 20-mm antiaircraft guns shattered the sleepy noontime lull of riverfront Saigon, firing red and green tracers that crossed in midair above the ship. Sprays of bullets nicked the coconut palms that lined the riverside highway, then stitched across the plush front lawn of naval headquarters to either side of the flagpole. The rebel soldiers ran for cover.

Within a few minutes it appeared that Kiem's men had taken control of the situation. "Cease fire!" he ordered. "Await further instruction."

Ten minutes passed. Then four figures emerged from the two-story CNO building, just to the right and front of the five-story main headquarters building. In front was a naval officer with his hands in the air; behind him, with rifles trained at his back, were three ARVN soldiers marching him down to the pier. Through his binoculars Kiem identified the naval officer as Dang Cao Thang, the VNN chief of staff—Kiem's senior by two years at Brest. When they got within shouting distance of HQ-06, the four men stopped. "Don't shoot, Kiem," yelled Thang.

"What's going on?" Kiem yelled back.

"I can't tell you, but please don't shoot." Then the army goons turned Thang around and marched him back into the CNO building.

A little while later, two A-1H combat planes belonging to the South Vietnamese Air Force made a pass at the presidential palace. One, two, three explosions followed, but Kiem was unable to tell where the bombs had landed. The A-1Hs banked sharply and made a second pass, and Kiem gave orders to shoot. One other ship began firing, too. But it was Kiem's men who scored, hitting one plane smack in the tail. Smoke poured out of the hit, although the plane didn't lose altitude. Both aircraft broke away and disappeared from view.

More time passed. Kiem tried to call up the other ship captains on his radio. He learned that Sea Force commander Dinh Manh Hung was aboard HQ-500, having hopped on the LST at the shipyard at the start of the coup. But even Commander Hung, whom Kiem respected, seemed to be biding his time, waiting for more information before making a move. Since Kiem was in the best position to see what was going on, he promised to keep the others informed.

After awhile two soldiers emerged from the CNO building carrying a large, framed painting, which they dumped unceremoniously on the ground. *Probably President Diem's portrait*, thought Kiem, though he couldn't quite make out the face through his binoculars.

More waiting. Finally, around five o'clock in the afternoon, two petty officers in a launch began buzzing around from ship to ship, picking up the skippers for a "meeting"—or so they said—at naval headquarters.

"Don't go, sir," Kiem's sergeant at arms urged. "They'll kill you."

Kiem answered with a gesture that was more French than Vietnamese: a sort of loose shrug that meant *Well, what would you have me do?*

"Then I'm going with you!" his man insisted.

"If they're planning to kill me, you're not going to stop them," said Kiem, starting to laugh at the absurdity of the situation. It took a bit of arguing, but his protector finally agreed to stay behind.

A short boat ride, a measured walk across the lush green lawn, and then the sudden cool indoor gloom of naval headquarters. Trying to remember the faces of Thom, Khai, and Kiet around the breakfast table that morning, Kiem braced himself for what was coming: would he *hear* the shot, he wondered, before the back of his head blew off? *Oh, the things they never told you in Midshipmen's School. . . .*

Outside the conference room Kiem was frisked and disarmed. Inside he saw a half-dozen of his fellow Saigon ship captains sitting around the long conference table. Two high-ranking naval officers slumped at the far end, digging into plates of *nem*, a hamlike snack, and washing it down with beer. *For courage*, Kiem thought disdainfully. He recognized one of the men as Capt. Chung Tan Cang, commander of the navy's River Force. *And the other, his face dark red as betel spit, was . . . was. . . .* Kiem knew he had seen the florid face somewhere before.

Suddenly he remembered. As commandant of the Vietnamese Naval Academy, Kiem had once made the mistake of assigning three of his cadets to Lt. Comdr. Nguyen Van Luc, also of the River Force, for practical training. All three had come back sick and shaking, telling the same story under repeated questioning. Luc had ordered the cadets to change into their dress whites, handed them rifles, then ordered them to shoot at anything that moved—which they'd taken to be a figure of speech. But a few minutes later their patrol boat had rounded a bend in the river, exposing a small boy with a stick in his hand, tending a water buffalo. "Shoot," Luc had hissed. They had looked at one another in confusion, thinking it some sort of test. "Shoot!" Luc had screamed at them again, so loudly that even the boy at the river's edge had cocked his head and stared. Then Luc had raised his own gun and fired, killing both animal and child.

Mercifully there weren't many officers like that in the navy—knowing nothing about the sea, only how to kill. Luc was more like an army than a navy man.

Now Luc banged his fist on the conference table and glared at each one of them in turn. "Who did it?" he asked. "Who fired on the revolutionaries?"

"I did," said Kiem.

"I did, too," said Lieutenant An, the captain of HQ-500.

"Why? Why did you do it?" roared Luc.

"They were attacking naval headquarters. They were wearing army uniforms," Kiem explained.

Luc cursed and muttered something too low for Kiem to hear.

"You should have told us what was going on," Kiem persisted.

That was a mistake. Luc slammed his beer bottle down on the table.

Captain Cang bent in close to him and whispered something, as if trying to calm him down. Still scowling in Kiem's direction, Luc announced that Ngo Dinh Diem was no longer in power and that a revolutionary council had taken control of the government. The leader, he said, was Duong Van Minh—"Big Minh"—a popular Southern army general who had fallen out with Diem. Another of the key figures was Ton That Dinh, the foul-mouthed general who had styled himself as Diem's "son"—now, *that* was a motherfucking surprise! Luc, Cang, and Hoang Co Minh—Kiem's homesick compatriot from the Naval Postgraduate School in California—were the chief conspirators from the navy.

Diem and Nhu were in hiding, having fled the presidential palace, Luc said, but Capt. Ho Tan Quyen, their naval commander in chief, was dead. Luc knew what he was talking about on that score, having lured Quyen into the murder car himself that morning. It had been Quyen's birthday, and Luc had told him that they were going to a "surprise party."

After the briefing the captains were allowed to return to their ships. Kiem sat up all night listening to scratchy military music on the radio. Every so often he heard the record-arm drag screechily across the disk, and then the voice of an army general would come on, advising people to remain calm. One by one, the generals "came up for air," revealing their affiliation with the revolutionary council and calling to their units to join them. Three or four times Kiem heard bursts of gunfire coming from the direction of the presidential palace.

In the morning the generals announced over the radio that Diem and Nhu had committed suicide. But the true story traveled mouth-to-mouth: hours after the coup the president and his brother had tried to surrender to the revolutionary council from their hiding place inside a Catholic church. They had been helped into the back of an armored vehicle, then shot and stabbed so many times that their bodies were scarcely recognizable.

Kiem's advisor, Lieutenant Peterson, reappeared that afternoon. He didn't try to explain his absence during the coup, and Kiem thought it wise not to ask.

"I think I see a hairy hand behind recent events," one of the other captains had whispered to Kiem on their way out of the meeting with Luc and Cang. "Hairy hand" was a racial slur against Caucasians: the backs of their own Asian hands were as smooth and hairless as the palms. In particular, Kiem knew, his friend had meant the hairy hand of the American CIA. Given that his advisor had apparently been tipped off in advance,

Kiem supposed now that his friend must have been right. The Saigon generals weren't well enough organized to have planned the coup on their own. Their motivations were too different, too personal, and most of them lacked the guts.

Immediately after the coup Kiem's ship was ordered to sail to nasty Phu Quoc Island with a "special guest" on board: Lieutenant Tuyen, commander of the Saigon Naval Garrison, who had been a member of Nhu's political party. Kiem knew it was partly punishment and partly a ruse to keep them out of the main action until things simmered down in Saigon, but he also knew they were lucky not to be under house arrest like Thang or dead like Quyen. Kiem had to laugh, though, at Hoang Co Minh's "reward" for plotting to kill Quyen: he was promoted and whisked off to Korea along with Luc as a member of South Vietnam's diplomatic corps, where Kiem knew he would be utterly miserable with the foreign food and cigarettes.

Three weeks after the coup, while Kiem's ship was still killing time off the coast of Phu Quoc, U.S. president John Kennedy was assassinated in Dallas, Texas. Kiem didn't understand the politics behind it, but he was sad that his country had lost a friend.

Now that the Saigon generals had tasted political power, they were no longer content to sit back and take orders from each other. In January a coup toppled the revolutionary council. Then coup began to follow coup with dizzying speed. After a four- or six-week tour at sea, it was not unusual for Kiem to come home to Saigon and find that the government had changed while he was gone. By then he had moved his family from the rental house near the Buddhist Institute to officers' quarters, but he himself was sleeping on his ship when it was in home port. He had to be prepared for middle-of-the-night phone calls from Khanh or Khiem or whoever was in power that month, concerned about the latest coup rumor. Then, when the president's entourage arrived at the darkened pier—cabinet members, bodyguards, wives, relatives, little children in pajamas rubbing sleep from their eyes—Kiem would be ordered to race for Vung Tau, the cape at the entrance to the South China Sea.

In August of 1964 the USS *Maddox* was attacked by North Vietnamese torpedo boats while patrolling off the coast of North Vietnam. The attack may not have been unjustified: Kiem had heard rumors of extra pay for VNN fast patrol-boat captains willing to provoke the North Vietnamese Navy into firing at them, and one such unit had been stirring up trouble near the *Maddox*'s position only days before. But it was all the justification U.S. president Lyndon Johnson needed to ask his Senate and Congress to pass the "Gulf of Tonkin Resolution" authorizing the use of U.S. military force to prevent further communist aggression in Southeast Asia.

In response Viet Cong terrorists lashed out at Americans in Vietnam several times the rest of that year, killing two and injuring twenty-five with a bomb at a casual American baseball game in Saigon, then killing two U.S. Embassy personnel and wounding more than a hundred with a Christmas Eve bomb in the lobby of the Brink Hotel in Saigon. The violence spilled over into calendar year 1965. On 7 February an American barracks at Pleiku was attacked, and on 10 February the VC blew up a hotel in Qui Nhon where U.S. soldiers were billeted, killing twenty-three and wounding twenty-one. By then, President Johnson was putting pressure on the Saigon generals to come up with a stable government if it killed them, and he was making plans to bomb North Vietnam with U.S. planes under an operation that would eventually be known as "Rolling Thunder." In March, Johnson sent in the first American combat troops: sixteen hundred marines.

In June of 1965 a ten-man military council led by Air Vice Marshal Nguyen Cao Ky, commander of the South Vietnamese Air Force, and army general Nguyen Van Thieu took control of the South Vietnamese government. Ky was named premier, while Thieu became chairman and chief of state. Chairman Thieu was a Southerner and an old friend of Rear Adm. Chung Tan Cang, the Diem coup participant who was now "chief of naval operations"—a title change from "naval deputy" reflecting a rise in the navy's status since the coup. The two men had been classmates at the Merchant Marine Academy in their youth, although Thieu had flunked out and been forced to settle for a career in the army. Premier Ky, a Northerner by birth, was very friendly with the naval chief of staff, also a Northerner. So it was only a matter of time before the navy became involved in the power struggle between Ky and Thieu— who, even though they were heading up a "compromise" government, avoided each other like the sun and moon.

CNO Cang was making sure that only Thieu loyalists were getting choice staff positions on shore, while the navy's Northern officers, who he feared would be loyal to Ky, found themselves stuck on semipermanent sea duty. It didn't take long for Kiem and the other Northerners to get fed up. It wasn't just their own careers they were upset about: they resented the fact that the navy was being used as a political tool. Their mission was to fight the communists, not their own air force! Meeting secretly aboard their friend Captain Thu's ship, Kiem and some of the other Saigon-based ship captains decided to align themselves with Premier Ky and push for Cang's ouster. Most of them were from the North, although there were a few Southerners who had gone to school in France with them, and a few young officers who had studied under them at Nha Trang.

The next day they moved their boats inside the shipyard and barred the entrance. They would no longer open the gates to CNO Cang, they announced, and they intended to strike until he was removed from the navy. Premier Ky, who loved publicity, had promised to back them up. With an eye to what would look dramatic on the TV news, he announced that he'd be dropping one of his deputies behind the shipyard gates by helicopter. Ky's choice for the insertion was Col. Nguyen Ngoc Loan—who would later become famous for shooting a Viet Cong suspect in the head while a photographer snapped pictures.

In the meantime, while waiting for reinforcements, Kiem was chosen by the other ship captains to step outside and negotiate with his least-favorite VNN commander: buffalo-boy-killer Nguyen Van Luc, recently returned from his post-coup diplomatic tour in Korea. Luc was on Cang's side of the standoff, and he'd been dispatched to try to get them to back down. Kiem made sure that his right hand was hovering above his gun and that three crack-shot sailors hefting M14 rifles were lined up behind him.

"What are you doing?" snarled Luc. His face was redder than ever, as red as a raw pig's heart.

Kiem did his best to explain, and Luc stared back at him for what felt like several minutes. "OK, I'll remember it," Luc snapped, and he wheeled on his boots to go.

On the third day of the strike, Rear Admiral Cang was removed from the navy and reassigned to the Armed Forces Staff College in Da Lat. Premier Ky selected Captain Van—a Northerner and a graduate of the French Naval Academy—to be the next chief of naval operations. Kiem and the other rebel ship captains called off their strike and began to celebrate.

But Captain Van took the precaution of consulting an astrologer about the promotion. And glumly the astrologer reported that the stars were just not right for it. So Van went back to Ky and declined. Ky was so furious that he threw the ill-starred Van into jail for a couple of weeks.

The end result was that the navy wound up getting another merchant-marine-trained Southerner in place of Cang: Capt. Tran Van Phan. He was a little better than Cang, but not by much.

One evening the new CNO made a personal visit to Kiem's ship to tip him off about an upcoming coup. "Don't let the rebel tanks breach the naval compound," he warned Kiem. "Don't hesitate to shoot."

"Aye, aye, sir," said Kiem. But privately he wondered how in hell he was supposed to distinguish a "bad tank" from a "good tank." He made up his mind not to shoot without written orders, no matter what the CNO might say when nobody was listening.

Fortunately, no tanks rumbled down to the docks that night, and the compromise government held together, putting an end to the two-year eruption of coups—although Thieu eventually prevailed in the power struggle with Ky and became the president.

CHAPTER 12

U.S. Steps Up Combat Role

Pacific Stars & Stripes, 10 June 1965

In February of 1965, there were no American combat troops in Vietnam; in March of 1965, there were sixteen hundred; in April, eighty-two thousand; and in August of that same year, one hundred twenty-five thousand. By the end of 1967, there would be half a million. For Vietnamese families like Kiem and Thom and their children, the American troop presence was a mixed blessing. Without it, they had very little hope of winning the war, but because of it, their way of life was changing almost beyond recognition.

It wasn't just that the gracious old sidewalk cafés of Saigon were giving way to bars and "massage parlors" or that shade trees were being cut down to widen Saigon's avenues for American vehicles. It wasn't just the influx of beggars and prostitutes into the city, making their curbside pitches to GIs, nor the barbed wire "uglifying" every public space where Americans might gather and tempt a VC grenade. It was more pervasive than all that. Suddenly anyone who could perform a service for Americans was getting rich—maids, chauffeurs, cooks, baby-sitters, laundresses, bellhops, shoeshine boys—while middle-class professionals like Kiem and his fellow naval officers found themselves poor and getting poorer on account of dollar-fueled inflation. Young people's values were changing: why should they sacrifice for their country when they could bribe their way out of the draft imposed in 1964 for all men aged twenty-four to forty-five and get rich selling orange pop to GIs on the sidewalk? When Kiem put out to sea now, it was with the fear—no, with the certainty—that Thom and the children would run out of food before he got back. If it was that bad for him, he wondered, how much worse was it for his men, who were paid so much less?

He had a crew of ninety under him now as commanding officer of PCE 07, the *Dong Da II*, and whenever he docked the escort ship in or near Saigon, at least a third of the men would go AWOL. He knew exactly what they were doing—not drinking or womanizing, for you couldn't light a fire under them to get them off the ship when they were in a strange port—but just checking up on their families, making sure they had enough to eat. He had tried everything he could think of to discourage absenteeism, from putting letters in the men's personnel files to depriving them of liberty the next time they were in port. But nothing worked. Fining them might have been effective—but that would have meant taking food from the men's families, and Kiem didn't have the heart.

Absenteeism was the least of Kiem's problems, though, one day in 1967 as sailing time approached. Having just given birth to their third child, a little girl named Thuc, Thom wasn't quite back on her feet yet, and Kiem hated to leave his wife alone with two active boys and the baby for a whole month. On top of that, he'd advanced his men their month's pay, out of his ship's allowance—in violation of rules—and now he didn't have the cash to buy fresh groceries for the trip. Plus, they were going to have to limp out to sea with the generator on the blink and the refrigeration system dying, and the only reason their radar would be working was that the technician was a genius at patching it with wire and junk metal. As usual, the toilets would be stopped up, the heat in the crew's bunks suffocating, and the sea so rough that it slammed them into walls, rails, and ceilings when they tried to sleep and let them work only between spells of vomiting. There'd be scarcely enough fresh water to drink, let alone wash with. If they were lucky, they'd locate a sea squall on radar and set their coordinates for it; then the deck officer would announce "shower stations," and they'd get to strip off their clothes and stand naked in the cleansing rain—and wring out their uniforms, too, while they had the chance.

Part of the reason Kiem's ship was always sailing "crippled" was the U.S. government's obsession with figures. Time spent in port for repairs or maintenance was time "idle," according to their fleet availability statistics, so the whole Sea Force had to stay out as much as possible. But even if Kiem's men had been granted the time to repair the ship, they couldn't get the parts. HQ-07, the ex–USS *Crestview* of World War II service, was so old now that many of them weren't even being manufactured anymore. That left two choices: "cannibalizing" the parts from other ships or trying to fabricate them. If by some miracle a part was still in stock in the United States, it might take a year or more to get the item, since the Americans naturally supplied their own ships first. Sometimes the VNN would send a survey team out to take a parts inventory. Then Kiem and his men would scramble to hide their best pieces under bunks and in footlockers: valves, circuit boards, chunks of piping. If their own navy knew they had anything good, they'd grab it.

Kiem's latest American advisor, Lt. Sam Carrado, had sized up the spare-parts situation pretty quickly. He had no qualms about boarding an American ship to beg its supply officer for parts while Kiem exchanged ritual greetings with the other captain—pretending not to know what was going on, to save face. When there was a chance at a real prize, like an engine or a generator part, Lieutenant Sam would swap for VC trophies captured by Kiem's sailors: flags, pistols, Russian-made rifles. The American sailors went nuts over that stuff.

Lieutenant Sam also knew enough not to bug them to maintain equipment they had no use for, like the sonar for spotting "enemy submarines." The advisor before him had insisted that they keep everything up and running, even when it was a waste of their resources.

But helpful, tactful Lieutenant Sam was fast becoming one of Kiem's biggest problems. It had started Lieutenant Sam's first time out with them, when he'd spotted a boatload of fishermen working in the nude. He'd asked a junior officer why the men weren't wearing any clothes. "Because they're so poor," the junior officer had answered.

"His eyes got all swampy when I told him that," the Vietnamese explained to Kiem later. In fact, the American had gone down to his cabin, gathered an armload of socks and T-shirts, and tossed them to the fishermen, who scooped them up smiling and waving.

But the junior officer had told Lieutenant Sam only half the story. It was true that the fishermen were poor, but not so poor that they didn't have any clothes at all—only so poor that they had one or two changes of clothes and no more. To keep their precious clothes from getting all wet and fishy-smelling while they worked, they would take them off and stash them in a waterproof bag.

The next time they put out to sea, Lieutenant Sam brought a whole cardboard box full of gift clothes with him, and it was obvious to Kiem that word was beginning to spread among the fishermen. As soon as they spotted "07" on the side of the ship—like James Bond's number—they stripped and came flocking around. The congestion was starting to interfere with their surveillance activities.

They were taking part in a joint operation with the U.S. Navy and Coast Guard called "Operation Market Time." The Vietnamese coastline from the seventeenth parallel to the Cambodian border had been carved into eight patrol zones stretching sixty-six kilometers out to sea. With the help of U.S. aerial and "spy ship" surveillance, VNN crews were boarding suspicious vessels to search for enemy cadres, weapons, and supplies. When they'd started in 1965, most of the Viet Cong's weapons and supplies had been coming into the country by water, but over the past two years the navy had cut that traffic to a dribble—even though the VNN disagreed with the Americans about the right way to search.

Searching a hold full of fish was a slimy, smelly task: plunging their arms in up to the shoulder to make sure nothing was hidden under the catch, while rats scuttled over their legs or cockroaches flew in their faces. And the American government expected VNN crews to search thousands of junks a month, even when there was no cause for suspicion—treating the poor fishermen like criminals, tearing holes in the junks' delicate hulls just by pulling the big ship up alongside, angering the fishermen into withholding information when they had it—*pushing* them into the arms of the Viet Cong, in Kiem's opinion.

Though the Americans thought the VNN crews were lazy for not wanting to search all those junks, that wasn't the case at all. The fishing junks all looked alike to the Americans, but Kiem and his men knew which boats to finger: those that moved around instead of staying in one spot to fish or headed to sea or shore at odd times of day or seemed to be avoiding them. Through binoculars, other clues revealed themselves: narrow "eyes" painted on the prow of a boat in an oval-boat-eye area like Vung Tau or a round-boat-eye area like Phu Quoc—"eyes" to look down underwater and see fish with, some said, or to look ahead and see danger with, said others; fresh haircuts and too-pale skin on crew members; or Chinese junk-type sails on a "local" boat. Once his ship was alongside, Kiem could spot phony accents, too-soft hands, even the absence of the normal ripe "fishy" smell a junk should exude. He kept an eye out, too, for young men who appeared to be draft-aged. And he was wise to the VC tricks for hiding contraband, such as towing weapons or containers under the boat by a string.

Lieutenant Sam was already beginning to "talk back" to Saigon Naval Headquarters, lobbying Kiem's CO to let Kiem's men search most junks with binoculars only. Would Kiem lose his ally, though, on the day Lieutenant Sam lost face in front of the entire ship, when he finally learned the truth about the naked fishermen? All Kiem could do was pray that a natural opportunity to set his advisor straight would present itself before the communists took advantage of the navy's distraction.

At least there'd be a detour this trip, before they got out to the islands where men were so poor they fished naked. At the request of local shore authorities, Kiem and his crew would be providing backup fire support in a "free-fire zone": an area of coastline infested with VC and therefore off-limits to fishermen. Kiem was happy to oblige. He knew that his men got bored with their daily routine of stopping fishermen and checking their papers, then searching the holds: the expression "looking for a needle in a haystack" was the same in Vietnamese as in English. There was nothing quite like manning battle stations and firing a couple hundred rounds of ammo at the shoreline to get the navy men's blood fizzing again.

As usual, the free-fire exercise was a welcome diversion. As a bonus Kiem's crew hauled in an off-limits fishing junk whose crew kept protesting that they were working for an ARVN general. No doubt it was true, for Vietnamese fish were extremely intelligent, able to sense which zones were off limits to their human predators and then migrating there in huge schools. Nobody but a high-ranking army officer would have had the nerve to send his own junk in to scoop them all up. Kiem made arrangements to have the junk towed into headquarters, where it would be impounded for a week to ten days. He'd have towed it in himself if they were closer to the end of the patrol tour, but they were just starting out.

Then it was just as he had feared. As Kiem's ship approached the barrier islands where men from the mainland went to fish for months at a time, drying their catch there in the sun and threading the fish-leather on strings—even growing vegetables to supplement their diet, if a particular island were big enough—boatloads of naked fishermen appeared out of nowhere and converged around HQ-07. "Hey! Hey! Over here!" they called to Lieutenant Sam, standing up in their boats and waving to him. *Well*, thought Kiem with grim humor, *for once, we don't have to worry about hidden VC weapons getting pulled on us.*

Lieutenant Sam went below deck, came back up with two cardboard boxes, and tossed the shirts and socks and underwear to his fans. When he held up his palms to show he'd run out of clothes, the fishermen just ringed their boats in closer—still hopeful. Kiem made up his mind that he'd have to say something, then and there, before his ship ran over one of the junks. But Lieutenant Sam turned to him, all swampy-eyed again, and said, "The need is so great, Captain Kiem. I only wish I could do more."

"Lieutenant," blurted out Kiem, "the men have clothes. In their ditty bags. No way they're going to wear the stuff you're throwing them, when they can sell it for big bucks."

Then, to his astonishment, the American began laughing. He laughed so hard that the laughter turned into hiccups. "Oh! Oh! Hic!" was all he could get out. Kiem's crewmen watched in mingled horror and fascination. "Oh! Oh! Hic!" And for days afterward, Lieutenant Sam went around the ship retelling the story, in pidgin Vietnamese, to any crewman who hadn't actually seen him lose face. With every retelling, the fishermen got craftier and he himself more gullible. Kiem even heard him relating the story in English over the ship's radio!

Kiem would never understand the American mind, *never:* if he'd been in Lt. Sam Carrado's place, he'd have wanted to vanish from the face of the earth.

M E T A L

Weapons are the tools of violence,
all decent men detest them.
Weapons are the tools of fear;
a decent man will avoid them
except in the direst necessity.

Lao Tzu, *Tao Te Ching*

CHAPTER 13

March on Pentagon
Mob Hurled Back by GIs, Marshals

Pacific Stars & Stripes, 10 October 1967

Toward the end of 1967, Kiem was appointed deputy fleet commander. "Fleet Command" or "Task Force 215," formerly known as the "Sea Force," was the central organization responsible for staffing, repairing, maintaining, and arming the sixty-five seagoing ships of the VNN's fleet. The ships themselves were functionally assigned to VNN coastal and riverine zone commanders.

The new position was a "shore job" based at Saigon Naval Headquarters. Thom was happy that Kiem wouldn't be going to sea anymore, Kiem was happy that his career finally seemed to be getting back on track, and the fleet commander was happy to have somebody to dump the technical requirements of his job on. The other officers called Kiem's new CO "Cowboy" behind his back, because of his taste for flashy guns, medals, and cars. Cowboy loved any kind of a ceremony, with one exception: funerals for Saigon-area sailors, which had become too frequent and too depressing since the naval war had spread to the rivers. So he delegated that duty to Kiem, and Kiem and an accomplice soon learned to track down sorrow all around the capital, folding and unfolding their worn street maps, stopping their jeep at curbside to peer at house numbers in unfamiliar neighborhoods.

Once they had located the funeral, Kiem and his assistant would go inside and introduce themselves, and Kiem would make a short speech about the sailor's sacrifice. Then he'd award a medal by pinning it to a small, decorative pillow, which he placed atop the coffin; the dead man almost always received a posthumous promotion, since it cost the navy nothing. Finally, Kiem would step back and salute, and his companion would begin playing "Taps" on the bugle he'd carried in under his arm. By the third or fourth bar of music, the whole family would be sobbing.

Before leaving—sometimes to attend a second funeral that same day— Kiem would seek out the widow or the parents and offer his personal condolences. Usually the wife or mother would brighten at the sight of him, looking so official in his white dress uniform. But every now and then she'd collapse and start screaming "Why? Why? Why?" Especially when the young man had been Kiem's student at Nha Trang, Kiem would be screaming the same question himself, inside.

The second-hardest thing, after burying a young officer, was having to jail one for illegal activities. Year after year the newly commissioned officers came bursting out of the Vietnamese Naval Academy, full of idealism about whipping the communists and cleaning up the government. Then gradually their idealism would begin to erode. They'd see rich men bribing army officials so their sons could be either *linh kieng*, decorative soldiers, doing something safe and superfluous in Saigon, or *linh ma*, ghost soldiers, on a unit's rolls but never really there, while they, as officers, and drafted men with no political connections, would be facing live ammunition for many years to come. They would start to question why a gardener or houseboy employed by Americans was making three times as much money as they were. They'd look around and see a petty officer's wife sporting diamond earrings while their own wives were having trouble stretching the rice supply. And then, looking more closely, they'd see that the petty officer was dealing in the black market. The lowest of the low were even selling to the enemy.

About that time the young commissioned officers would begin to realize that the glorious naval victories they'd studied at the Naval Academy had nothing to do with this war. The goal of this war was just to hang on. The best possible outcome would be to drive the communists out of the South and just go back to life as before.

If such an officer had a philosophical bent, he might even find himself envying the communists for their vision of a "workmen's paradise." No one could dispute it; no one could "prove" that, should the communists win, the reality would be very different. Meanwhile the enemy's soldiers could go to their deaths without ever waking up from their dream. On the South's side, men knew they were dying to preserve the status quo— when they could look around and see that it was rotten.

A naval officer had plenty of opportunities to steal—or to look the other way, for a fee, while others stole. American goods were pouring into the country, and VNN ships made frequent runs to Da Nang, Cam Ranh, and other cities with big American supply depots. It was easy to divert a shipment here or there, with the help of a crooked GI. But there was always a chance that somebody would find out and tip Kiem off by phone or radio before the ship returned to Saigon. The honest officers didn't like to see theft and smuggling going on in the navy, and they knew that Kiem wouldn't stand for it, either.

When Kiem had reason to suspect that a ship had black-market goods on board, he'd be waiting at the docks to greet it in Saigon. "Unplanned inspection to evaluate shipboard conditions," he'd announce. It was a legitimate excuse: the deputy fleet commander had such authority. Then he'd inspect the ship with the captain, praising its cleanliness and asking for a door or hatch to be opened here or there. The men had plenty of tricks for hiding things—but Kiem knew the layout of his ships.

One favorite hiding place was the captain's cabin. For some reason they never believed Kiem would go poking around in there. Sometimes the goods would be wedged behind ammo in the storage area: pyramids of toilet paper rolls or walls of cigarette cartons. Kiem had found boxes of laundry detergent, insect repellent, and even hair spray back there. The most popular hiding place of all was the void ballast, the empty space between the keel and the floor of the deck. It was supposed to be kept free of water leakage, so Kiem always had a good excuse for making the captain open it.

Sometimes the black-market goods would be right out in the open. Kiem would never forget the sight of a PGM that had come in with its broken boom dangling and five cows lumbering around the deck, munching on the fallen safety rope their hooves had knocked down. Thousands of farm animals were loose in the center of the country, where fighting had been thick. The captain must have thought he could round up a few, float them back to Saigon, and turn a quick profit. If he got caught, it would mean fifteen days in jail, but if he got away with it, it would bring him more money than he could earn in salary in a year.

Every ship had an American advisor on board; the smuggling was going on right under their noses. With the cows, for example, the captain could have said he was bringing them back for a government banquet. He couldn't very well hide them, so he'd have to come up with some plausible excuse for his advisor.

One time when Cowboy was out of the country and Kiem was the acting fleet commander, he caught one of the navy's biggest ships, an LST, with a load of black-market items on board. Disciplining a man who outranked him went against Kiem's Confucian principles, but he still imposed the maximum sentence. "I respect your rank, sir," he told the captain, "but you are dishonoring the navy."

Kiem's "counterpart" at that time—the U.S. Navy had wisely decided to change the term "advisor" to "counterpart," implying a relationship of equals, so that Kiem's counterpart now referred to Kiem as his "counterpart" as well—was Gene Erner, an Annapolis graduate. Kiem was impressed with the young lieutenant commander. Besides being smart and good at his job, Gene had a knack for putting people at ease. Nobody else could smooth things out between counterpart-pairs who were itching to kill each other or could sweet-talk the shipyard authorities into speeding up ship repair schedules.

Thom had met Gene socially several times, and she liked him, too. It was her idea to invite him to the family's Tet celebration dinner on 30 January 1968. Since Thom, like Kiem, had grown up believing that the first guest to enter one's house in the new year determined the family's fortunes for the year ahead—for good or ill, depending on that person's character—the invitation had not been extended lightly. Kiem suggested that they include Bob Dickinson, his American supply officer, and a third American who was Bob and Gene's friend.

Nine-year-old Khai, five-year-old Kiet, and one-year-old Thuc were a little wary of the "giants" at first. But Gene was as good at charming children as grownups, and he soon had the boys calling him "uncle" and the baby playing with his car keys. He'd brought Thom a bunch of peonies and Kiem a bottle of champagne; each of them had a glass of it with dinner, even Thom, and it brought a pretty pink flush to her cheeks. Hearing her talk politics and current events with the Americans, Kiem was reminded of how smart his wife really was. Most of the time when he was home in the evenings, they just talked about money or the children.

While Thom was putting baby Thuc to bed, the men brought Khai and Kiet outside to see the fireworks. The curfew had been lifted for Tet, and hundreds of people were milling in the streets. Kiem could feel the exhilaration in the air: everybody wanted the old year gone and a new one in its place. Sparks rained into the Thi Njhe River behind their officers' barracks, nearly setting fire to a wooden bridge that arched across it. More sparks fell and sputtered out on the roofs of the *maisons sur pilo-*

tis, the houses of the poor, perched on stilts on the opposite bank.

Back inside, the group sat talking over coffee and tea, comparing their two countries' New Year customs. Thom laughed at the idea of Baby New Year in his diaper and people dancing with lampshades on their heads, while the Americans were curious about the swarms of people headed for the Lang Ong Temple. Was it something like their Midnight Mass at Christmas? Did Tet have religious significance, they wanted to know.

Kiem and Thom explained that the temple had been built to honor a human war hero, Le Van Duyet, who had died defending Saigon; it had nothing to do with the official religion of Buddhism. But the "Great Man," as they called him, had begun to take on a supernatural reputation after his death, as people came to believe he could intercede in their problems and bring them luck. It was the same all over Vietnam. A poor man might die and be buried in a field. The next day his grave would swell up because of ants or termites, but the villagers would take it as a sign and begin to worship him. Or a dead person might appear in the village chief's dream, telling him do this or that to avoid a fire or flood, and the dead person would become a god because of it. Sometimes all you had to do was drop dead at the right astrological hour on the right day, as a certain prostitute in North Vietnam did—becoming the guardian-spirit of her small village.

"Is there any chance we could visit the Lang Ong Temple tonight?" asked one of the guests.

"Oh, please, Anh"—a term meaning "Big Brother" or "dear" in Vietnamese, and a sign that Thom was in a wonderful mood—"let's take them there! I could ask my friend downstairs to watch the children. . . ."

"Most Americans never get to see the *real* Vietnam," one of the Americans was saying.

Kiem hated to be a killjoy, but just that morning there'd been an attack on Nha Trang. Rumors of more VC trouble to come had been buzzing all day long. The Lang Ong Temple, with so many people in one place, was just too logical a target for a VC bomb. "Next year, Em"—meaning "Little Sister"—he said.

The pink flush slowly faded from Thom's cheeks. She looked tired now, like a little girl trying to stay up late for Tet. All five of them sat there in silence.

"I guess we should be going," said Gene. "We've kept you good folks up late enough."

As he held the door open for his guests, Kiem looked up to see if Ke Do, the bad-luck star with his name, was out—his name the way the Americans used to call it on their rolls in California: "K. Do." But the star was not in the sky.

"Em," he relented, "I'll take you to the temple. But only for half an hour. Tell your friend to listen for the children, and then we'll go."

Kiem had never seen so many beggars lined up on either side of the temple gates: at least a hundred of them, looking hopeful on account of the holiday. He tugged his wife past them, through the ornately carved wooden gates and across a long courtyard studded with incense burners. The outdoor air was so thick with incense he could almost chew it. Out of the swirling haze rose three low buildings with dragon-sculpted roofs. He guided Thom into the middle building, the temple proper. It was dense with people and smoke.

"If we don't have much time, I'll skip the Great Man's altar," said Thom. "I want to get a New Year's fortune." They took seats on square rush mats on the concrete floor, praying and waiting for the others to pass them the bamboo cup filled with wooden chopsticks. *Chook-chook, chook-chook:* now it was Thom's turn. She rattled the cup until one chopstick shook out above the rest. It was engraved with a number in Chinese and Arabic. Taken into the room of the fortune-teller, off to the side, it would be exchanged for a colored paper slip of the same number, with a verse written on it. Then the fortune-teller would interpret it.

Suddenly Kiem had no air. "Em!" he said. "We have to go."

"But. . . ."

"Now. Hurry."

"You're so *serious*," she complained, scurrying to keep up with him. "You don't believe in fortune-tellers, do you? I know what you're thinking: the verse is ambiguous. It could mean anything. The more you can afford to pay the fortune-teller, the better your fortune. Right? That's what husbands always say. . . ."

"I'm thinking that we may be in danger, serious danger. I don't know what possessed me to come here, over my good judgment." With that, the conversation between them came to an end.

The trip home was uneventful, making Kiem feel a little foolish. Thom undressed with her back turned and claimed her side of the bed without speaking to him. He smoked a cigarette to delay getting in on his side for a while longer. When he finally lay down, he fell into sleep like falling down a well. Not thirty minutes later, a window-rattling burst of firecrackers made him sit up straight in bed, Thom stirring beside him. "Those aren't firecrackers," he said. He jumped out of bed and crossed to the window.

Peering into the darkness in the direction of the Thi Nghe River, a tributary of the Saigon, he could just make out the shape of the wooden bridge across it. Then he saw them: a dozen or so black-clad Viet Cong, shouting and waving their guns and flags on the opposite bank. He backed up to the dresser and retrieved his pistol. Then he inched along the wall to the window and looked out again.

The VC didn't seem to be advancing: maybe, he thought, they didn't know about the naval housing on this side. In addition to Kiem's building, which housed five officers and their families, there was a bachelor petty officers' barracks next door. It could be that the VC were just wary of the bridge guard. The guard had nothing to do with the navy; his job was to search produce trucks entering Saigon from the countryside, since the bridge linked the city with a two-lane highway. From time to time he would have found some strange vegetables tucked among the bitter cucumbers and dishcloth gourds: long and cold and silver-colored or round and hard with a stem you wouldn't want to pull yourself. Of course if a farmer didn't want to unload a hundred watermelons on the sidewalk, he could always shake the guard's hand with a few piastres tucked inside his own.

Kiem hurried to the phone and dialed Cowboy's home number. No answer. *Probably out celebrating the New Year at Madame's house.* So Kiem rang up Fleet Command and reached the duty officer. "We've had a report of trouble at headquarters, too," the man told Kiem. He promised to send a boat out to investigate and pick Kiem up. Then, before Kiem had a chance to dial headquarters, *kaboom!* Kiem had heard VC rockets land before—but not in his side yard. He could hardly believe the building was still standing.

Thom came running out of the bedroom, headed for the children's rooms, just as the baby began to wail.

"VC," he told her. "Quick, get the children and crawl under the stairwell. Don't come out until I tell you to." He quickly changed from his pajamas to his uniform, then took up his position at the window. Pretty soon he heard the boats' engines: the navy had sent two LCVPs. But they were beaching on the other side of the river—the VC side!

"Over here!" he yelled out the window. "Commander Kiem here!" Apparently the sailors couldn't hear him. Then the VC began shooting at the boats with pistols and AK-47s. The boats lashed back with their 20-mm Oerlikons and .30-caliber machine guns. Back and forth, for about fifteen or twenty minutes, the two sides traded fire. When it had been quiet for a good five minutes, Kiem ran outside and signaled to the LCVPs with a flashlight. They crossed to his side of the river, keeping their weapons trained on the VC side. Nobody on board had been hurt.

Telling them to wait, Kiem ducked back inside to check on Thom and the children, still huddled under the stairs. Then, leaving three sailors behind to secure the bridge, he gave orders to proceed to headquarters.

As they approached the pier, he saw with relief that the main gate to headquarters was still closed, although two cars were positioned at odd angles outside it. Then he noticed that their tires were flat, giving them the quaint look of elephants kneeling in the road, waiting for their riders to board. Kiem adjusted his binoculars. Security lighting revealed one man-sized form slumped over the wheel of a Simca and several others lying on the ground beside the second vehicle, a taxi. A burst of gunfire startled him, but it was only a neighboring ship firing at the lifeless tableau.

He radioed headquarters and was told that a quick-thinking guard had banged the alarm and started shooting when the vehicles tried to breach the gate. The VC had been caught in the crossfire between the men inside headquarters and the gunships docked at the pier. Two or three of them had escaped on foot. So far, there had been no VNN casualties.

"Hold your fire," he radioed to the other ships. "I'm going ashore." He took half a dozen crewmen with him. One man scouted the scene while the others trained their weapons at the vehicles.

"Don't shoot at the Simca!" the scout yelled back. "It's loaded with explosives!"

If it hadn't been for that gate guard. Next year, Le Van Duyet, Kiem thought, *I might even splurge and buy you a joss stick. . . .* Just then, a shot rang out from the direction of Hai Ba Trung Square. The scout dropped to his knees.

"The fountain, sir," said one of Kiem's men. "They're in the water tank."

At the junction of two major streets a stone's throw from naval headquarters stood one of the few public monuments not yet blown up by VC terrorists: a statue of Tran Hung Dao, the Vietnamese naval hero known as the "Sea Lord." The patron saint of the navy now reigned over a gurgling water fountain, looking stern in his funny helmet and armor.

Couples liked to meet at that statue. Children were always trailing toes and fingers in the delicious coolness of the water.

Kiem hesitated for a long, painful moment. "Small arms only: commence fire," he ordered. Drawing closer to the square, they began sniping at the tank with newly issued M16 rifles, taking care not to hit the statue. They seemed to be getting some extra help from the direction of the American compound. Kiem winced as a chunk of the Sea Lord's armor flew off.

But they were just wasting their ammunition. Kiem hated to make the next decision: "Hold rifle fire," he commanded. "Ready the grenade launcher. One, two, three: *launch*."

The sailor carrying the M79 grenade launcher pulled a 40-mm "grenade"—actually a big, short bullet called that for the way it explodes—from his chest bandolier. He loaded it into the single-shot weapon and fired it at their target as Kiem and the other sailors hit the ground face down. Shock waves crashed in their ears as the earth shook them like flopped puppets. Even before they blinked and stood up, they could taste the grit of concrete dust sifting out of the air.

The explosion hadn't destroyed the statue; it had only damaged it. But the two VC were lying as still as statues under Tran Hung Dao's raised sword. Kiem crept up to one of the bodies and beamed his flashlight down on it. Though it was lying facedown, he could see that it had the square, stocky build of a countryside fellow. He nudged it with his foot to turn it over, and a tangle of intestines spilled out of the stomach. But what sickened Kiem was the face: no more than sixteen or seventeen years old, with the mouth gaping stupidly open. Not a man but a boy, and a simpleton at that.

Ten years at war, and this was the first time he'd seen the dead enemy's face. In the navy, shooting at the seam of water and sky or water and land with long-range guns, you didn't often get the chance to see what you had hit.

Kiem knew that he should feel something for the boy; after all, a mother and a father would soon be wailing at his funeral. He could almost picture the rural coffin with its bowl of raw rice and three sticks of incense on top, to keep the corpse from rising. But he felt nothing inside, nothing, and the nothingness frightened him. *I deserve a better class of enemy* was all he could think, kicking the corpse back over on its slime of intestines.

"That's enough of this shit," he snapped. "Let's go."

Inside headquarters, the wire machine was chattering like a monkey in the new Year of the Monkey. If its reports could be believed, the communists had attacked every major city at once. The strategy made no sense: spreading themselves that thin, there was no way they could gain any ground. *What were they up to?*

Just after sunrise, Kiem's men captured two more VC. Bare-chested, dressed only in cheap black cotton shorts, with that same dumbfounded expression on their faces, they'd been discovered hiding in a culvert that led to the river. Under interrogation they confirmed that they were rural VC, told to go in and hold headquarters for a short time, after which the "regulars"—the Northern communist People's Army of Vietnam (PAVN)—would come down to finish the job. Their cadres had assured them that the people of Saigon would rise up to join them in their cause. But when their operation failed and they'd tried to escape, they'd found themselves trapped: they didn't know their way out of the big city. Their leaders hadn't wasted maps nor compasses on them.

It was the same all over Saigon, with pockets of VC holed up in houses and schools, struggling to hang on. ARVN soldiers marched around from house to house trying to flush them out. Neighbors stood watching the army fight the communists at the end of their block as if they were watching a movie. Thousands of other residents grabbed whatever belongings they could and fled their homes and their burning neighborhoods.

Suddenly, by the default of other civilian or government relief organizations, Fleet Command found itself in charge of a Saigon refugee camp. Twelve hundred people had crowded into three huge hangars full of rusted machinery—the remnants of a sugar mill that had been financed by West Germany under Diem but never completed. They unrolled their bamboo mats on the floors and hung bedsheets from ropes for privacy.

Recruiting volunteers from ships under repair in the Saigon shipyard, Kiem and Cowboy formed an "action team" to cope with the mass of demands: food, water, sanitation, blankets, milk for the children. The most pressing problem was food. The four main supply arteries into Saigon had been pinched off because of the fighting, and the city was operating under a twenty-four-hour curfew. Before shutting down altogether, Saigon's grocery stores had been picked clean of fresh, dried, and canned foods.

While Kiem's sailors fed the refugees naval C rations of dry rice and noodles, Cowboy's American counterpart used his pull with the U.S. supply depot at Long Binh, twenty kilometers outside Saigon. Long

Binh promised him all the food he could want if the VNN could make it there.

But that was a big *if,* since the road was closed and VC were all over the place. Cowboy ordered Kiem to organize an expeditionary force of three command jeeps carrying Kiem, Gene Erner, and Bob Dickinson; two eighteen-wheeler flatbeds for the food; and three truckloads of VNN sailors outfitted in helmets and flak jackets and armed with M79 grenade launchers, M16 rifles, and mounted machine and submachine guns on top of the trucks.

The sailors were jittery: it was the first time they'd ever had to fight on land. Every time they heard the familiar *pop pop* of the enemy's AK-47s, they jumped off the trucks and fanned across the highway, probing the ambush area with grenades. Most of the houses along the way had been destroyed—some were still burning—and the stink of death was in the air. Except for the AK-47s and one burst of machine-gun fire from behind a bamboo hedge, the countryside was almost surrealistically quiet.

Bob Dickinson loaded the two flatbeds to the brim with C rations, milk powder, dehydrated shrimp, steaks, fruit, and cabbages and then stacked the overflow in the jeeps—leaving little room for their occupants. By some miracle they got back to Saigon unscathed.

The next day the atmosphere in the camp was almost festive. A long line of people stretched to the food distribution table, where Cowboy and his counterpart stood joking heartily with the refugees as they handed out cabbages and oranges for treats along with the C rations. Kiem stood off to one side observing, happy that he'd get a chance to see Thom and the children now that the crisis was over.

It took a month for the South Vietnamese Armed Forces to shake out the last pockets of resistance. When it was all over, the communists had lost more than fifty thousand men in their "Tet Offensive"; the South Vietnamese and Americans combined, fewer than ten thousand. "Just give us one or two more Tets, Uncle Ho, and this war will soon be over!" was the feeling inside naval headquarters, especially among the younger officers.

But when Americans looked at their TV sets, they saw killing in the streets of Saigon, dead marines lying inside their embassy. They perceived that they were losing a war that had cost them thousands of lives and billions of dollars. In March of that year, U.S. president Lyndon Johnson announced that he was halting the bombing of the North and calling for peace talks with the communists. The Tet Offensive haunted his decision not to run for reelection in the fall and led the way for Richard Nixon to win the presidency with a "secret plan" to end the war.

Early one morning in the year after Tet—so early that the sky was still black and the river gulls behind the barracks not yet cawing and diving for fish—Kiem dreamed that his brother Nam was preparing to walk backward in front of their father's coffin. Suddenly aware that he was dreaming, he tried to claw his way to consciousness, up, up, out of the dream and toward his wife's warm body in the bed beside him. But the nightmare wouldn't fade. He found that his face was wet and that ugly, strangled crying noises were coming from his throat. Thom was awake now, too, leaning over him. "Kiem, Honey, what is it? What's wrong? Are you sick? Say something. Please, Honey. . . ."

It was hard to get the words out, with his breath coming in shallow gasps. He hadn't cried in over twenty years—not since he was a little boy. "My father," he whispered. "He's dead. He died this morning."

She didn't try to talk him out of it. A dream like that was as certain as a telegram—to the day and to the hour.

Kiem's mother (*left*)
with Thom's mother
in Haiphong, 1953.

Thom at age sixteen,
Haiphong.

Midshipman Do Kiem on a French training ship.

Vietnamese midshipmen at L'Ecole Navale (the French Naval Academy), 1955; Kiem is third from the right.

Kiem (*center*) with a U.S. advisor on a fighting junk, 1965.

Thom and Kiem in
Phu Quoc, 1969.

Thom posing in
Phu Quoc, 1969.

Thom and Kiem
with their sons,
Kiet (*left*) and Khai
(*right*), 1969.

Kiem swimming at An Thoi with his daughters Thuan (*left*) and Thuc (*right*).

Kiem pinning a medal on his U.S. counterpart, Capt. Maurice Shine, 1971.

Kiem (*center*) with VNN chief petty officer Hai and USN chief of naval operations, Adm. Elmo Zumwalt, admiring a rooster raised under Zumwalt's assistance program for VNN dependents.

Admiral Zumwalt chatting with Kiem during a visit to Phu Quoc.

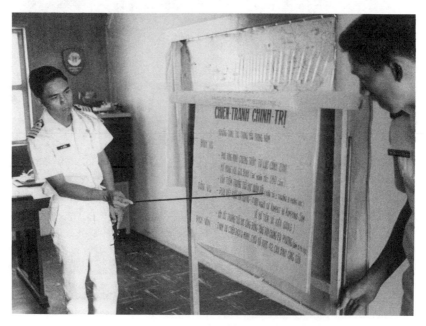

Kiem giving a briefing as commander of the IV Coastal Zone.

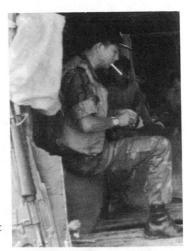

Kiem taking a break
during an operation at
Nam Can, 1971.

Kiem (*pointing*) on a combined coastal operation with Cambodian Navy officers. *Peter Swartz Collection, Naval Historical Center*

Flying the U.S. flag, HQ-229 is tied up at harbor in
Subic Bay in May 1975, following the evacuation of the
Vietnamese naval fleet. *Naval Historical Center*

Former Vietnamese Navy ships (*left to right*) HQ-471, HQ-07, HQ-08, and
HQ-11 are tied up at Buoy 1, Subic Bay, after bringing in refugees. Cambodian
Navy ship P-112 can be seen to the far right. *Naval Historical Center*

CHAPTER 14

4 Kent State Students Killed by Troops
8 Hurt as Shooting Follows Reported Sniping at Rally

New York Times, 5 May 1970

Nixon's "secret plan" to end the war centered on "Vietnamization," a policy by which U.S. bases and equipment would be transferred to South Vietnam as U.S. troops were withdrawn. Though it was not unlike the French policy of *jaunissement*— the "yellowing" of its forces, late in the First Indochinese War—the men of the Vietnamese Navy forgot their history lessons and reacted to Vietnamization with joy and renewed optimism. The younger naval officers under Kiem could hardly wait to begin fighting the war themselves, without American supervision. And everybody from the newest enlisted man to the starriest admiral was thrilled at the prospect of getting "new" warships—even if they were relics from World War II.

In February of 1969, Kiem had been named district commander of the IV Coastal Zone, becoming one of only eight territorial zone commanders holding the navy's highest field-command positions. There were four coastal and two riverine zone commanders, plus commanders of the Rung Sat Special District and the Capital Military District, Saigon. The IV Coastal Zone was the southernmost "wedge" of the country, with the Gulf of Thailand to one side of its peninsula and the South China Sea to the other. Inland, it contained a segment of the Cambodian border. Although technically a coastal zone, its rivers were strategically important, making it a hybrid of sorts. Forced to juggle the demands of coastal and riverine warfare, Kiem helicoptered back and forth between the coastal command station at Phu Quoc Island and a floating base at Nam Can, on the Cua Lon River. While on blue water he reported to two different navies, Vietnamese and American; while on brown, to his country's army and his own navy. It was confusing, to say the least. And whenever Kiem's fourth boss, President Thieu, decided to fly down for a weekend of sportfishing on one of the beautiful islands in Kiem's district, Kiem would have to lie to the army, the navy, and the Americans all at once, saying he had a "special mission to accompany the president"—which usually meant making up a fourth at card games with the wives and girlfriends of Thieu's ministers.

On the morning of Lunar New Year 1970, Kiem lay in his bunk at Nam Can smelling the coffee filtering through the air-conditioning system. The bugle had not yet sounded, but he'd been up most of the night, thanks to the anti-sapper concussion grenades dropped into the Cua Lon River every ten to fifteen minutes. His American counterpart, Lt. Comdr. Ricky Petre, USN, was still snoring in the bunk next to him, and Kiem tried not to disturb him as he rose and dressed. Ricky was a "Mustang"—slang for an officer who'd risen from enlisted man—and he'd been in-country for only a few months.

Kiem strode the length of the dock through the early-morning fog, sticking his head into the mess to beg a cup of coffee from the breakfast cooks, then continuing on to the CIC (Combat Information Center). It was his habit to go there first thing in the morning when he was on base, to review the intelligence reports from the night before. Settling into his swivel chair, he grabbed a stack of printouts and began scanning them for signs of enemy troop movement, sipping the coffee that was hot enough to burn his tongue.

Lieutenant Canh, Kiem's aide, stuck his head in the door: "Good news, sir. We intercepted an ambush party at Ganh Nho last night. Killed one VC and captured a female agent. One man jumped overboard before we could grab him."

"Good work!" said Kiem. "Where's the prisoner?"

"In custody, sir. I'm afraid she's playing dumb. We also got one Czech VZ 52 rifle and a cache of VC documents. They're in that knapsack on your desk. I thought you might like to see them."

Kiem grinned: the junior officer knew his habits. "Thanks," he said. "Why don't you give me an hour or so, then bring the agent around?"

"Aye, aye, sir."

Kiem set the stack of printouts aside and unbuckled the tan cotton knapsack, pulling out a sheaf of letters and notebooks. Once, he recalled, his men had captured a whole roomful of notebooks from a secret VC training outpost. Kiem had read through them with disgust and fascination. "I didn't feel like standing guard in the rain today. Tomorrow I will stand an extra shift, to make up for my insolent thoughts," one soldier had written. "I thought of my wife today, when I was supposed to be concentrating on our cause. I will burn her picture so that I will not be distracted from my duty," another had confessed. And another: "Today I felt resentful that my portion of rice was so small. Tomorrow and the next day I will give my portion to another so that I may grow in the self-discipline necessary for our cause." How, Kiem had wondered at the time, could his own freethinking men—dreaming of dry uniforms, full stomachs, nights stolen with their wives—prevail over minds washed clean of every thought but sacrifice?

Now, cracking open a notebook, he traced with one finger the words of a familiar poem copied out in blue ink:

If you are a flower, be the sunflower.
If you are a stone, be the diamond.
If you are a bird, be the white paloma.
If you are a man, be a communist.

As Kiem was reading, Ricky came limping in: tall and rangy, with white-blond hair and eyes like ice cubes in his sunburned face. "How'd you get the coffee before breakfast, Man? Jeez, do I need a cup. The longest I slept in one stretch last night was about eighteen minutes."

If any other counterpart had dared to call him "Man" instead of "Commander," Kiem's fingers would have curled into fists. But Ricky just made Kiem laugh. He was like an exasperating younger brother. Kiem and Ricky had both been friends with "Pinocchio," a young American petty officer with a soft spot for the Nam Can villagers. Pinocchio had dug the villagers their first freshwater well. He used to spend most of his paychecks on gum and candy for the village kids; sometimes the bolder kids would come right up onto the base, looking for him.

As blind to danger as a child, Pinocchio had paid no attention to the crude "floaters," lashed together from banana trunks and carrying red-lettered warning signs, that the VC would set adrift just upriver from their base: "Prepare for Your Death," "We Kill Americans," "Get Out of Here." One day, managing to dodge his little fans, Pinocchio had gone for an early-morning walk outside the village limits. It was a foolish risk for him to have taken—and he did not get away with it. Later that morning, somebody found his head on a stick by the village gates.

By the time the naval base had been alerted to incident and Kiem had sent a man out to cut Pinocchio's head down, it had been too late to spare the children: they were all out there staring at it, some of them screaming. No more bubblegum now.

That night Ricky had blundered into the CIC with a bottle of whiskey under his arm. Out of politeness Kiem had accepted glass after glass, dumping it into the wastebasket when Ricky wasn't looking. With Pinocchio gone, Ricky said, Kiem was the only real friend he had left. He said that he believed in friendship but not in love, that love was just a crock of shit and he hoped Kiem's wife was a fine lady and faithful, because his own ex-wife was a no-good whore. Kiem sat up late with him, just listening.

After the horror of Pinocchio's death and that night of crazy camaraderie, Ricky and Kiem had been friends and not just counterparts, although they were often at odds with each other. Recently, for example, one of the Vietnamese maids on base had given several U.S. sailors a case of VD. "Do something!" Ricky had yelled. "Get that slut out of here! She's a goddamned Typhoid Mary!" Kiem had tried to explain that the maid was married to one of *his* sailors and that an accusation like that would ruin the man's life. The two of them had shouted back and forth at each other until they'd arrived at a compromise: Kiem would fire the woman with no explanation.

This particular morning Kiem filled Ricky in on the events of the night before, then returned to skimming the knapsack's contents. One of the letters moved him so strangely that he read through it a second time, then decided to share it with Ricky. "Listen," he said. "It's from our friend Hoang The Binh to his wife. Tell me what you think." Ricky recognized the name at once: Binh was, in a sense, his and Kiem's "enemy counterpart": district commander of Dam Doi, a region named for the fruit bats that swarmed around its biggest lake. Kiem translated as best he could. "Dear Tam," it began, "This is to inform you of my promotion to district commander. I am very fit for my position, and I am putting all my efforts into fighting the Americans and their puppets. The victory of the people is near at hand. When the mission is near your area, I will have someone get in touch with you. I hope that you and the son whose face I have not seen are well. Signed, District Commander Binh."

"Man—what a lady-killer," said Ricky dryly. "Oh, Romeo. Oh, Romeo, wherefore art thou—Dam Doi?"

Kiem started to laugh. It was exactly what he'd been thinking.

"The prisoner, sir." It was Lieutenant Canh, looking surprised to find them laughing. "Would you like to see her?"

"Send her in," said Kiem.

How many dozens of prisoners had the two of them seen before this one? Male or female, they all looked alike: skinny, ragged, and filthy from living in the swamps. But this young woman made them suck in their breaths. She was tall for a Vietnamese, slim but full-breasted, with light skin and full pink lips. Though she was wearing black VC pajamas, there wasn't a dab of swamp mud anywhere on her trousers, ankles, or slim pale feet. Even her shoulder-length black hair looked clean and freshly combed. *What was that poem about the lotus flower rising from the mud but not stinking of the mud?* Kiem tried to remember but couldn't quite put his finger on it. The "white paloma" poem and Shakespeare must have put him in a literary mood.

Conscious of their stares, she made a slight bow in Kiem's direction. Then she turned and bowed deeply to Ricky.

"What's your name, Miss?" asked Kiem.

"My name is Cau," she lied.

"And how's Binh. Is he doing all right?" asked Kiem.

She blinked, and her pink lips opened slightly; then she recovered her composure. "I don't know any Binh," she said.

"Mr. Hoang The Binh, district commander of Dam Doi? Your husband? You don't remember him? That's a little odd, don't you think?"

"I was only hitchhiking a ride on a boat, sir," she said. "I had to get medicine for my father, so I asked two strangers to take me in their boat."

"They were taking you to see your husband," Kiem corrected. "He's in the area now, isn't he, Tam? Why don't you tell. . . ."

"Hey! Hey! Kiem!" Ricky cut in. "Go a little easier on her, Man."

Shit! There goes any chance of getting intelligence. And just when Kiem was starting to get somewhere with her, too. Kiem summoned Lieutenant Canh. "Get the paperwork ready to transfer prisoner to Phoenix Bureau," he told him.

"Aye, aye, sir. We'll have to delay a day, though, because of the holiday." Kiem had almost forgotten that another Tet had rolled around: 1970, the Year of the Dog.

"Correct. That will be all, Lieutenant." The prisoner bowed to each of them before leaving.

"She can't possibly be a communist!" Ricky exploded. "She's so clean, so . . . so . . . *pure!* Why'd you have to be so hard on her, for Christ's sake?"

"You sound like her defense attorney," said Kiem. "Don't fool yourself, Ricky. She could have been the one who killed Pinocchio. It could have been her machete."

"No way, Man. No fuckin' way. Did you see her eyes? You almost made her *cry*, Man. . . . But, shit, Man: I didn't mean to piss you off. I'm sorry."

"That's all right," said Kiem. And it was all right—because Ricky was his friend.

Later that day Kiem stood out on the dock watching a Saigon Civic Action Team distribute New Year's gifts to the villagers, who were flocking around HQ-401 in hundreds of small sampans. Some of them were knocking on the hull of the LSM, not yet convinced that steel could float. Doctors Vong and Giao, dentist Phi, and the nurses were handing out cakes of soap, boxes of powdered milk, sacks of Chinese noodles: "luxury items" that the villagers hadn't seen in years.

He was proud of what had been accomplished here. Before the war the district of Nam Can had bustled with several thousand residents. But the VC had chased them into the surrounding swamps, then burned and razed their huts. U.S. admiral Elmo Zumwalt, commander naval forces, Vietnam, had come up with the idea of going back in and establishing a joint American and Vietnamese military presence under Task Force "Tran Hung Dao." Besides wresting control of the Cua Lon River from the VC and making naval and chopper raids against them, the two countries' navies would build schools, dig wells, and provide health care for the region's residents. They would retake Nam Can by caring rather than by force. Many South Vietnamese officials had thought Zumwalt's idea was crazy; many U.S. officials, too, said Ricky. Sooner or later, the doubters thought, they'd have to send their armies in to rescue the "pioneers." But Kiem, the project's official commander, had believed in it from the start. And now, just look at the results!

The floating base, resting on eleven giant pontoons, had been towed upriver by barge in June of 1969 and anchored on the outskirts of what had once been Nam Can. Then from their foothold, the American and Vietnamese navies had begun trying to lure the former residents back. Borrowing army helicopters, they'd airdropped thousands of leaflets over the region, carrying the message that it was safe to return. Boats with public address systems had ventured into the smaller canals. And their strategy had worked: never wanting to abandon their ancestors' graves in the first place, the residents had rushed home, once they knew it was safe.

Zumwalt's support of the project had meant that Kiem's men could get the villagers almost anything they asked for: U.S. Seabees to clear the land for two new settlements, corrugated metal to roof every hut in style, two dozen baby chicks and feed for every family—even a black-and-white TV for the communal pagoda! Once a week Kiem would fill a portable electric generator with gas and pull the string so that people could watch Vietnamese soap operas. On the floating naval base, Kiem's men opened a sampan repair station and an ax-sharpening shop.

In the old days, most people had earned their living peddling charcoal made from a local hardwood tree. But the war had made traveling dangerous, and the igloo-shaped kilns had fallen into disuse—one could sell only so much charcoal to one's neighbors. Then Kiem's men cleared a trade route to Ca Mau, the nearest city, keeping it open and safe with frequent patrols, and the charcoal industry was revived. From Ca Mau the charcoal could be transferred to barges and shipped to Saigon, where people preferred it to wood for cooking.

Kiem chuckled at the sight of an elderly woman begging the Civic Action Team for a calendar of Mai Le Huyen, the big-busted Vietnamese singer. No sooner did she get one than she stashed it in the bottom of her boat and started begging for another. "Hey there, Grandmother," he called to her. "One picture ought to be enough to keep your husband home all day!" She laughed good-naturedly in his direction, showing her black-dyed teeth. The exchange made Kiem realize that most of the people out that day were women and children. *Where were the men?* Without their trust, Operation Sea Float would never succeed.

Just then he glanced to the end of the dock and saw the prisoner leaning over the cable, half-thinking, half-observing. *She's a sharp one,* he said to himself, *always calculating, never resting.* He nodded in her direction, and she nodded back.

After a dinner that was more festive than usual, Kiem and the other officers met to plan the next day's schedule. They were just about ready to adjourn when Lieutenant Canh poked his head in the door. "Sir," he said, "the prisoner has asked to see you."

"Bring her to the CIC," he said. He turned to Ricky. "You come, too." Then, to the rest: "The meeting is adjourned. Happy New Year, all of you."

It was already dark outside. As the prisoner hesitated in the doorway to the CIC, harsh electric light spilled over her hair and shoulders, making her black eyes sparkle and her skin and lips look feverish. Then another gleam caught Kiem's eye, and his gaze dropped to her breasts. Two slick black circles of cloth were clinging to her nipples.

"Yes, sir," she admitted, "my name is Tam, and I am District Commander Binh's wife." She told Kiem and Ricky that she was from Ganh Con, "Little Junction," but had been working as a teacher in Ca Mau before her marriage. She hadn't wanted to marry Binh, she said, but he had threatened to hurt her parents if she refused—with that, she'd caved in. Late in her pregnancy Binh had been transferred, so she'd gone back to Ganh Con to live with her parents. Her father had tried to support them all with his sampan and fishing net, but armed forces helicopters had been everywhere, and then he'd cut his hand on a trap. The wound had become infected. He could no longer fish.

Yesterday Binh had sent two agents to take Tam to him, but only for a short visit. She had fed the baby first, then pressed the rest of her milk into a jar. She hadn't counted on being captured.

"Please," she said, "my baby is hungry. He's going to die if you don't help him. Please, please have mercy on him. This war isn't his fault. He's just a baby. . . ."

"Are you asking me to release you?" Kiem asked sternly.

"Oh, no, sir," she cried. "I don't want to go back to Ganh Con. The cadres are crazy, bloodthirsty. I saw them slit an old man's stomach open, trying to scare the rest of us into obeying them. All they care about is punishing the village 'comeback' people. . . ."

"Then what have you come here to ask me?" he demanded.

"To rescue my b-b-baby, sir," she said and began to cry.

Ricky went over and put his arm around her shoulders. "Don't you worry about a thing, Sweetheart," he said. "We'll get that baby, won't we, Commander Kiem?" And the next thing Kiem knew, he and Ricky were plotting an operation that could have gotten them both court-martialed if the wrong people found out.

After grilling the prisoner about their target's location, the terrain, and enemy troop strength, Kiem and Ricky sent her to the medical team for attention. Then they pulled out area maps and plotted their strategy.

They would set out shortly after midnight with ten fighting junks, two "Alpha" gunboats, and twelve assault frogmen, planning to snatch the baby just before sunrise. They had just enough time left to notify the others, then catch an hour's sleep.

But Kiem couldn't still his racing thoughts. The enemy's strength shouldn't be a problem: their own intelligence reports, corroborated by the woman prisoner, showed a platoon of fifteen men maximum. The prisoner claimed they were separated into smaller groups of three or four, gathering once a month for indoctrination training. And Kiem saw no reason to doubt her. The enemy's weapons consisted of two sub-machine guns, five B-40 rocket launchers, and individual AK-47s—no match for the navy's firepower, which included straight-shooting 60-mm mortars, 12.7-mm machine guns, and 40-mm grenade launchers.

"As long as we don't run into an ambush, we should be okay," he told Ricky, tossing restlessly in the next bunk.

"Amen, Bro," came Ricky's voice in the dark.

At thirty minutes past midnight, they jumped out of their bunks, put on combat gear, and smeared their faces and arms with mud. Kiem took the added precaution of tucking a piece of checkered shawl under his cap, to ward off mosquitoes: in this part of the country, even the buffaloes had to be draped with mosquito netting. Then he joined Ricky in the CIC.

The two of them briefed the boat captains and lead frogmen: "This is a rescue operation. Our goal is to get the baby back to his mother. We're not planning to attack. If we're shot at, that means they're waiting for us: so shoot back, then get the hell out of there. Understand? Roll in and roll out."

The first few times Kiem had gone out on patrol with his men, he'd insisted on flying the command flag from his boat—not for bravado but to convince his men that the VC didn't pass their lives waiting in ambush for them. When the VC knew the navy's movements in advance, they had time to dig trenches; but the VC were an easy target for the navy in an open field. Their second time out, Kiem and his men had killed two VC and captured their weapons. The very next day Kiem had helicoptered to the battle site to hand out gallantry medals by the freshly dug graves. U.S. Coast Guard commander Paul Yost, Ricky's predecessor as Kiem's counterpart, had stood gamely by.

"Good luck to everyone!" Kiem added now, glancing over at the prisoner. She was staring down at her bare feet, looking patient, enigmatic, almost resigned. If he'd been a single man like Ricky, he might have fallen in love with her himself.

They set off, scanning the tree lines for movement through green-glowing "starlight scopes" and observing radio silence. Two-thirds of the way into their thirty-kilometer journey, they came across a log barricade across the main canal. Trusting the prisoner's word that it was unguarded, they found a way to slip around. They stationed both gunboats at Big Junction; then, between there and Little Junction they strung out eight combat junks in groups of two. On coded orders the junks cut their engines and drifted toward the banks, beaching slightly on the soft clay or securing by tying a rope to an overhanging tree.

Kiem and Ricky were riding in the last two junks. The sky was just beginning to lighten when Kiem, spotting Little Junction and then the house, gave the coded order to stop. The advance boat had been towing two sampans with Japanese "shrimp tail" motors, noiseless and easy to steer. At Kiem's signal the frogmen helped Ricky, Lieutenant Canh, and the prisoner into one sampan and started its engine, then hopped into the other and started its engine as well. Casting off their tow lines, the sampans glided toward shore like two slick eels. Kiem ordered his own boat to move in closer.

He pressed his walkie-talkie to his lips so that his voice would be barely audible. "Tell her to be quick," he reminded Ricky. "Just the baby, nothing else."

"Roger," came Ricky's whisper.

The sampans beached. Holding onto Ricky's hand, the prisoner stepped out of the boat and waded ashore. Half-running, half-walking, she crossed the yard. It was an ordinary-looking house, with a flowering bush to one side and a clay water jug to the other. The prisoner sprang onto the front stoop. Her fingers reached out to touch the stressed-bamboo door-covering.

Suddenly Kiem felt the hairs on the back of his neck stand up. "Stop her!" he shouted into his mouthpiece. But the prisoner's hand kept reaching forward.

There was a flash of pure white light, then orange flames, and the whole earth shook with a roaring noise. Pieces of burning wood and thatch rained into the boat, stinging Kiem's arms like bees. He could smell burning flesh and hear Ricky's anguished sobs through his headset: "Oh, my God, no, no, no. . . ."

Somebody had booby-trapped the door, knowing she'd be back for the baby. Not Tam's father: he was too old and too sick, and it was his house—and a father is a father. Not the VC cadres acting on their own, knowing they'd have to answer to Binh's wrath. It could only have been Binh himself, perhaps assuming that Kiem's men would search the house after interrogating the prisoners. But would he have gambled his own wife's life on those odds? Was it true that the enemy's brainwashing destroyed a man's attachment to his family, his religion—everything but the state? "White palomas, my ass!" spat Kiem. "Precious diamonds! Showy sunflowers! You pieces of shit."

From then on, there was no controlling Ricky's drinking. Kiem tried to talk him into taking R&R, but he wouldn't listen. Within a month Ricky was gone, his tour of duty foreshortened.

In his place the U.S. Navy sent a temporary counterpart named Gerry, an old commander who'd risen through the ranks without ever making captain. Now that he was close to retirement age, he didn't want to jeopardize it. Just staying alive from March to November was ambition enough for him.

That May, Kiem dumped Gerry behind on an island before entering Cambodia from the sea-side, threading his way up a small inland river to the city of Kampot. Preceded by a junk force that cleared a path for them with small arms, and followed by landing ships carrying ARVN ground troops, Kiem commanded three 28-knot PCFs, or "Swift boats," carrying military supplies into the besieged country. The waterway was unfamiliar, and they threaded their way carefully, the junks planting red-flagged poles to alert the convoy to shallows. Several midstream barrages had to be probed with M79s, but they turned out to be nothing but fishing traps. A second contingent of riverine assault craft and Vietnamese marines was making its way up the Mekong River into Phnom Penh. Prince Sihanouk of Cambodia, who had been letting Vietnamese communists use his country as a staging ground, had been ousted by his minister Lon Nol in March. Now the new government was battling the North Vietnamese Army, Viet Cong, and Khmer Rouge all at once. Kiem felt a strong sympathy with them, not only because they were fighting the communists but because some of their top navy officials had been his classmates at Brest.

Landing at Kampot, they were greeted by the regional commander, a Cambodian Army colonel. He lifted a flak jacket out of its carton as if it were made of gold. "Life," he whispered to Kiem. "Do you understand? You have given us the gift of life." He grabbed Kiem's hand and held onto it for an hour, making Kiem want to light a cigarette—or scratch his nose.

Later that day Kiem's force left Kampot and sailed to the sea-resort city of Kep, the site of the prince's summer palace. The streets were deserted. Accompanied by a dozen of his sailors and Cambodian naval commander Sam Sary, an old friend from Brest, Kiem walked through every room of the sumptuous palace. But with his mind on suffering, he hardly noticed the jade, ivory, and gemstones, except to scold a Vietnamese Navy nurse for fingering a little statue. Two days later Kiem's own army would pull up in trucks and armored tanks and clean the place out, carrying the booty back to Vietnam.

The night before Kiem's sailors returned to Vietnam, the Cambodian Army colonel brought out baskets of durian fruit, the best he could do to thank them. Durian was sweeter than candy, and very rare, but eating too much of it could make one's skin break out in a prickly rash. Though they'd curbed their greed for Cambodia's jewels, the sailors could not do the same for its durian. They sailed home scratching like monkeys, Kiem among them.

CHAPTER 15

U.S. Gives Saigon Base at Longbinh

New York Times, 12 November 1972

Kiem could not put his finger on it exactly, but at some point during his years as district commander of the IV Coastal Zone, Nam Can and Phu Quoc began to feel like "home" to him, and his home in Saigon began to feel uncomfortable and strange. He spent less and less time there.

Saigon was so different from the rest of the country, so insulated from the reality and hardships of war. In Nam Can, in Phu Quoc, people looked up to Kiem for fighting for his principles, but in Saigon nobody admired him. To Saigoners the war was just a way to make easy money—and if you weren't getting rich from it, you were a fool. The war was something being fought by the government, the military, and the Americans, but not by the Saigon middle class. Thanks to bribes and political connections, most of the conscripts were coming from the countryside or from the poorer urban class.

Even though Kiem had been promoted to captain, his family was still living in the same old cramped officers' quarters on the banks of the Thi Nghe River in Saigon. Thom's uncle had come to the house one day and looked disdainfully around him. "A crappy place like this, for a big shot like you?" he'd asked Kiem. Kiem had tried to make a joke out of it, but the remark had cut him deeply.

Their fourth child and second daughter, Thuan, had been born in 1969, and Thom had gone to work as a telegraph operator for Shell Oil while her mother watched the two baby girls during the day. When she'd asked his permission to take the job, Kiem had felt devastated: now *everybody* would know that he couldn't make enough money to support his family. But he'd put his family's comfort ahead of his own vanity and said yes.

Taking the job had also been rough on Thom, Kiem knew. She'd had enough to do managing the house and four children with his being gone most of the time. Her old classmates from the Lycée Yersin had married doctors, lawyers, businessmen, or bribe-taking army officers; they spent their days shopping, gambling, riding in chauffeur-driven cars, having their hair and nails done, fretting about the laziness of their servants or about which French or American schools to send their kids to. Once Thom had started working, those old friends had begun to shun her just as the navy wives did, for being "different"—and, to tell the truth, Kiem had been glad. Their trivial chatter made him sick.

It was as if a chasm had opened up between himself and his wife and children. He had beautiful kids, as beautiful as their mother—but all they ever did when he was home was pester him for toys. When Thom rounded up Khai and Kiet for their after-dinner study time and stuck him with the babies, he felt hurt and a bit neglected. After all, he was only home two or three days a month—she should be spending time with *him*. Something had changed in the bedroom, as well; he was hungrier than ever for his wife's slender body, but she seemed slower to arouse and respond. After almost fourteen years of marriage, he knew Thom well enough to know that something was troubling her. She couldn't "compartmentalize" her problems the way he did: they leaked out into everything she said and did.

One morning in Saigon he'd awakened late to find his favorite breakfast steaming on the table: coffee and a bowl of *soi lap suon*, sweet rice with Chinese salami. Maybe everything was all right after all, he'd thought—the recent "chill" just a passing mood on Thom's part. He could hear Thom getting the boys ready for school in the hallway. "Mommy, Kiet doesn't want to go to school today," he heard Khai say.

"Don't try that stuff with me, Kiet!" said Thom. "Get on your brother's bike. This minute! Come on!"

Kiem set down his bowl and chopsticks and pushed his way through the kitchen door. "Come here, Son," he said. "Are you feeling sick?" He reached out and patted Kiet's cheek, which felt cool to his touch. Kiet looked down and shook his head.

Thom raised her voice one notch. "Hurry up and get to school, then," she said. "Your father has to leave for Phu Quoc this morning, so don't act up. He won't want to come home to a bad boy, now will he?"

Kiem flinched. "Kiet," he said, "you're a good boy, and I'm proud of you. Do you know that?" He caressed the soft black hair on the nine-year-old's head.

"I don't want to ride to school on Khai's bike," said Kiet. "The other boys laugh at me. They say it's cheap."

"What's cheap about riding on your brother's bike?" asked Kiem. "Your brother thinks riding a bike is fun, doesn't he?"

"Sure, Dad," said Khai, who was thirteen, tall and lanky for his age.

"When I was your age," said Kiem, "I had to *walk* five kilometers to school and back every day. I would have loved to ride a bike. . . ."

"I want to go to school in your jeep!" announced Kiet. "All my friends ride to school in jeeps—but they aren't fighter's jeeps like yours. Yours is cool!"

So Kiet had noticed the new jeep, parked outside and rigged for the long trip to visit inland combat units. "You're right," said Kiem, "it's a fighter's jeep. That's why it shouldn't be used to carry children to school, OK?"

Kiet seemed to be ready to concede, but Thom intervened. "Your driver could take him to school while you finish your breakfast," she said.

Kiem tried to keep his voice even. "Government property is not for personal use, Thom. You know that as well as I do."

"But everybody does it," she said. "I even see jeeps at the market, carrying officers' wives or their maids. So why can't you bring *my* son to school in yours?"

Kiem tried to ignore the stress on *my*. "*Nobody* is allowed to, and that's the law," he said. "The military is no place for permissive attitudes, Thom. People's lives depend on orders being followed."

"Well then, if you feel so strongly about it, why don't you do something about it?" she taunted.

"I do, in my own command," he said. "And it starts with my own example. But I don't have the time or the business to preach to the goddamn army."

"You and your stupid integrity," she said. "That's all I hear from the other navy wives: how strict you are, how *dedicated*. What good does it do your family? Where are we going to be at the end of the war—if we even live to see it? I can tell you one thing for sure, Kiem: if anything happens to you, we'll be out of this place and out in the street in the blink of an eye. Nobody's going to take care of this family—least of all your precious navy."

Kiem cringed at the truth behind his wife's words. Seeing that she had the advantage, Thom pushed harder: "We've sacrificed enough of our love life for this war. I'm not going to sacrifice our children's futures. Khai will be finishing high school in just a few years, and we need to start saving to send him to college. Please, Kiem, all I'm asking is that you *bend* a little. Just do the same things everybody else is doing to help their families."

"Corruption! War profiteering!" he exploded. "You think that kind of thing is *normal?* We may be at war, times may be difficult—but at least we still have our ancestors' principles to hold onto! What else is there? What else is worth believing in?"

"You and your lousy *principles*," she screamed. "It's nothing but your big fat *ego!*" She stopped and covered her mouth with her hand, then let the hand drop. "Kiem," she said in a softer tone of voice, "when I married you, all I saw was you. I didn't stop to think how we were going to make it on your salary as a second lieutenant. I trusted you with my whole heart. But you've changed. Your principles are more important than your wife and children. And I've had enough."

Kiem listened with a shearing pain in his heart, watching the tears roll down his wife's flushed cheeks. *What,* he asked himself, *would my father have done in such a situation?* But Kiem's father hadn't had much success with wives, either. Kiem would have to figure this one out for himself. He pulled her to him and hugged her tightly. "Em," he said, "I love you and our kids more than anything else on earth. I don't always say it, but it's like this air I'm breathing: I don't go around announcing it's what's keeping me alive, either. We have a future together, you and me and the kids. Just hang in there a little longer. I know how much you've sacrificed for us, and, believe me, I appreciate it. Now, I'll tell you what I'm going to do. I'm going to take Kict to school in my jeep, and then I'm going to leave on my inspection trip. So could I have a good-bye kiss?"

Thom stood up on tiptoe to kiss him, but there was something resigned in the gesture. "I'll be back in three weeks," he said. "Next time, I'll stay longer. I promise."

Kiet's round, friendly face was all smiles as he pulled up to school in his father's jeep. He called out to his classmates by name, making sure they noticed. Just before disappearing behind the gate, he yelled, "Next time, Dad, you'll have to take me in your helicopter!" Kiem gave the thumbs-up sign—*what the hell.* He could learn to bend a little.

It was lonely without Thom and the children in Nam Can and even lonelier on Phu Quoc Island, inside the "dream house" Admiral Zumwalt had ordered built for Kiem after seeing the shabby apartment he was sharing with three other officers. Constructed by the U.S. Seabees of sturdy concrete blocks and planted all around with pine trees and flowers, the three-bedroom house looked out to a view of An Thoi Bay. If Kiem squinted, he could even block the sandbags and barbed wire from the postcard-perfect sunsets.

Kiem's house was a favorite gathering place for American naval officers in Phu Quoc, who had few other options for their entertainment. Admiral Zumwalt himself used to drop by whenever he was in town, before he went back to the United States to be CNO of his navy. One night, sitting on the breezy veranda with Kiem, he'd confided that he was worried about his son Elmo III, who was under Kiem's command at Nam Can. Elmo III was a talented young naval officer, the captain of a Swift boat—and a real daredevil. He'd been the first man to "make the loop," as they called it—passing through the Ganh Hao River mouth to the sea, then back to the floating base through the Cua Lon River mouth, through some pretty hairy VC stretches. "He's trying to make a name for himself, independently of me," said the admiral: "but I'm afraid he's going to get himself killed in the process." Kiem promised the admiral he'd talk to the young man, and he did. Elmo III tried hard to curb his wild streak after that.

Capt. Maurice Shine, the successor to Paul Yost and Ricky and Gerry as Kiem's district commander counterpart, was another honored guest. He'd stood up for Kiem after Tet of 1971, when the U.S. Navy had ordered Kiem to observe the holiday cease-fire, but Kiem's own navy had failed to confirm the order. Kiem had kept on patrolling throughout the truce, to the wrath of his U.S. commander, and Maurice Shine had risked his own naval career to defend him. When Shine later came down with hepatitis, the same commander had tried to replace him with a rude, insulting counterpart in smelly battle fatigues—permanently, not just until Shine recovered. Kiem had raised hell, phoning Zumwalt in the United States, then threatening to resign from his own navy. And Captain Shine had been reinstated. So now they had each other to thank, or blame, for their futures in the navy.

Kiem liked Bill Ackerman, too. A former schoolteacher in the States, Bill was a helicopter pilot with the U.S. Air Combat Service Group, always willing to help Kiem out when no VNAF chopper was available. He and Kiem had gone spearfishing in An Thoi a few times and had watched a dozen sunsets from the veranda of Kiem's house.

Kiem never knew when "Tran Van Phu" was going to pop up, either. Not a Vietnamese at all, but a tall, blond, husky U.S. Naval Intelligence officer who reminded Kiem of Marlon Brando, Phu seemed drawn like a moth to flame to the "hot spots" of the naval war: bedding down on the ground with Vietnamese commandos, sharing their rations and hot sauce, telling jokes in flawless Vietnamese. Instead of a uniform, Phu wore VC black cotton pajamas, and Kiem would never have known he was a lieutenant commander if somebody hadn't tipped him off. The American's real name was Richard Lee Armitage, but his VNN commando friends had given him their own moniker: "Tran," the family name of their greatest naval hero, Tran Hung Dao; "Van," the most common middle name for Vietnamese males; and "Phu," meaning "rich," as in "wealthy."

But even with all those people around, the house on the bay seemed empty. Kiem's security guard slept in the back bedroom that should have belonged to Khai and Kiet. Thom kept promising to come visit, but her job and the boys' schooling left little opportunity. When the house was finished, she'd sewed curtains for it and sent them back with Kiem—but they'd been the most of herself that she could spare.

On Kiem's next trip "home" to Saigon, Thom gave him troubling news: a man in a suit with a Thai accent had been flashing Kiem's picture to the neighbors, asking if they knew him. Kiem could guess what it was about: the Thai were eager to fish in Vietnamese waters and had already tried to bribe him twice, once through a distant female cousin and once through a corrupt underling. They didn't seem to understand the meaning of the word *no.*

Vietnam had plenty of fish—too many in fact, with the big fish eating the little ones and upsetting the chain of generations. But the VNN just didn't have the resources to monitor the Thai fishing fleet. Letting the Thai in would be like handing the Viet Cong a new disguise for their infiltration. So the navy kept telling the Thai *no, no, no,* but the Thai paid no attention, sending thirty to fifty trawlers at a time into Vietnamese waters. So what if the navy chased them and one or two got caught? The Thai kept an agency in Saigon just to bail their boats out of trouble at the Rach Gia customs house.

What Kiem wasn't prepared for, this time around, was his own admiralty's taking him aside and saying that "someone with an interesting plan to propose" wanted to meet him. The man turned out to be a Saigon councilman with a sleazy reputation. He came on smoothly, though, talking to Kiem at length about "fundraising strategies" to be used for "charitable causes." Kiem understood that the "donors" would be the Thai.

Kiem told the councilman to give him time to think about it. Then he went back to naval headquarters and pleaded his case: "If we close our eyes, sir, the communists are going to take advantage. The enemy is like one robber determined to break into a man's house. Sooner or later, when the man lets down his guard, the robber is going to get in." Kiem's superior seemed to agree with him, but the next day he sent a second "businessman" over to see Kiem. And this time, the Thai talked money: a thousand bucks per trawler for one week of casting their nets without VNN persecution.

Fifty thousand dollars! That was more than five years' worth of salary—in just one week! Thom could quit her job and bring the girls to live with him on Phu Quoc. The boys could go to private schools with diplomats' children. . . . After all, everybody else was doing it. What was the good in being a martyr, a sanctimonious prig? If the Thai could have guaranteed Kiem, on the spot, that no harm would come to his men because of his actions, he might have taken the money. But they could not, and he did not.

He didn't dare tell Thom the size of the offer or confide in her about headquarters' involvement. Whether because he was keeping secrets from her or because she had recently blown up at him, the chill between Kiem and his wife got colder.

Not long after that, his morale down to almost nothing, Kiem was skimming over Binh Thuy in a UH-1 Huey helicopter. He flew surveillance for at least three hours every other day he was in Phu Quoc, alternating with his XO, to monitor his ships' deployment. Usually he went up in a two-seater observation plane, but that day he had his chief of staff with him, and they needed the extra room. When his pilot acknowledged positions with a nearby U.S. Army helicopter, Kiem recognized Bill Ackerman's voice. Happy to be in the sky with Bill, he switched his radio frequency for a quick private chat.

"OK, Captain!" Bill concluded. "I'm going to swing to the river mouth, then take a new approach to that outpost. Last time we got shot at going in and coming out. Bye now!"

"So long, Bill. Watch out!" Kiem knew how a heat-seeking land-to-air missile could lock onto a chopper's exhaust stack.

Kiem's sharp eyes spotted a sampan full of black-clad people down below in the river fork, a second or two before he heard Bill's voice reporting a sampan in the free-fire zone and saying he was going down to investigate. Bill took a sharp turn and dropped so low that Kiem could hardly distinguish his friend's chopper's camouflage from the green jungle-canopy rolling by beneath the Huey's open sides. All at once, orange fire flashed from the sampan, followed by smoke and a loud, sharp noise, and Kiem watched helplessly as Bill's aircraft exploded and went down in a ball of flames.

Kiem's pilot angled almost straight up, rising like an elevator until they were out of danger, while Kiem gripped the mike and tried to call for an air strike. He stumbled on his English so badly that he had to repeat the coordinates twice. As their Huey circled the crash site, he overheard a nearby "spotter" plane calling in the same request. Minutes later two U.S. Marine OV-10 Bronco planes came screaming in and dropped their 3,600-pound payloads into the sampan, blasting it out of the water. The turboprop craft made a few more bombing runs for good measure, then disappeared as fast as they'd come.

Kiem had seen plenty of friends die, but never one who'd seemed so alive just minutes before. Bill had been about to repatriate soon, Kiem remembered. He closed his eyes and stretched his neck backward, trying to shake the bad dream. But it was reality, unshakable.

Kiem's pilot touched down in Can Tho, headquarters for the Army IV Corps. Ducking under the still-whirling blades of their Huey, the three men were taken into custody for debriefing. When the interrogation was over, they found themselves back outside on the airstrip, blinking under the westward-slanting sun. For once in his life, Kiem didn't know where to go or what to do.

"I don't know about you guys, but I need a drink," said the pilot. "Any takers?"

Kiem wasn't a drinking man. But he said yes.

Inside the nightclub it was cool and mercifully dark. Colored spotlights beamed down on a small stage where a glamorous older woman was singing into a microphone. Kiem asked the pilot for a cigarette. His hands shook as he lit it. Then the waitress came over. Kiem ordered a Coke, and the pilot laughed at him. The pilot ordered a double scotch. A new singer, even more beautiful than the first one, had begun to perform, but the song couldn't hold Kiem's attention. The pilot got up to dance.

One by one, hideous memories began to detonate in Kiem's brain. The little street-kid who'd attached himself to their unit in Phu Quoc, who'd been "caught" by a booby-trapped knapsack in the act of stealing from them. Scraping the twelve-year-old's flesh off the walls with Ricky. . . . A slim, pale, beautiful young woman, half-walking, half-running across a yard and up a stoop. . . . A North Vietnamese hospital, aswirl with the smells of shit and blood and pus: "Anybody here named Tri? Is my brother Tri here?". . . . Kiem's high-school buddy Long, an air force lieutenant, dredged from the Saigon River with his body puffed up so badly he wouldn't fit into the coffin they'd brought along. . . .

The emcee introduced another singer, and Kiem glanced in her direction: younger than the others, plainer. If not for the bloom of youth, he wouldn't have looked at her twice. Then she opened her mouth to sing, and the first few notes raised snail-horns on the skin of his arms. The voice was as strong and honest as her face:

All I have left in my life
is a long chain of heartaches.
No, no, I have nothing to believe in,
nothing to hang onto—
and I don't love you anymore.

Kiem had heard the song on the radio many times before, but this was the first time he'd listened to the words. When it was over, he stood up and applauded wildly.

And she must have noticed, because she made her way over to his table. The pilot was still off dancing. Kiem invited her to sit down.

She told him that her name was Hoa and that she was twenty-one and a war widow, with no education. Only that powerful singing voice, he knew, was shielding her from a life of prostitution.

"You don't drink," she observed, surprised.

He shook his head, surprised that she would notice.

"When you came in here with your friend, I said to myself: that man has a faraway look in his eyes. I wonder why."

His hand flew up to his cheek. He always thought of himself in action. He never thought of himself being seen. It felt strange.

Without intending to, he found himself telling Hoa about Bill Acker-man's death. "I'm so sorry," she said, reaching to touch his arm. But when the pilot returned and told her that Kiem was the commander of the IV Coastal Zone, she jumped up and tried to leave the table. "You don't want to waste your time with a nobody like me," she protested.

"Don't go," he begged her. "Please."

He did not sleep in Can Tho bachelors' quarters that night.

The next day he was disgusted with himself. How could he have risked a fourteen-year marriage for one night's pleasure? He swore to himself he'd never see the girl again.

But the sampan incident wound up being splashed all over the newspapers, and an American with a briefcase full of tape-recording equipment flew down from Saigon to take Kiem's deposition. Women and children had been riding in the sampan. The pilots involved were in big trouble, regardless of who'd killed first. On his next trip to Can Tho, Kiem found himself wandering into Hoa's bar and sliding into a seat.

Things went on like that for two or three months, even after his men started winking and smirking at the mention of Can Tho. Sooner or later, he knew, the rumors would float back to Saigon. To the wives. But his own behavior was baffling to him. He didn't love Hoa, really—not the way he loved Thom. She wasn't nearly as smart or as pretty. He could have lived without the sex—indeed, he had, for months at a time. But a man and woman reaching for each other—it was something natural, something warm and human in the middle of an inhumane war. That was as much as he could understand.

But after that first crack in his moral code, what next? *Why not succumb to the beauties of Saigon, to the thrills of the bribery circus?* He could feel himself crumbling into fragments: mentally, physically, morally. After fourteen years at war he wasn't even sure what he was fighting for anymore. Not for "freedom," "truth," "justice," the ideals that had sustained him for so many years. For himself, for his own pride: that was all that motivated him now. Pride that he had not succumbed. Pride that he could not be beaten, on the battlefield or in his soul. Thom was right: his "moral principles" masked a big fat ego. He had to get out of that adulterous relationship and that sleazy atmosphere before it was too late. Before he lost what was left of his self-respect.

He went to Thom and confessed. "You deserted me just like my father and stepfather," she told him. "I thought you were different, but I was wrong. Get out."

Then he went to naval headquarters and asked to be sent to the U.S. Naval War College in Newport, Rhode Island. He was offering his superiors the chance to replace him with somebody more malleable—and they grabbed it, as he knew they would. He took the entrance exam for the Naval War College and got the top VNN score. Everything seemed set.

But then the CNO ran into a bind. He had to kick out his chief of staff, the member of a rival clique, and the only way to do it was to stuff him in the U.S. training slot. "It's true you had the highest score, but the chief of staff has more seniority than you," he explained feebly. So Kiem had to swallow his pride and ask to be sent to the Vietnamese Armed Forces Staff College at Da Lat. His request was granted. All he could do was wait and pray that Thom would take him back.

CHAPTER 16

U.S. Forces Out of Vietnam; Hanoi Frees the Last P.O.W.
War Role Is Ended after Decade of Controversy

New York Times, 30 March 1973

By the summer of 1972, when Kiem was about to graduate from the Armed Forces Staff College, the United States had withdrawn most of its ground forces from Vietnam, and peace talks had resumed in Paris after having broken down twice that year. Kiem went to his CNO in the position of a beggar. "Please," he said, "send me anywhere but Can Tho. My wife won't stand for it." After months of refusing to see or speak to him, Thom had agreed to give the marriage a second chance. She was three months' pregnant with the child of their reconciliation, due in January.

Admiral Chon's response was to name him chief of staff of the Mobile Riverine Force, based in Can Tho. *You big clown,* thought Kiem as he grimly accepted his new orders.

The ARVN and the VNN had joint responsibility for the MRF, which operated in the IV Riverine Zone—the notorious Mekong Delta. Right from the start of his new assignment, Kiem found himself butting heads with the Army IV Corps over the navy's role. Under "Vietnamization," the VNN had inherited a two-hundred-boat assault fleet of well-armored monitors, ASPBs, CCBs, and patrol minesweepers for providing close-in fire support to the army, plus three hundred PBRs for patrolling the rivers and canals and interdicting enemy supply lines. There were also ATCs for transporting infantry and "mobile base" support ships for billeting troops until they were launched. Kiem wanted to keep all of those formerly successful activities going—but to the army, the Brown Water Navy was nothing but a bunch of floating supply trucks.

The army's far-flung "regional force outposts" were the pride of the Saigon generals. There must have been a thousand of them altogether. On a briefing map, with colored pushpins marking their locations, they gave the impression that the South Vietnamese Armed Forces were still in control of the whole country. But Kiem knew the truth: many of those outposts were just "islands in an enemy sea." They were manned by the regional forces, ill-trained and ill-equipped—boys who were too attached to their families to leave home and join the regular army. Living inside these compounds with their families camped out beside them, they didn't dare venture outside because of sniper fire. They weren't "protecting" anyone but themselves.

Isolated like that, the regional force outposts had to be resupplied with food and ammo several times a year—a job the army assigned to the navy. Getting in was no fun for Kiem's sailors: tearing down mud barricades, blasting their way through felled trees, setting off explosives to dredge the channel deeper when they couldn't get enough draft, the men grunted and poured sweat and swatted insects every step of the way. But getting in was easy compared to getting out because, unlike the army, which could march back any way it chose, or the air force, which could fly away in any direction, the navy always had to sail out the same way it had sailed in. On the way back, though, the enemy would be good and ready for them. Sometimes the line of ambush would be two kilometers long: machine guns, Russian B-40 rocket launchers, grenades. It only took one well-armed rocket to sink a ship, and when one ship got hit, the others couldn't afford to stop and hunt for survivors. Just shoot and run. Any crewmen not killed outright in the explosion would have to swim to shore and be taken prisoner by the VC.

The resupply missions were costing Kiem the lives of ten to fifteen sailors every week. When he tried to protest that the military objective wasn't worth it—why not use cargo helicopters instead, or get rid of the worthless outposts?—the army just laughed at him. They were losing hundreds of men a week. But it took only a month to train a new infantryman. Kiem's sailors were *technicians*, men with high-school diplomas; it took a year to train one.

While Kiem found the resupply missions insane, the requests from local government officials for their own private naval protection were just plain stupid. The province chiefs were all colonels or lieutenant colonels in the army, in charge of the regional forces, and they all seemed to want a pair of navy boats tied up in front of province headquarters to scare off VC. But the stationary boats were too easy a target for enemy sappers. And Kiem didn't like for his men to sit idle: it was bad for morale. After awhile they began to pick up vices from the regional forces. They'd sell their boat fuel on the black market, spend the money on gambling and alcohol, get into fistfights with the army. . . .

Kiem knew that if he could just keep his mouth shut and do what the army wanted, he could make admiral in less than two years on this job— it was that visible, that influential. But instead, he found himself playing the "barking dog" at every meeting: meetings with province and district officials, meetings with the Army IV Corps, debriefings after every ambush, meetings to speed up the repair of damaged ships. When he wasn't actually sitting around a table at a meeting, he was usually bouncing on the seat of a jeep, riding to the next one. But all he seemed to be accomplishing was acquiring a reputation for being "difficult." *Well, what did he expect?* He was a mere captain in the navy, lacking strong support from his own admiralty, up against a three-star army general with political pull in Saigon.

After awhile, although the army didn't care about Kiem's human losses, it began to fuss about his equipment losses. One downed ship could be worth anywhere from two hundred thousand to a million dollars. And week by week the fleet availability percentage kept decreasing: bad publicity back in the number-crazed United States, where most of the Vietnamese Navy's bills were still being paid.

Instead of cutting back on the outpost resupply missions, the government decided to mount salvage operations to raise the sunken boats, tow them in to a base, and repair them. It was eerie work: chains creaking, mud sucking, water gushing, decomposed bodies popping up along with the ghostly vessel. But at least it went so fast that the enemy didn't have time to dig trenches and prepare a decent ambush. On the way back Kiem's men could shoot it out with them on an equal basis.

Kiem's fifth child, a delicate little girl, was born in January 1973. He and Thom named her "Nhu Thuy," meaning "pure like water." Just five days later, representatives of the United States and North Vietnam initialed a peace treaty in Paris. There was no celebration in South Vietnam, however. Thieu had been strong-armed by the United States into going along with it. Under the terms of the agreement North Vietnamese troops would continue to occupy the territory they had seized prior to the accord: about a fifth of South Vietnam's land mass. As with the false truce ending the First Indochinese War, everybody knew that it was only a matter of time before those forces would be reactivated.

This time around, it only took a month for the communists to begin attacking at the multidivision level. Then it was right back to war as usual, except that the West shut its eyes and pretended the situation did not exist.

Kiem did such a terrible job as chief of staff of the MRF, alienating so many influential people, that in June of 1973 he was promoted to the navy's third-highest command position: deputy chief of staff, operations. He should have caught on long ago: do a good job and you threaten those in power; do a bad job and you shoot right up to the top. Almost unbelievably the VNN had swelled to forty-two thousand officers and men and over fifteen hundred ships and craft, making it among the top ten navies in the world, at least numerically. Kiem was responsible for the operational deployment of those men and ships; the navy's coastal and riverine zone commanders reported to him, and only the CNO or deputy CNO could overrule his decisions and orders.

Even though the Americans were now technically out of the fighting, Kiem still had a U.S. counterpart, though the latter's role had changed considerably since the signing of the treaty: the new man was an observer, rather than a helper, and so quiet that Kiem had trouble remembering his name. He reported to the Defense Attaché Office, an arm of the U.S. Embassy located at Tan Son Nhut Air Base. Prior to the treaty Kiem had been able to contact the U.S. Seventh Fleet directly, but now he had to ask his counterpart to ask the DAO to ask the U.S. Navy whatever it was he wanted. It was a cumbersome procedure, to say the least. But Kiem didn't fully understand its implications until January of 1974, when Red Chinese warships seized the Hoang Sa or "Paracel" Islands that had been claimed by Vietnam since the early nineteenth century.

The Paracel Islands lay about three hundred fifty kilometers east of Da Nang, in the South China Sea. They were small, desolate, treeless, covered with crusted bird droppings—which Madame Nhu had tried unsuccessfully to mine for fertilizer a decade earlier—and ringed with jagged reefs that made beaching a gamble. The biggest island, called "Pattle" by Westerners, had a weather station that beamed typhoon warnings to the mainland and a single squad of what had to be the loneliest regional forces in Vietnam. The VNN ran routine patrols around the island, and Kiem himself had visited them several times between 1963 and 1965. Once he'd even made arrangements to buy a goat, as a treat for his sailors, from the Pattle Island army garrison. The soldiers raised them but let them run free, since the sea was their fence. "Listen," the squad leader had chuckled, "if you can catch them, you can have two goats for the same price." Kiem's whole ship had turned out to chase the goats around the island, slipping and sliding in the gooey new bird-droppings until, hours later, the men and the goats had just fallen down on top of each other, exhausted.

Northwest of the Paracels, the sea had spit back three or four equally desolate islands that had been occupied by Chinese fishermen for as long as anyone could remember. The Chinese had never given the Vietnamese any trouble; in fact, whenever a storm blew one of their fishing boats down to the Paracels, the Vietnamese Navy would tow it back as a courtesy. Three hundred kilometers due north of the Paracels lay Hainan Island, a vast Chinese landmass with its own air force base and fleet of MIG-21 bombers. But it was so far away, nobody gave it much thought.

According to reports received by I Corps in Da Nang, however, Pattle Island was now flying the Chinese flag, with two armored Chinese trawlers anchored nearby. And Duncan Island, second in size to Pattle, had a Chinese bunker with soldiers milling about and a Chinese landing ship moored right on the beach! Their presence had been discovered by Captain Thu of HQ-16, one of seven WHECs (high-endurance U.S. Coast Guard cutters) turned over by the United States to the VNN under Vietnamization. Thu had been asked by the U.S. Consulate in Da Nang to run an American civilian out to the islands, as a "special favor"—a request that should have been routed through naval headquarters, under the terms of the treaty. After dropping off the American and half a dozen Vietnamese Army officers who were accompanying him, Thu had decided to patrol for a day or two before heading back. Now the captain was desperately radioing I Corps, asking what to do next.

I Corps had notified naval headquarters in Saigon; headquarters had started meeting with President Thieu, Thieu's cabinet, National Assembly leaders, and the heads of the other armed forces; and Thieu's foreign minister was sounding out the reactions of the international diplomatic community.

"If we act fast, we can retake the islands," Kiem was urging Admiral Chon. "But we have to rush more ships in *now*, while we still have the firepower advantage. If we knock out the Chinese ships, the shore force will surrender easily." The longer they delayed, the more likely was the chance that the enormous Chinese Navy would be sending in reinforcements.

In response, Admiral Chon ordered Kiem to dig up proof of Vietnam's historical claims to the islands. While Kiem was slamming and banging through library shelves and file drawers like a lawyer conducting a title search, he learned from his counterpart that his request to the U.S. Seventh Fleet to set up a "line of interdiction"—to keep the Chinese Navy from moving south—had been refused. Of course it was possible that the DAO had killed the request without ever forwarding it to the U.S. Navy. There was no way to know.

While Kiem was trotting in and out of briefings lugging an overhead slide projector and a suitcase full of papers, Radar Picket Escort HQ-04— the sleek, fast ex–USS *Forster*—was gliding toward the Paracels from Da Nang. Late in the morning of 17 January 1974 she landed a team of Vietnamese Navy commandos on Cam Tuyen ("Robert") Island to yank up additional Chinese flags that had been reported there. But the trawler had moved, and there were no Chinese anywhere on the island—the commandos couldn't have missed them, on a stretch of bird poop only five hundred meters long. Having returned to their ship, the commandos were just finishing lunch and dealing out cards when they spotted two fast-moving, Komar-class motor torpedo boats churning up the sea to starboard. The captain sounded the alarm to man battle stations, but as the men scrambled to their positions, the Chinese Navy ships suddenly changed direction and disappeared.

With Chinese reinforcements on the scene, there was no longer much hope of retaking the islands. But the Vietnamese Navy could still go in there, slap the Chinese Navy on the face, and run back out again. If only the damn government would *hurry*.

Permission to attack finally came through on the morning of 18 January, with one stipulation: President Thieu wanted the navy to try to "parley" with the Chinese first. Hearing the news, Kiem cursed: more time wasted. But now the flagship of the looming sea battle—HQ-05, another WHEC—began racing toward the scene at top speed, 18 knots. HQ-10—an MSF with its minesweeping gear removed and about the size of one of the enemy's motor torpedo boats—set out a couple of hours behind her. Kiem couldn't help noticing that all four of the battleship captains—Thu, San, Quynh, and Tha—had been his students at Nha Trang. He wondered how Captain Quynh of HQ-05, who tended to be nervous, was going to do with On-Site Commander Ngac on board.

Vice CNO Tanh flew to Da Nang to direct the battle from the I Corps CIC. Kiem and Admiral Chon would be monitoring communications from the powerful CIC at Saigon Naval Headquarters. They were trying to secure air coverage for the operation from the Vietnamese Air Force, without much luck. The VNAF's jets flew too fast to be able to "see" a target with human eyesight; over the ocean they had to rely on CAP radar ships for guidance, which wouldn't be available in time. What's more, by the time their short-range CF-5s and A-27s reached the Paracels, their fuel tanks would be half-empty; they'd have to wheel right around and head back home. "That's good enough," the navy told them. Finally the air force agreed to make one overhead pass during the battle, to shore up the fighting men's morale.

Near midnight on 18 January, Captain Ngac positioned HQ-10 and HQ-16 close to the bunkered shore of Duncan Island, and HQ-04 and HQ-05 on the island's other side. The Chinese were now up to *four* torpedo boats; this way, each VNN ship could cover one Chinese boat, north to south, while they waited for reinforcements to arrive from Da Nang. With their steel hulls and hidden machine guns, the Chinese "fishing" trawlers were still a threat, though. And the landing ship was also sure to be well-armed.

As the tide crested on the morning of 19 January, HQ-05 lowered a brace of rubber landing boats over her side. Twenty Vietnamese Navy commandos—looking sleek as otters in their dark wet suits—steered the motorized craft toward the shore of Duncan Island. Clambering to their feet in the wildly crashing surf, they began staggering toward high ground. Their leader, a lieutenant junior grade, went first, waving a white flag. Blinking salt spray from his eyes, he saw that the Chinese ground force, bigger than expected, was advancing from several different directions. He called out in Chinese for them to stop, but they kept coming. Conferring with Captain Ngac by radio, he ordered his men to retreat.

As the Vietnamese began nudging their boats into the water, the Chinese opened fire on their backs. The lieutenant and two of his men fell over dead in the raging surf. As the survivors scrambled to get back to their mother ship, Captain Thu of HQ-16, on the opposite side of the island, notified Captain Ngac that one of the Chinese ships had just made a move to ram him.

"Request permission to shoot," Captain Ngac radioed I Corps. Pacing the length of the Saigon CIC—wood-paneled, softly lit, crammed with electronics equipment, with a central Plexiglas plotting board and pull-down maps on the walls—Kiem wondered where Admiral Chon had gone. He asked a communications officer to ring him. After calling around, the officer reported back that Chon had boarded a flight to Da Nang. Kiem tried not to let his surprise show on his face. "All right. Well then, call up the Vice CNO at Da Nang," Kiem ordered. A few minutes later, the same officer reported back that the Vice CNO was on his way to the airport to collect Chon.

"Oh, *mia madre*," said Kiem. *Could it be possible that Chon was hiding out to save his skin?* He could believe it of Chon but not of Vice CNO Tanh, one of the navy's most highly respected officers. But why hadn't Tanh sent a *driver* to the airport, which was a good hour's drive from I Corps?

Thinking it best not to start a war with Red China all by himself, Kiem sent one of his junior officers to fetch the chief of staff. Although he hadn't been involved in planning the operation, the middle-aged admiral was thrilled to jump in: every Vietnamese schoolboy grows up dreaming of sea battles with China. "Are you sure that President Thieu has authorized force?" he asked when Kiem had finished his on-the-spot briefing.

"Yes, Admiral," said Kiem.

"Well then, give them the order," said the chief of staff, breaking into a big smile.

"What order, sir?" asked Kiem.

"Shoot!" said the admiral.

"Yes, sir!" Kiem called up Captain Ngac and told him that "Hometown," the Saigon CIC, would be taking over controls from "Solar," its counterpart in Da Nang. "Report to us directly," he said. "Your orders are to retrieve the landing party, if possible; then get out into the open and shoot."

"Hometown, this is Shark-5," crackled Ngac's voice. "Roger. Out."

Next, Kiem contacted the air force and gave them the signal. Waiting for something to happen, he began to worry about the condition of his ships. Because of the pressure to keep them out on patrol no matter how bad their condition, HQ-10 was going into battle with only one engine working. And the forward 3-inch gun on HQ-04 was out. Like a skunk or a porcupine, she'd have to point her rear end at the enemy to shoot. Where were the two backup ships coming from Da Nang? Why was the air force taking so long?

Kiem recontacted Ngac: "Shark-5, this is Hometown. Are you in position? Over."

"This is Shark-5. Affirmative. Out."

"Then shoot. Over." There was no immediate response from Ngac.

"Shoot!" Kiem prodded. "Over!"

In the course of the next forty-five minutes, the Vietnamese Navy sank one Chinese Navy motor torpedo boat and one trawler. But HQ-10 took a direct hit from a Chinese surface-to-surface missile and, spewing smoke and fire from her bridge, went dead in the water with eighty-two men on board. And HQ-16, listing twenty degrees from a hole under the water level in her engine room, lost her radio, electricity, and automatic governing system. Only her main engine was still maneuverable.

Sweating like crazy, despite the air-conditioning, Kiem asked his counterpart—who'd been sitting there so quietly that Kiem had almost forgotten about him—to recontact the DAO. With two VNN ships in trouble, would the Seventh Fleet reconsider setting up a line of interdiction? "I'll try, Captain Kiem," he said. A few minutes later, he notified Kiem that U.S. radar was tracking an apparent Chinese MIG launch from Hainan Island. A Chinese guided-missile frigate was bearing down right behind the planes, in the direction of the Paracels.

"Looks like we're going to have to terminate, sir," Kiem advised the chief of staff.

HQ-10 was going under. The three remaining warships were given orders to retreat. At first Captain Thu of HQ-16 thought he was going to have to beach in order to save his crew, but his engineering officer persuaded him that they could make it back to Da Nang on one engine, even though they were now listing forty degrees. Kiem ordered HQ-04 to escort the wounded vessel. HQ-05 would head south and begin an "expanding square" search for survivors.

For the third time Kiem asked his counterpart to ask the DAO to get in touch with the Seventh Fleet. This time, all he wanted was assistance in picking up survivors. But the request was turned down.

On the heels of the battle Kiem had to fly to Phan Rang to brief vacationing President Thieu. He didn't dare tell him that the CNO and Vice CNO had missed the only sea battle in modern naval history, although he mentioned the no-show by the air force. The briefing took place under the shade of a brick gazebo built right on the beach, while Thieu's family members came and went, looking for towels or cigarettes.

"Don't worry, Captain Kiem," Thieu soothed, "we'll get you another ship." He was almost giddy, riding the wave of the battle's astonishing public popularity; for even though their side had lost the islands and even though HQ-16 turned out to have been hit by a "friendly" shell stamped "Made in U.S.A.," they had sunk two ships to their two-thousand-year enemy's one! The TV, radio, and newspapers were going crazy. Homemade banners were flapping in the streets of Saigon and Da Nang. For a few days everyone seemed to have forgotten the communists, who'd only been an enemy for sixteen years. Even the communists were keeping their mouths shut, loath to remind people that they were allied with the ancient enemy. President Thieu ordered a champagne reception for the returning heroes in Saigon.

Kiem didn't want another ship. He wanted the lives of his missing men. Four days after the battle, a Dutch tanker pulled twenty-three HQ-10 survivors on life rafts out of the ocean. They said that Captain Tha had been killed on the bridge of his ship but that the other crew members had escaped to rafts. Five days after that, a Vietnamese fishing boat picked up a raft containing fourteen more survivors and one corpse—a former petty officer of Kiem's, who had died of exposure and dehydration just hours before. That still left more than three dozen men unaccounted for. The Chinese government announced that they had captured forty-eight prisoners, including one American—but those included the Pattle Island Regional Forces and the six ARVN officers who had accompanied the American civilian out there in the days preceding the battle. The U.S. government explained to the world that the American had been "visiting the islands at the invitation of a South Vietnamese Navy commander"—to Kiem's astonishment, as no commander would dare take an American out there without U.S. and VNN authorization.

The United States had fed Kiem bad intelligence, too: there hadn't been any "Chinese MIG launch," though Kiem had called off the battle on account of it. *What the hell was going on?* Did it have anything to do with President Richard Nixon's historic trip to China the year before or with the rumors of deep-sea oil reserves near the Spratly Islands and the Paracels? Was the United States going to sacrifice South Vietnam as an ally in order to set up a lucrative trade with China? *I can't believe it. The DAO must not have passed my requests to the Seventh Fleet,* Kiem told himself for what must have been the fiftieth time. He could believe that the U.S. government would let him down—but never the U.S. Navy.

WATER

I feel so bitter about my flotsam condition:
a bubble in the sea of misery,
a seaweed on the beach of illusion.

On Nhu Hau (pen name of Nguyen Gia Thieu),
A Song of Sorrow inside the Royal Harem

CHAPTER 17

House Bars Cut of 100,000 Troops Stationed Abroad But $474
Million in Saigon Military Aid Is Pared As Arms Budget Is Passed

New York Times, 23 May 1974

One of Kiem's responsibilities as deputy chief of staff, operations, was drafting the navy's annual budget. A few days before
the naval CNO was scheduled to present the budget for the fiscal year 1975 to the Americans and the army, he sat down with
Kiem to go over the details.

The picture Kiem painted was bleak. Following the 1973
Paris "peace" treaty, the United States had slashed the Vietnamese Navy's budget by a quarter. For the upcoming fiscal
year, which stretched from 1 July 1974 to 30 June 1975, the
United States would be chopping that meager sum in half.
Already the VNN had cut back on patrols, stopped replacing
lost ships, and started rationing ammo. Their only remaining
option, short of not meeting payroll, would be to mothball a
chunk of the fleet.

"Captain Kiem," said the CNO when the briefing was over,
"since you're so familiar with the budget, I'm going to let you
make the presentation all by yourself this year." Kiem understood, and he couldn't blame him: the CNO didn't want to lose
face in front of the Americans.

So on a swelteringly hot spring day in 1974 Kiem found himself pacing alone outside the DAO compound at Tan Son Nhut
Air Base, waiting for his counterpart to escort him past the
security checkpoint. Feeling something jabbing into his foot,
he looked down and noticed that the sole of one shoe was peel-
ing loose from the upper. A rock had become sandwiched in
between.

"What's the matter, Captain Kiem? Hurt your foot?" asked his latest counterpart, striding toward him. The sun bounced off his glasses, making his blond hair look almost white.

"Just a pebble," said Kiem, flushing with embarrassment. Since the treaty, officers and men had been cut back to one pair of shoes a year instead of two. The cheap imitation leather tended to fall apart the first time it got wet—and it rained almost every day from May to November. Of course, somebody high up must be getting a nice kickback from the manufacturer.

They cleared security and stopped to ask directions from the secretary, another cool-looking American blond. Entering the conference room, Kiem saw with relief that it had a chest-high podium for him to hide his feet behind. The fifteen or so attendees wouldn't be able to see his disintegrating shoe, but they would have to listen to a speech about a disintegrating navy.

As the first few speakers gave their presentations, Kiem found himself unable to concentrate. He tapped his pencil, fiddled with the lock on his briefcase, took a few deep breaths. When he heard his name called, he took his place behind the podium and scanned the faces: mostly Americans, with a few representatives from the ARVN. He tried to guess what they might be thinking, but their expressions were blank. "The navy has had to make some hard choices for the fiscal year ahead," he began. Two or three minutes into his speech, he paused and looked to the faces for reassurance. Some of them were yawning, some watching a fly tiptoe around the rim of a coffee cup. That's when it struck him: his men's *lives* were at risk on account of the budget cuts, and these people weren't even paying attention! Water rose in his eyes, and bitterness choked his throat. He forgot the rest of his speech.

As he stood there fighting for composure, the faces tipped up at him, intrigued. It was a thousand times worse than if they'd noticed his shabby shoe. At last, a puff of air in his lungs, and then a sound forming in his mouth: "Therefore, the navy proposes taking six of our amphibious ships out of service," he resumed. The army representatives sat up straight in their chairs, startling the fly into taking wing.

Sheer navy pride, and not common sense, had made him try to hold on to his fighting ships at the expense of the landing ships that only lugged troops and supplies for the army. He had known that the navy's budget wasn't going to be accepted, but he had made his point. The ordeal was almost over.

After the meeting, as chairs were scraping and emptying, Kiem's counterpart draped an arm around his shoulders. "It must have been rough on you up there, Captain Kiem," he said.

"Yes, thank you," said Kiem. Sympathetic in private, aloof in public—that was the style of his new counterparts, ever since the treaty.

He couldn't understand it: the Americans seemed bored with the war, though not with other aspects of his job. They had named him chairman of their Cambodian Relief Tripartite Commission: once a month now he had to organize a convoy, with a joint Vietnamese-Cambodian naval escort, to run shipments of rice and salt up the Mekong River to Phnom Penh. International drug smuggling also piqued their interest—shipments of black opium from China, funneled to a growing pool of post-treaty, despondent Vietnamese, or white heroin from Bangkok, repackaged in Vietnamese ports for shipment to the United States. Twice now, U.S. officials had ordered Kiem to board and search foreign vessels in international waters—which was absolutely illegal—but fortunately his men had found heroin both times.

Maybe, he thought, *the Americans still had good intentions toward Vietnam, but just no experience with a long war.* Their own civil war and their role in World War II had lasted only four years. Maybe their attention had begun to wander to other things.

In August of 1974 U.S. president Richard Nixon resigned. "Voluntarily, because his aides were caught in a burglary?" asked Thom when he told her the news by phone. "No way! There must have been a coup."

Quickly, before the new U.S. president could build a coalition, the antiwar U.S. Congress voted to trim three hundred million dollars from the already-approved fiscal-year 1975 aid package to Vietnam. Along with that development came news that the Vietnamese Armed Forces had overspent their 1974 budget allocations, meaning that the shortfall would have to be subtracted from 1975 funds. Minus cost overruns and DAO expenses, all four armed services were going to have to operate on five hundred million dollars for fiscal-year 1975—about what the army had spent on ammo the previous year. The navy would be left with a total of twenty million dollars—down from a hundred forty million a year in pretreaty days.

The VNN, one of the top ten navies in the world, was on the verge of turning into a joke, a "bathtub flotilla." The signs were everywhere. It used to take a truck to load one of Kiem's patrol ships; now two sailors could carry a month's worth of supplies in their arms. To keep their pumps and motorboat engines running, ship captains were having to send crewmen ashore to siphon gasoline from unguarded jeeps. *Well, the navy could keep going with no gasoline and no toilet paper. But what about the day they ran out of ammo, or rice?* And meanwhile the Northern communists were getting richer and stronger. They were sitting on huge stockpiles of Chinese and Soviet military equipment, raked in during the last few months before the treaty. And according to reliable intelligence, the Soviet Union had recently stepped up its monthly arms shipments by a factor of four.

Surely now, the United States would come to the South's rescue—at the least, allocate more aid money; at the most, come back with their troops and B-52 bombers! After all, before his resignation President Nixon had promised President Thieu in writing that the United States would intervene militarily if the communists violated the cease-fire agreement. Kiem's hopes soared in January of 1975, when U.S. president Gerald Ford asked his Congress to restore the three hundred million dollars they had just cut from the current Vietnam budget. With that infusion of cash, the Vietnamese Armed Forces could survive through the end of the fiscal year in June, after which they could begin to draw on fiscal-year 1976 funds.

One month later, still waiting for the U.S. Congress's response to President Ford's request, Kiem unfolded a letter typed on Thieu's crisp presidential stationery. It said that a U.S. congressional delegation would be visiting Vietnam to assess the need for more aid. VNAF contact persons were being asked to be open, frank, and cooperative in responding to their questions. Above all, stressed Thieu, strive to demonstrate how we are "tightening our belts" economically and using U.S. aid money to become more self-sufficient.

Acting CNO Lam Nguyen Tanh—who had stepped into the navy's top position following Chon's forced "retirement" in 1974—selected Kiem to give the navy's presentation to the delegation. Kiem wasn't quite sure what to expect, but he was grateful for the chance to be able to plead the navy's case directly to the American government, without having to go through counterparts and the U.S. Embassy.

At the end of February 1975, three members of the eight-person delegation showed up at Saigon Naval Headquarters with their aides and translators. Kiem recognized one of them right away, from pictures in *Time* magazine. Short and fat, wearing an enormous straw hat from which a feather poked up like a punji stick, Congresswoman Bella Abzug folded her arms in front of her chest and scowled at him. As Admiral Tanh began making his welcoming remarks, she rolled her eyes toward heaven.

Also familiar to Kiem was the youthful black-haired man who'd been introduced as Senator "Pete" McCloskey of California. His politeness did not quite mask his stand on the war—but at least he was listening, unlike Abzug. Kiem regretted not having caught the name of the third congressman, a tall, gray-haired gentleman whose enthusiastic hand-shake had let Kiem know at once that he was on their side.

Admiral Tanh turned the proceedings over to Kiem. For half an hour, moving through the pages of a flip chart, he demonstrated how the navy was deploying its patrol ships to conserve fuel, upgrading preventive maintenance training to reduce the need for long-term repairs, and so forth. McCloskey and the gray-haired man asked follow-up questions while Abzug studied the cracks in the ceiling.

They moved to the shipyard. "These men are building a ferro-cement patrol boat to replace one of the aging junks in our coastal patrol unit," Kiem began. "Unlike the traditional wooden hull, ferro-cement can withstand the marine borer. Notice how the cement is being applied to a framework of chicken wire." One of the men said something about cement shoes, and everybody laughed. Kiem didn't understand the joke. "When completed, the hundred-foot boat will be equipped with mor-tars, 12-mm and 30-mm machine guns, and radar. She'll carry a crew of six to eight men."

The gray-haired man raised his hand: "Captain Kiem, you stated that this boat is going to replace an obsolete junk. Wasn't the purpose of the junk force to blend in with ordinary fishing boats, so that the com-munists wouldn't know they were VNN vessels?"

"Ah, good question," Kiem said. "Yes, that was the original intent, but it never fooled the communists. After the junk force was incorporated into the coastal command, we stopped dressing the men in black paja-mas, and so forth."

Kiem thought he had answered the question "frankly," as President Thieu had wished, but the Abzug woman shot him a look of such hatred that he took a step backward.

"Pssst," said the gray-haired congressman, "I'd like to ask you some-thing."

The others had begun to walk around the half-built boat or were straining to catch a breeze from the Saigon River—all except for Mrs. Abzug, who was observing cloud formations. "Certainly," said Kiem.

"Suppose we had to move a large number of men from Da Nang to Saigon. What's the maximum number of troops your fleet could carry?"

Kiem wasn't sure he'd understood the question. "Our transport squadron is small, by your navy's standards," he hedged. "We're not really equipped to handle large armored divisions."

"No," he said. "No armor, no trucks, no artillery—just personnel."

Now Kiem was even more confused. If the army left its artillery behind, what was it going to fight with? He tried to stall for more time, to better grasp the congressman's meaning. "*All* my ships?" he asked. "Or just the transport ships?"

"I said *all* the ships."

Suddenly Kiem shivered, despite the late-February heat. "You have to include the men's families," he said. "Otherwise, they're not going anywhere—believe me." He clicked through the numbers in his head, ran them through once again to make sure, and gave the congressman his answer: "About two divisions, including dependents. Thirty-five to forty thousand people in all."

The congressman seemed satisfied. But the question continued to gnaw at Kiem. That night, while Thom and the children were sleeping, he paced up and down the hallway with the equally restless baby on his shoulder, trying to puzzle it out. The next morning he dropped by Admiral Tanh's office and translated the question for his ears. "What do you think he meant by it?" Kiem asked.

"Nothing at all, Captain Kiem. He was just trying to test your computational skills."

"The question makes no sense," Kiem insisted.

"So what? They ask all kinds of questions. Disregard it," said Tanh.

"It wouldn't hurt us to pull the patrol ships closer to shore, just for a couple of weeks. Just until we see if something is up. . . ."

"Eh, Captain Kiem, they're making you paranoid. Let it go."

So Kiem let it go. Since the beginning of the year, the South had been losing chunk after chunk of territory to the enemy: first Phuoc Luong province, then the Binh Tuy province capital, then a strategic mountain pass in Tay Ninh province. Early in the second week of March, the communists launched an all-out offensive in the Central Highlands, and ten days later President Thieu made the stunning decision to abandon a fifth of the country's landmass to the enemy.

It was a strategy that had been discussed for over a year, even pushed strongly by the United States at one point in time: rather than spread themselves too thin, the army could regroup north of Saigon and focus on defending the Mekong Delta, where nine-tenths of the South's population lived. But the decision had been made so fast that there'd been no time to plan an orderly evacuation. Thousands of government troops and tens of thousands of civilian refugees were surging toward the seacoast, begging for the navy's ships to pick them up as enemy shells and rockets pounded Quang Tri and Hué. The navy's transport ships swung into action, picking up one regiment of marines and an entire army division. A wave of refugees, hundreds of thousands strong, flooded the coastal highway to Da Nang.

In the midst of the pandemonium, the navy got a "new" CNO—Adm. Chung Tan Cang, who'd been thrown out as CNO nine years before, after Kiem and the other Northern ship captains went on strike and seized the shipyard. Coup rumors were beginning to swirl like a waterspout on the South China Sea, and President Thieu wanted a proven loyalist in control of Saigon's gunships. If conditions had been different, the working situation might have been awkward. But Kiem respected Cang's intelligence: his only grievance against Cang had been political, and that hardly mattered now. And Cang—who during his absence from the navy had headed up the Armed Forces Staff College, the Defense Ministry's antismuggling program, and the army's Capital Military District—needed Kiem to brief him and seemed to bear him no ill will.

Cang sent all of the navy's seaworthy ships, but it wasn't enough. Tens of thousands of government troops and refugees piled onto the piers, pushing and shoving, trampling some of their number to death, knocking others into the water. Thousands more tried to wade out to the ships, preventing them from getting close enough to dock. The U.S. Military Sealift Command joined in the effort, chartering private vessels to scoop and shovel up civilians. But the U.S. Navy was powerless to help because of the treaty's ban on "military intervention."

Kiem worked virtually around the clock, sleeping a few hours a night on the fold-out cot in his office. The rest of the time, he was on duty in the CIC. He'd beefed up its staff to man all backup radio lines and four extra telephone lines in an attempt to gather any and all information from army, navy, and air force bases, remote regional outposts, VNN ships, U.S. Liberty ships, commercial frequencies—even fishing boats in the region. He moved from one desk to another in the well-lit, spacious room, keeping his eyes riveted on the Plexiglas board where the latest known positions of his ships plus any army units or air bases still in existence were being plotted.

It was as if the CIC's radios had been tuned to broadcast the entire range of human emotions:

"Please send the air force. The VC are everywhere. . . ."

"So we made the looters remove their flak jackets and they were lined with gold. . . ."

"We couldn't even get close. We had to leave a whole battalion behind. . . ."

"They say his wife refused to evacuate. He turned the gun on her, then himself. . . ."

"Thirty to forty died on the trip down, mostly children. Suffocation, diarrhea. . . . They're stacking the bodies on the docks. . . ."

"Another U.S. civilian ship has been hijacked by army deserters. It's being forced to change course from Phu Quoc Island to Vung Tau. . . ."

"Fuck all of you, whoever you are! And shut up if you can't help. . . ."

"We're going to stand and fight. You can tell the world that Company 3, Battalion 5, 'No Fear,' will never surrender. . . ."

"Where are our *Co Van Vi Dai* ['Great Advisors']? . . ."

Kiem's purpose in listening was to gather information: there was nothing, absolutely nothing, he could do to help those abandoned troops if his ships couldn't reach them. But calm or panicked, detached or begging, the voices kept getting to him, and he had to keep stepping out on the balcony to light a cigarette, inhaling its smoke as if he were swallowing his own frailty and powerlessness.

Worst of all was the report from the captain of a ship with orders to pick up an armor unit. "I can't beach," he complained. "There are thousands of people waiting in water up to their necks. I've never seen anything like it." Before Kiem could tell the captain anything, he heard the sounds of a scuffle and then a second, menacing voice: "You see this gun pointed at your head? Now, beach! *Beach*, you motherfucker!" Hours later, when the captain was able to resume communications, he could hardly speak for weeping into the microphone. "The crunching, the crunching! I'll never forget that crunching sound as long as I live. . . ."

On 30 March, all radio contact was lost with Da Nang. The navy abandoned its sealift. And still the communists rolled relentlessly southward—whole battalions of them in mile-long lines of tanks and trucks that could have been knocked out easily with American B-52s. As they advanced, they shelled the refugees now surging for their lives toward Qui Nhon.

Then a peculiar thing began to happen. City by city the districts south of Da Nang began to surrender without a fight, before the communists had even arrived! Kiem saw a pattern emerging. First a U.S. Seventh Fleet ship would pull in within a mile or two of shore, advising all Americans in the area to leave immediately. Seeing his counterpart packing to go, the Vietnamese district commander would panic, gather up his family, and flee along with him. With the district commander gone, the district force would abandon their posts, leaving the regular army's flank wide open. Then the army men would retreat to the shore and call the navy to pick them up. One minute Kiem would be checking with a district commander: "No trouble here," he'd be told. An hour later he'd call back and the phone would ring with no answer. Kiem's coastal patrol ships, sailing along the chaotic shoreline, didn't know what to do. "Request orders. Request orders," they radioed repeatedly.

Around the clock, every twenty to thirty minutes, Kiem conferred by phone with Lt. Gen. Dong Van Khuyen, chief of staff of Joint General Staff. The army and air force had lost their communications capability when they'd lost their bases, but the navy could still call up its ships, so Khuyen was using Kiem to track the locations of his units and key officers as best he could.

"We've got to do something to turn this situation around, General Khuyen," Kiem urged. "At least have our air force knock out the bridges behind us. That would be better than nothing."

"I want to stand and fight," growled Khuyen in his distinctive voice, coarse as a he-duck's. "But how? I can't talk to my officers."

"The navy can communicate with them—that's no problem. But we have no authority over them." Kiem struggled to clear his mind, foggy with lack of sleep. An idea had begun to form: "Suppose we could get a high-ranking naval officer promoted to army district commander? I'm thinking of Commodore Hoang Co Minh. There's still a whole ARVN division waiting to be picked up in Qui Nhon. Instead of evacuating your men, Minh could combine them with his own forces and set up a perimeter defense around the city."

General Khuyen agreed that the plan might work, and after hearing Kiem out, Admiral Cang petitioned President Thieu, who approved the promotion at two o'clock in the morning. But when the newly appointed district commander arrived in Qui Nhon, he found his troops in no mood to stay and fight. Two-thirds of the division had deserted, and the rest of the men, demoralized, were clamoring to be evacuated as soon as possible. Minh directed them to regroup at Cam Ranh Bay to set up a defense there. But Qui Nhon fell, then Tuy Hoa, then Nha Trang, and the government decided to abandon Cam Ranh Bay and ring the South's forces above Phan Rang and Saigon.

Meanwhile, at the Plexiglas plotting board, the duty officer kept drawing and erasing and redrawing and erasing the imaginary line that might stop the pattern of collapse. Maybe Xuan Loc. Maybe Phan Rang. Maybe. . . .

Midway through the third week of April, Kiem's U.S. counterpart summoned Kiem into his office to listen to the news on his radio, in English. The week before, U.S. president Ford had upped his Vietnam emergency military aid request to seven hundred twenty-two million dollars. He'd also asked for hundreds of millions in "humanitarian" aid, plus permission to use American troops if U.S. allies had to be evacuated from the country. Tens of thousands of South Vietnamese would be at risk from a communist takeover, Ford had told his country; he believed that the United States had a "moral obligation" to rescue them. He asked Congress to rule on his aid package no later than 19 April.

Now Kiem and his counterpart sat staring at the radio as if it were a TV set. But the voice coming out of the plastic holes had terrible news: not a penny more in military aid would be granted to Vietnam. A moderate sum would be designated for "evacuation and human relief purposes." U.S. troops could be used to evacuate Americans, but not large numbers of Vietnamese.

Kiem's counterpart scraped back his chair and gathered up a few photographs and knickknacks. Under the fluorescent light fixture, his face was the color of ashes. "I have to go now, Captain Kiem," he said.

Hours later he returned with an affidavit authorizing Kiem and his family to leave the country. "I'm on my way to the airport," he said. "Sign this, and we'll stop and get your wife and children."

"No," said Kiem.

"Believe me, Captain Kiem, it's all over."

"I'm not leaving ahead of my men. No way."

"Jesus Christ. . . . All right. You stay. But let me take Mrs. Kiem and the children with me. Please, Kiem."

Kiem wavered. "No," he finally said.

Kiem's counterpart asked if there were anything else he could do before he left, and Kiem's thoughts flashed to the counterpart's car, a chauffeured Ford with smoked-glass windows and U.S. Embassy plates. But Kiem had no papers; it would do him no good. "I don't think so," he said.

His counterpart hugged him. "God bless you," he said. Then he was gone.

Xuan Loc fell, after a brave thirteen-day defense in which Gen. Le Minh Dao's 18th ARVN Division came within a silk thread of turning back three NVA divisions. The communist tanks crunched on, toward the wall of defensive forces thickening around Saigon, five divisions strong.

Kiem took his jeep to check on his family. Saigon was operating under a twenty-four-hour curfew now, and he had to pass through several military checkpoints on the way, though his apartment was not far away. He ate an early dinner, keeping one eye on the black-and-white TV set he'd lugged back from California in 1961. Suddenly an announcer interrupted the program to say that President Thieu was going to make an important statement.

"I'll bet there's been a coup," said Thom. "Everybody knows there's been a coup brewing."

"No," said Thom's brother-in-law, a lawyer named Nguyen. He and Thom's sister Thao and their children had moved into the apartment when the fighting got fierce around Saigon. "No, he's going to announce the resumption of American bombing. I'm sure of it."

"I hope you're both wrong," said Kiem. "I hope he's going to do what's right for his country."

"What's that, Kiem?" asked Thao.

"Resign. With somebody else in power, the communists might negotiate—and, right now, that's our only hope."

Kiem's guess turned out to be right. When, halfway through his resignation speech, Thieu began blaming the United States for "flip-flopping" on the war, railing at Henry Kissinger for "betraying" him, Kiem whooped and thumped his brother-in-law on the knee. That was just the way he felt. He hated that two-faced German, too. But as the speech rambled on, Kiem began to see that all Thieu cared about was his ego, not his country. He was resigning in anger, as a challenge to his critics: *après moi, le déluge*. As quickly as Kiem's hopes had surged, they fell.

The next day American transport planes began airlifting thousands of Vietnamese out of the country. There was still time for Kiem to get his family out, if he pulled strings. But he couldn't bring himself to do it. That would be putting his family ahead of his country and community— an instinct his father had warned him against, long ago.

"Fool," he told himself. "What are you hoping for? A miracle?"

On 25 April, the miracle arrived. "Telephone," said a CIC communications officer. Kiem reached for the receiver.

"Hey, *Dai Ta* Kiem, this is Rich. Rich Armitage."

"Phu!" Kiem cried. "I mean, Rich! Is it really you?" With every other American scrambling to leave the country, it was just like unconventional Phu to be flying back in after years away. Kiem hoped that the former U.S. Naval Intelligence officer wasn't wearing his black pajamas this trip; they weren't the most popular outfit in Saigon at the moment.

"I need to talk to you, Captain Kiem. As soon as possible."

"Now is fine," said Kiem. "Over here, or at your place?"

"In your office. Half an hour from now," Armitage told him.

When they were alone in Kiem's office, the American explained: "I'm here to draw up a plan to evacuate the fleet, to keep the major ships from falling into the hands of the enemy, if and when they capture Saigon. I'm going to need your help. What do you say?"

CHAPTER 18

It's Over

Most Yanks Got Out

Pacific Stars & Stripes, 1 May 1975

"Don't mention the evacuation plan to anyone but Admiral Cang," Rich Armitage cautioned before he left. "I'll get back in touch with you soon."

What if Cang refused to go along with them or turned Kiem in to the police? Plotting for the navy to leave the country was an act of treason: treason against the existing government as well as treason against the communists, if and when they took over. Cang had been back in the navy only a month, and he would have only Kiem's word to vouch for Armitage and the legitimacy of his mission.

But Cang saw at once that it was the navy's only honorable choice. Evacuate or surrender: those were his options. If the navy got its ships out and discovered that the government was going to stand and fight, they could always turn around and sail back. But if they missed their one chance to escape, they weren't going to get another one. Bringing four other officers in on the secret, he delegated the job of planning to Kiem.

Over the next three days Kiem wrestled with the logistics of the E-Plan. Pulling the Sea Force into the Saigon River too soon could set off a mass panic. But there were other preparations that could be made without attracting attention: shortening the coastal ships' axis of patrol so that even the southernmost ships could be called back to Saigon within five hours; halting all long-term shipyard repair overhauls so that the navy could concentrate its labor on the most seaworthy vessels; and calling all naval personnel and their families to return to their bases "for reasons of security," as Armitage had suggested. Armitage understood that the ships' crews wouldn't budge without their families. In Saigon, the Naval Training Compound would serve as a temporary shelter.

At the time of the treaty, the VNN could count ninety-seven ships in its Sea Force. But that figure included twenty PGMs and twenty-six WPBs—small coastal patrol ships, captained by lieutenants or lieutenants junior grade, with crews of only seven to ten. Although technically "blue water" vessels, the coastal patrol ships' normal patrol schedule was two days out, one day in; they couldn't stay out much longer without replenishing fuel and water. They'd be out of the planning, as would the navy's three MSCs—wooden-hulled for protection when dragging up mines, but now used mainly as coastal supply ships because of their large, open decks—underarmed and broken down to boot.

The VNN's two *Edsall*-class DERs were their pride and joy: sleek, fast, beautiful, and second only to the WHECs in firepower. HQ-01, the navy's flagship, was in good condition to go, but HQ-04, a veteran of last year's Battle of the Paracel Islands, was laid up in the shipyard. Leaving her behind would be like leaving a person—but there was no other choice.

Six of the seven WHECs were fit for the journey, but HQ-15 was in the shipyard and would be a no-go. HQ-06, the last of their PCs, or "submarine chasers," had been decommissioned the year before. Kiem had been one of her captains; he felt sad that she would not be around for the final dash to freedom.

Kiem counted the MSFs with the PCEs, since the United States had removed the ships' proprietary minesweeping gear prior to turning them over. The navy had possessed eight MSFs and PCEs at the time of the treaty, but HQ-10 had been sunk during the Battle of the Paracels, and two more were in dubious condition. That left five as likely candidates.

The navy's landing ships were in terrible shape, having been either cannibalized for spare parts or damaged while escorting supply runs to Phnom Penh. Two LSILs had been sunk in 1974 alone. But four of the navy's six LSTs were seaworthy, as were three LSMs, four LSSLs, and three LSILs. A fourth LSM, HQ-402, would be a question mark: shipyard personnel would be working on her right down to the wire. The VNN's two AGPs and one ARL looked good: LSTs that had been converted to repair ships, they would be able to carry thousands out.

Kiem had to smile at the thought of a YOG "racing" to safety. Those cumbersome oilers could do ten knots in theory but only seven in reality. Still, if the communists weren't right on their tails, a few might make it out. One had been mothballed since the treaty, leaving five.

The final list tallied pretty well with the estimate Kiem had given Armitage. At least thirty of the VNN's forty-five big ships had a shot at getting out. Those thirty ships could also carry tens of thousands of human lives—but no one had mentioned people yet. Just ships.

On the second day of planning, the whole thing nearly fell through. Word leaked back to Kiem that Fleet Comdr. Nguyen Xuan Son, who was in on the E-Plan, and one of his skippers had let their families move on board two very well-stocked, well-fueled ships. The crew members weren't stupid: they'd started threatening to mutiny unless their own families could be brought on board as well. To make it look to the rest of the navy as if Son had been acting on his own, Admiral Cang publicly relieved him as Fleet Commander. *Damn it to hell.* Son had been a good officer, and his loss was going to hurt.

Kiem broke from his desk only once, to check on his family. He'd decided not to move them into the Naval Training Compound with the other dependents. Thom would be sure to fuss about her children sleeping on the floor, and they lived close enough to headquarters that it wouldn't make much difference: Kiem could scoop them up quickly when the time came. This way he could also make sure, before he put his family on board ship, that the first few vessels to leave Saigon didn't sail into an ambush.

Before returning to headquarters Kiem took his eldest son aside. Khai had grown up to be a tall, quiet, thoughtful boy. "You're sixteen years old now, Son," he said. "I'm going to speak to you as one man to another. In the next few days, things could get hectic. There's a chance that you and the others might have to leave home suddenly—and I might not be there to help. If I'm not there, be the man of the family. Look after your mother, brother, and sisters until we're together again. And don't say a word about this conversation to your mother. Understand?"

The boy's thin face look frightened. But he nodded. Kiem left for headquarters with his mind more at ease.

Armitage came back on 27 April, bringing a man he introduced as Erich Von Marbod, deputy assistant U.S. secretary of defense. Kiem gathered that Von Marbod was overseeing the evacuation of the air force. Kiem and Armitage roughed out the rest of the E-Plan, with Von Marbod listening quietly. They settled on Con Son Island, two hundred fifteen kilometers south of Vung Tau, as their rendezvous point. Besides providing a sheltered harbor, it would be accessible to small craft fleeing the country from the Mekong Delta's many river mouths. Once at Con Son, they could transfer their passenger loads to the big LSMs and LSTs. Armitage left it up to the VNN to select the exact date and time to start loading, but he warned them that U.S. intelligence was targeting 2 or 3 May as the date of the final NVA assault on Saigon.

Armitage wanted the navy to destroy two key facilities before moving out: the CIC and the dry dock. Kiem agreed to disable the CIC computer, but he spoke out against blowing up the dry dock. It would take at least a ton of dynamite, he argued, and the explosion could frighten Saigoners into thinking the communists had arrived. It could hinder their escape. Armitage thought otherwise, but he didn't push.

Everything, Kiem knew, would depend on the cohesion of his men. He'd seen the army, air force, and marines fall apart during the retreat from the Central Highlands. But he believed his sailors would be different. Living together on small, cramped ships for months at a time, they'd forged a bond that just might hold together through the coming crisis. Because, once they were on the ships, there would be no more Republic of Vietnam, no more government, no more navy. Nobody would have to answer to anybody else. "Phu" nodded as Kiem voiced his concerns.

Now here came the showdown. It was obvious from the way Armitage had been talking that the Pentagon hadn't thought beyond skeleton crews piloting the ships out, whereas Kiem saw a chance to get tens of thousands out alive, ahead of the communists. He knew from reading *Time* and *Newsweek* that America didn't want large numbers of South Vietnamese refugees admitted into its borders—living, breathing reminders of a war it would just as soon forget. He took a deep breath: "Of course we have room for more, besides just the crews and their families," he said as delicately as he could. The held air whistled out with a slight squeak.

Rich Armitage didn't say yes and didn't say no, which was all the authorization Kiem needed to start planning for the maximum passenger load. For the time being, they adjourned.

Around midnight, sitting in his office with the lights burning, Kiem heard a muffled knock. His hand went to his .22 revolver. "Who is it?"

"Admiral Cang."

"Come in, Admiral."

Kiem's old adversary seated himself and rubbed his eyes. "I've just come back from meeting with representatives of the new government."

Duong Van Minh—one of the anti-Diem conspirators of 1963 and a powerful Southern army general—was being sworn in as president the next day. "Big Minh is willing to form a coalition government with the communists. He's begging the armed forces to hold on for a few more days, to give him bargaining power. What's your opinion, Captain Kiem?"

"I think it's too easy for a rosy government to turn into a red one. And once it's red, the navy will be stuck."

"I agree. I was only testing you," said the CNO.

They sat up for several more hours, hammering out the remaining details. Unless there was hope of defending Saigon and the Mekong Delta, they would activate the E-Plan at 1800 hours on 29 April. Estimating four hours to load the ships, that would assure them cover of darkness on the way out. Shallow-draft ships could proceed up the Soai Rap River, but most of the fleet would have to sail down the Saigon River—and pray that they didn't get shot at. If even one big ship went down, those behind would be bottlenecked. Some of the ships would have to be dispatched to Vung Tau, Nam Can, and Phu Quoc to evacuate the III, IV, and V Coastal Zones.

At three A.M. Kiem escorted Cang to the hallway and locked his office door. He piled his weapons on a chair next to the fold-out cot: the large-bore Smith & Wesson revolver, confiscated from a Thai fishing boat during Operation Market Time; his M79 grenade launcher, plus the chest bandolier with oversized shells for it; two antifrogmen concussion grenades that he'd carried since his time in Nam Can; and his ammunition case. Then he changed into the pajamas he now carried, along with a spare toothbrush, in his briefcase.

But he wasn't to get much sleep. First came a frantic phone call from a friend at school in California. "The Americans won't let me fly home," said the officer, near hysteria. "Promise me you'll look out for my family, Kiem. As one Brest graduate to another. . . ." That call was followed by several to the man's sobbing wife, Madame Quynh.

"I'm stuck here in Ban Co, just me and the kids. No, I can't make it to naval headquarters. There's no transportation. And there's a curfew. . . ."

"Use your wits," Kiem snapped at her. "There's bound to be some cash or jewelry in your house. Hire somebody. Offer good money. You can slip through the military checkpoints, if you use your wits. . . ."

Sleep finally knocked him out; and he slept past sunrise, since the morning dawned dark as an eclipse. Thinking that he smelled smoke, he opened his window and looked out. He saw a column of ash billowing from the American Embassy smokestack and scraps of paper fluttering to the ground like clouds of black butterflies. A greasy black haze hung low in the sky.

"Captain Kiem!" He wheeled around. "Captain, a Madame Quynh and her children are waiting to see you at the front gate."

He smiled. "Escort them to the Training Center, Lieutenant." Then he changed out of his pajamas and went down the hall to the Intelligence Bureau's photo lab to brush his teeth in the darkroom sink.

It was one flight up from his office to the CIC. "Planes are still taking off, low to the ground, but they're getting shot at." That was air force colonel Uoc at Tan Son Nhut airport. The airport lay to the west of the city, giving the air force responsibility for defending Saigon's western flank. The east, bounded by the Saigon River, was the navy's responsibility. The 21st River Assault Group was stationed there, plus gunboats from Harbor Command. The army was guarding the northern and southern fronts.

"The river is still secure. Hang in there, Colonel."

Next to check in was General Khuyen. "Good day, Captain Kiem," he growled. "I'm afraid I've lost communications with IV Corps."

"Yes, General. My coastal patrol ships are reporting that the main road south has been cut off. We picked up some of your men north of Vung Tau."

"Give me the status on the river if you would, Captain Kiem."

"Still secure, sir."

"Ha! hang in there, Captain."

Kiem wished that Rich Armitage would check in: the fighting seemed to be moving closer and faster than U.S. intelligence predictions. But unknown to Kiem, Armitage had just flown by helicopter to Bien Hoa air base, north of Saigon. At that very moment his chopper was touching down in the middle of an artillery barrage. The American jumped out, raced for a culvert, and jumped in. After awhile he began to notice a dozen or so ARVN soldiers and airmen crawling out of various hiding places. They told him that the base was surrounded and they were trapped. So Armitage struck up a deal with them: if they'd help him collect and destroy the items on his checklist, he'd get them out of there. They set to work, picking off the occasional NVA soldier who penetrated the compound.

Around noon Erich Von Marbod signaled Armitage on his PRC-25 radio. "New intelligence, Rich. You're going to have to evacuate. I've ordered a helo."

"Erich, if I try to leave my new pals behind, they're going to shoot me."

"Damn it, Rich, I'm serious. The helo will be there in. . . ."

"I gave them my word, Erich. We won't all fit on one helo."

Von Marbod called him a lot of names, not including "Phu," but finally scrounged up a reluctant CIA plane flying out of Thailand. Around 4:45 P.M. it landed, spun around, dropped its back ramp down on the tarmac, sucked up thirty-one bodies in a torrent of 130-mm gunfire, and took off again without ever having come to a complete stop. As the plane made a corkscrew spiral to altitude, NVA soldiers swarmed like ants over the base.

They landed at Tan Son Nhut airport just in time to have their wits rescrambled by four A-37 aircraft dropping five-hundred-pound bombs. "Look at this, Rich," snapped Von Marbod inside the DAO office. It was a transcript of an intercepted NVA communication: "We have the enemy surrounded in Bien Hoa. Kill him."

An hour later, hearing that a U.S. helicopter was landing by the flag-pole, Kiem hustled down several flights of stairs and across the naval headquarters lawn. He saw two Americans in smoke-blackened flight suits jump out.

"Captain Kiem! It's me!" yelled the taller one. Armitage's face looked sooty and streaked, even burned in patches. He was wearing a chest-hol-ster.

Kiem couldn't hear very well over the churning rotor. He moved closer.

"Get on! Hurry!" yelled Armitage.

Kiem raised his hands, palms up, in the universal gesture that meant *What's going on?*

"We're leaving! Board with us! You've done your part, the planning. Admiral Cang can handle the execution. . . ."

"I can't," Kiem shouted. "Sorry!" Armitage waved, and Kiem waved back. Then the two Americans ducked and raced for their chopper.

"Big Minh" was inaugurated as president that evening. Admiral Cang went to the ceremony, but Kiem was too disgusted. *Pomp at a time like this!* Rockets rained down on Saigon throughout the night. Flares and explosions lit the horizon.

E-Day dawned hot, sticky, and hazy—thunderstorm weather. Kiem splashed his face and brushed his teeth in the darkroom sink, then stopped in to see Admiral Cang.

"I've just come from a private meeting with the president," the CNO said quietly. "He told me the situation is hopeless—that further bloodshed would be pointless. I asked him what the navy should do, and he said that in this case everyone should make his own decision."

Kiem nodded, although he could hardly believe Cang's words.

Colonel Uoc checked in, saying that they'd lost two aircraft so far that morning. He didn't think the air force could hold on much longer, but he promised to let Kiem know before they abandoned base.

General Khuyen was as affable as ever. "Good day, Captain Kiem. Are you still in control of the Saigon River?"

"Yes, sir, I am."

"Ha! Is there anything you need? Anything I can do for you?" asked Khuyen.

"No, General, I don't think so," said Kiem.

"All right then. Good-bye." Had the general ever growled "good-bye" to him before? Kiem didn't think so. But just then, two hundred airborne soldiers began banging on the front gates, seeking asylum. Kiem put them to work guarding the perimeter fence, and then it was time for him to meet with the Saigon ship captains.

"We're going to leave. Very likely today," Cang and Kiem told the stunned circle of faces. "Pick out your most trusted men to serve as crew. Take the maximum number with you, but be sure to disarm all nonnaval personnel. Make sure you control the engine room and have a guard at the small-arms locker. Don't worry about food or water. Above all, if you're shot at, *don't shoot back*. Leave that to the Riverine Force. Our rendezvous point will be the southwest bay of Con Son Island. Any questions?"

"Yeah. What if we don't want to go?"

"Nobody's forcing anyone to go," Kiem clarified. "But please, if you're not going to go yourself, do what you can to help the others escape. Shoulder a rifle and help guard the perimeter fence so another man can see to his family."

Back in his office Kiem fielded a call from a panic-stricken colonel at the Joint General Staff. "Everybody's gone," he kept repeating. "I'm the last one here."

"What about General Khuyen?"

"Gone, gone. It's only me. Who's the most senior general you have over there?"

"That would be Admiral Chung Tan Cang, our CNO," said Kiem. "Three stars."

"Well, tell him to come over here at once and take over the function of commander of the armed forces."

"I'll tell him," Kiem said dubiously. He started to dial Cang's office but decided to drop by in person instead. *The army, gone?* It seemed impossible.

To his surprise Cang threw back his head and laughed until tears brimmed in his eyes. "So I'm a four-star general now!" he whooped. "My dream has come true!"

Kiem couldn't help it. He began to chuckle himself. "Hey, why don't you promote me?" he managed to get out. "Make me a three-star general, your chief of staff!"

Their helpless laughter mingled with the booming of artillery, the popping of small-arms fire, and the droning of aircraft. Feeling strangely refreshed, Kiem went back to work.

Around noontime, he donned helmet and flak jacket and rode out to his apartment. Thom and her sister Thao were distraught about a third sister's husband, who was trapped outside Saigon. "She says she's not going anywhere without him. Can't you send a boat out to get him, Mr. Navy Big Shot?" fussed Thom. The baby girl was screaming.

Then Thao's lawyer-husband, Nguyen, came rushing into the room. "Brother-in-law, listen to this! A man outside is willing to pay you *ten ounces of gold per person* if you'll take him and his family back to the docks with you."

"Get his father out!" Kiem shouted—a curse against an ancestor, which was the worst possible insult one Vietnamese could give another. "Do you hear me? That's just the kind of scum who made a fortune off this war, and now he thinks he can *buy* his way out."

"Kiem!" Thom scolded. "Your language! In front of the children! What's gotten into you? And why did you scare Khai so badly the other day, saying the family might get separated. . . ?"

Kiem stiffened. "Where's Khai?"

"Over here, Father," the boy said.

"When I was your age, I'd been to war. You've disappointed me, Son. I expected you to be tougher than that." Kiem raised his hand and slapped his son hard across the face. "Shut up, all of you, and listen to me. It's time to go. Pack one change of clothing and a toothbrush each—no more. No large sums of cash, no household possessions. When you're ready, wait by the phone. I'll call to alert you, then send the jeep to pick you up."

"Where are we going?" Thom was asking.

"I can't tell you that, Thom."

"What if the phone stops working?" she whined.

"If anything goes wrong," he continued, pulling a scrap of paper from his pocket, "I have a friend with a fishing boat close by, on the Cau Son Canal. This is how to get there." He scribbled a rough map. "Tell him to hoist the French flag and make a run for the river mouth." That would double his family's chances of getting out alive. His own and the navy's odds, he guessed, would be about one in five.

As he turned to go, he saw that they were all cowering and weeping: more afraid of him and his stupid anger than of the communists. *Harden yourself*, a voice said, *or no one is going to survive.* He turned and left.

On the way back to headquarters, Kiem's driver cleared his throat. "Excuse me, Captain Kiem, but I couldn't help overhearing. The man who tried to bribe you? I know him: he's a colonel in the military justice system."

Kiem shook his head. "If only he'd *asked* me, I would have helped him. The stupid son of a bitch."

Back at headquarters, Kiem found a message from Colonel Uoc. His hand shook, dialing the return number. No one answered. He tried again and again. "It appears that the air force has given up fighting," he told Admiral Cang. The two of them decided to advance the start of the E-Plan by four hours, even if it was going to mean sailing out in daylight.

Fifteen minutes later Kiem walked downstairs and outdoors to the courtyard where three hundred staff members were assembling after hearing an announcement on the public-address system. Kiem had to shout to be heard above the pounding of artillery and the roar of helicopters. "It's time to go! The enemy is closing in. You have two hours to gather your families and bring them to the ships. Don't panic. There's room for everyone. Take nothing with you, not even food."

"Does this mean we're leaving the country?" someone asked.

"Yes. We have no choice. It's either that or capture."

A cry of anguish arose from the crowd, three hundred people wailing as one. Some slumped to the ground, rocking and holding their heads. Some went rushing out. Most stared straight ahead, in shock. Then they began scrambling, colliding with each other.

Kiem went back upstairs to the CIC, where he dispatched orders to all naval units. Then he hurried down to the riverfront, where four big ships sat rocking on the current: three at Pier A and one at B. Pier C lay a little farther upstream; D and E were inside the shipyard, about a quarter of a mile away. By the time the Saigon ships had finished loading, the coastal ships would have arrived to take their places.

So far, things seemed to be under control. "Disarm, disarm!" he urged the ship captains. "Set up your security at the gangplank before the crowds arrive."

Back in his office, he dialed his home number, but nobody answered. He dialed again and let it ring thirty times. *Wait ten minutes*, he told himself; *they must have stepped outside*. But *all* of them? When he'd ordered them to wait by the phone? He tried again. *Maybe the line wasn't working.*

. . .

Lieutenant Su interrupted with the news that a colonel from the Four Party Joint Military Commission had phoned while Kiem was away. "'Borek' or 'Borck'—some Polish or Hungarian name beginning with *B*," said the junior officer. "He wouldn't leave his number. Said he had an important message for you and that he might call back later."

Kiem didn't know a soul on that worthless "multinational" commission charged with monitoring the terms of the Paris "peace" agreement. Why the hell would they be bothering him now? What could they possibly want from him?

But what if somebody on the other side was trying to get in touch with him? It would make sense for them to go through one of the communist members of the Four Party Commission. If so, then who? One of his brothers or half-brothers? Tuong, his best friend from the Naval Academy? And what could they possibly want from him now—to stay behind so he and they could meet?

Well, fuck him, whoever it was. Kiem had chosen his way, and he was going to finish it, dead or alive. "Thank you, Lieutenant. It was probably nothing," he said.

Since Lieutenant Su was then planning to stay behind, Kiem asked if he'd mind taking the jeep keys and collecting Kiem's family if they were at home. The aide said he'd be glad to.

As the door closed behind Lieutenant Su, the phone rang. Clumsy with relief, Kiem almost knocked it off the receiver. But it was Rich Armitage. The voice sounded strange and far away, as if it were bubbling up from the bottom of the sea. "It's too late, Captain Kiem, it's too late. . . ."

"Yes, Rich, we know. We're evacuating right now."

"It's too late. . . ." The American's voice faded out.

Lieutenant Su returned less than an hour later. "The door was standing open. The house was empty. But I found this." He held out Kiem's battered gray briefcase. Kiem managed to thank him, even though he'd gone numb inside.

Right after that, the power went out. The hallway was as dark as a train tunnel. Kiem had to run his hand along the wall, counting the doors to Cang's office. He found the admiral sitting alone at his desk. "Sir," he said, "there's nothing for us to do here. Go on down to the pier, see to your family. I've arranged for you to board HQ-01. You have a private cabin."

"Thank you," Admiral Cang whispered.

"I'm going down to check on the loading. Why don't you come with me?"

"In a little while, Captain Kiem."

Kiem left him there, surrounded by shadows.

Outside, thousands of civilians were surging against the compound fence. Some of the army soldiers were firing into the air to scare them back. Kiem stopped and gave them a good chewing-out, trying to make them see that they might hit somebody and start a riot. *People like to make a big noise when they're afraid, to dominate their fear,* he thought. He continued to the docks, where people careened uncertainly from one pier to the next.

Nearing Pier B, Kiem could hear jeering and cursing. Shielding his profile with one hand, a national assemblyman was attempting to board HQ-01, the navy's flagship. "You got us into this mess, you bastard!" one sailor was yelling. Another pushed him back roughly.

"Gentlemen, please! You know the communists will kill me if I stay behind. . . ."

Behind the assemblyman was an army colonel known for taking bribes. "You too!" the men shouted. "Get that diamond ring off your pinkie finger, or we'll chop it off with a machete!"

Kiem put his arms around the shoulders of the two chief rabble-rousers. "I hate those crooked bastards as much as you do," he said, "but let's not jeopardize the whole operation for their sake. The tanks are on their way. We don't have much time."

He left without waiting to see who prevailed. But he made a mental note to reassign Admiral Cang and his family to a smaller boat. The sailors hardly knew him. They might decide to blame him for the catastrophe.

He jogged along the riverfront, in the direction of the shipyard. Feeling strangely lightheaded, he realized that he'd forgotten to eat when he went home at noon. He slowed down to a walk. Sweat trickled down inside his uniform.

He pushed his way through the mob outside the shipyard to find the gates still locked and four ships sitting empty. When he ordered the captain inside to open the gates, the crowd stampeded. Cars and motorbikes were abandoned in the street with their engines still running. The traffic behind them stalled, and drivers blocks away began leaning on their horns.

Across the street, in front of the naval hospital, a band of white-coated doctors and nurses stood watching the madness from their front lawn. As members of the medical corps, they had less to fear from the communists than the others. Chances were they'd be staying behind.

Kiem crossed the street. "Want that car, that jeep, or that Vespa over there?" he asked the group. "Those vehicles are yours if you'll drive them away."

Some of them recognized him. "Are you sure, Captain?" one of the doctors asked.

"You bet I am. Their owners aren't coming back."

They ran for the cars, and within minutes the jam had cleared.

He reentered the shipyard, planning to check on the disarming procedures. But a cramp seized his left leg, and it buckled under him. He had forgotten to take his thyroid medication. The pill bottle was back in his office, in his briefcase.

"Captain Kiem, is that you?" Chanh, a chief petty officer, was kneeling by his side. "What's wrong? Are you hurt?"

"It's nothing," he said. "A leg cramp. It will pass."

"Here," he said, "let me massage it for you. It may be the last chance I have to serve you."

"You'd better see to your family, Chief."

"I don't know, sir. My whole life, I've been taught to fight and shoot. What sort of skills are those to take to a new country?"

Kiem looked at Chanh's pox-scarred face as if for the first time. How he'd aged from the husky young recruit at the Naval Training Center, thirteen years before. "You're still a young man. You could learn a new trade," Kiem told him. *But I'm forty-two years old,* thought Kiem suddenly.

"Eh, who knows? It's up to my wife's mother. She'll decide."

"Thank you, Chief," said Kiem, stretching the leg. "It feels much better now. I think I'll just sit here and rest for a few minutes before moving on."

How ugly people's faces looked, thought Kiem with surprise, peering up from his spot on the ground. Back in high school, he had liked to set up his easel on a busy Hanoi street corner, just to sketch passing strangers. How he'd loved to catch their movements, their expressions! Now all he could see were rude men and women knocking others out of the way; soldiers begging or cursing, oblivious to the uniforms they were wearing; elderly couples holding fast to each other with tears oozing down their wrinkled faces. Still others looked like zombies, eyes staring straight ahead, fingers mechanically gripping children. They moved on puppet-legs, jerking, twitching.

He got to his feet and limped back to headquarters, feeling his way up the stairs to Cang's office in the dark. "I'd like you to get your family now, sir," he said. "Meet me in front of HQ-601. The first plan isn't going to work."

But he'd forgotten who was captain of the PGM: the son of ex–CNO Chon. "There isn't any CNO anymore, and I'm not going anywhere!" he sneered, strutting up and down the deck.

"Please, Lieutenant. This may be the last time you'll be able to do something for your fellow sailors. . . ."

"I'm not doing anything for *him.* Not for the CNO."

"He's not the CNO anymore, Lieutenant. You're right about that. Today he's just another sailor."

Finally Chon's son softened. "I'll take a load out to Con Son Island, but then I'm turning back. And only because you *asked* me to, Captain Kiem. I don't take orders anymore."

Back at the CIC, Kiem was handed a mike by the watch officer: "Captain Kiem, the captain of HQ-11 wants to speak to you."

"Cobra-11, this is Hometown," he said. "Over."

"Hometown, Cobra-11 requests permission to make a swing into Phan Rang Bay." The confident voice of Lieutenant Commander San, one of Kiem's best students at Nha Trang, boomed excitedly over the amplified mike. "There are thousands of VC crossing the bridge at Highway 1. You should see those arrogant bastards, flying their flag on every truck. I have a couple of hundred rounds of big boys left. I could blow those bastards to hell with Ho Chi Minh. Over."

Kiem closed his eyes for a second, then pressed the mike. "Cobra-11, negative. Permission not granted. Too much risk for you in shallow water. Over."

"Hometown, but. . . ."

"Cobra-11, this is an *order*. Proceed immediately and at full speed to the main gate as planned. Stay in contact with Hometown. Out."

Poor Lieutenant Commander San: he must be feeling frustrated as hell. "But what's the use?" Kiem asked himself out loud, causing the watch officer to turn and stare at him—"What's the point of killing or getting killed now?"

Night was just beginning to fall when Lieutenant Su came rushing in to tell him there was trouble in the shipyard: mutiny! Kiem raced for the pier and grabbed a launch. Within minutes he was zooming into the shipyard bay. The same three ships that had been loading earlier that afternoon were still at Pier D, lined up abreast. *Damn their pokiness!* The inner and middle ships were crammed with bodies, but the outer ship, an LST, looked strangely empty.

Kiem boarded the middle ship and called over to the handful of sailors on HQ-503. "It's Captain Kiem," he said. "I'd like to speak with your captain." They told him that wouldn't be possible: the captain refused. "Not as his commanding officer. As one sailor to another." They told him the captain still refused. "All right. But why don't you cut the rope so the other ships can get out?" Because the captain refused, they explained.

Kiem took off his helmet and turned to face the audience he had gathered on the other two ships. "Ladies and gentlemen, your piastres will be worth nothing in the new country, believe me. But right now they can buy you your freedom. . . ." People began stuffing fistfuls of money into the helmet, then car and house keys. "Another hat! Who'll loan me his hat?" He passed the bribe-baskets over the rail to the sailors, who dumped them on the deck like a catch of fish.

It worked. The men cut the rope.

The next bit of excitement came from the commander in charge of the harbor. Staggering and reeking of whiskey, he pointed a pistol into Kiem's ribcage. "Why . . . did you tell . . . my shipsh . . . to go?" he wanted to know. Kiem tried to explain that the communists were coming. "Ish . . . that . . . true?" the commander prodded, stabbing him with the gun barrel for emphasis.

"You were my student in Class Ten at the Naval Academy. Did I ever lie to you?" The pistol clattered harmlessly to the ground.

They had planned to be underway by six, but toward midnight, as the last ships were loading, a jeep with its lights on came barreling up to the pier. A naval officer jumped out holding a portable loudspeaker. "Attention, attention! This is your new fleet commander speaking. All ships are to stay where they are. That's an order." Kiem was standing on the bridge of HQ-07, his old ship from coastal patrol days—the one that had inspired the local fishermen to take off all their clothes.

The ship's radio began to crackle. "This is Captain Binh, the new deputy chief of staff, operations. All ships are to return to Saigon immediately. Repeat: all ships report back to Saigon."

"No!" Kiem grabbed the ship's transmitter. "This is Captain Kiem. *I'm* the deputy chief of staff, operations, and you'd better shut up, Binh, you impostor! All ships are to get out!" But Binh was broadcasting from the CIC, where he could be heard all the way out to Phu Quoc. Kiem's transmission could only be heard in the immediate area.

"Attention. This is Captain Tan, your new CNO." *Oh, mia madre.* "I order the gates to the shipyard closed. All ships at pier are to remain where they are. All units are to report back to their stations."

"This is Captain Kiem. Shut up, all you phonies! All ships are to *go.*" Looking around the bay, he confirmed that the ships were continuing to load—but what would the rest of the convoy do?

A new voice hissed from the radio: "You who are leaving the country to chase after dollars: do you call yourselves Vietnamese? Slaves of Western capitalists, that's what you are. . . ."

"Don't listen to that communist propaganda!" Kiem shouted. "They're trying to trick you into staying! Liars!" No human voice could have seduced him, but the next voice wasn't human. It was the voice of a flute, playing a song every Vietnamese person knew: "The Sound of the Flute on the River Ngo." In the song an ancient warrior is about to cross the famous river to fight the enemy. Knowing in his heart that he will die in battle, he pauses before crossing to play his flute.

As the last eerie, silvery notes died away, Kiem could feel the strength ebbing from his muscles. He wanted to rest, to sleep—but he reached for the transmitter. "If you don't want to go, that's fine. But let the rest of us do what we want. This is Captain Kiem."

Then he sank down in the bridge chair. "Cast off all lines. Left rudder full. Engine one-third," he heard the captain cry. It was sometime after midnight, and they would be the third-to-last ship to leave. As they passed the east end of Saigon, they could hear the rumble of approaching tanks.

Small boats chased after them, their occupants begging to be taken on board. Some they stopped for; some they didn't. Kiem could hardly believe that no one was shooting at them, particularly with no more regional forces guarding the river. As they neared Vung Tau, he learned from a passing craft that the naval unit there had jumped the gun and exited the day before. Kiem had been counting on them to guard their passage to international waters: "You think *you're* mad, Captain! The marines were so mad they pointed their big guns at the navy ships and fired!" He ordered a ship and communications blackout till they were clear of the peninsula.

Now and then he spotted an abandoned junk burning like a "Zippo" flamethrower. He tried hard not to think about his family.

Daylight arrived. The South China Sea was as flat as glass but littered with chunks of flotsam and eerie, riderless junks. Time stretched, elastic, as Kiem's wristwatch ticked toward noon. Over the PRC radio came the news that the government had surrendered at eleven o'clock that morning.

Despite the danger from the enemy's air force and now from their navy—Kiem had to remind himself that the communists had just captured the South's naval bases and would have no more trouble refueling their gunboats—they slowed down to help direct small boats out of the river mouths into the open sea. Kiem picked up a distress signal from a launch that had run out of fuel near the mouth of the Soai Rap River. "I have three army VIPs on board, Captain Kiem! You should see them—all dressed up in their best suits! They went to the presidential palace to meet with 'Big Minh' this morning. But when he read his capitulation speech, they changed their minds. They went running out the door and down the block to naval headquarters. But by then everybody had gone. I just happened to be cruising by. . . ."

"You seem like a wordy fellow. How about telling me their names?"

"I'm afraid that's confidential, Captain Kiem."

"OK with me. Keep your secret and stay where you are."

The skipper blurted out the names of two generals and a colonel. Kiem recognized them: they were good men. So he radioed the captain of HQ-17, a WHEC heading out from the IV Coastal Zone, and asked him to swing around and pick them up. Kiem had to beg twice, but the captain finally gave in. The captain said he'd check around the other "Nine Dragons' Mouths" to see if any other small boats were stranded.

A little while later Kiem made radio contact with Rich Armitage. Looking like a bum, as usual, and not carrying any identification papers, Armitage had boarded the USS *Blue Ridge* and asked to speak to Adm. Donald Whitmire, commander of the Seventh Fleet. "Honest to God, sir. Just call up the Pentagon, and they'll confirm my identity," he had told the astonished admiral. By some miracle he had been taken seriously. The U.S. Defense Department had dispatched the USS *Kirk* and a tugboat to rendezvous with the convoy at Con Son Island and escort it to safety.

CHAPTER 19

Hostility Found across the Country As the First South
Vietnamese Exiles Arrive
Economic Impact Is Cited by Most

New York Times, 2 May 1975

As the lead ships approached Con Son Island and everyone
knew, at last, that they'd escaped from the communists, other
voices besides Kiem's piped up and began broadcasting orders
to the convoy. Suddenly Kiem was nobody, and the sense of
urgency that had been driving him for nineteen years rolled
away. He'd done his part by getting the fleet out of the country.
Now let somebody else worry about where they were going
next and the condition of the ships to make it.

As soon as HQ-07 dropped anchor, Kiem took a launch from
ship to ship, hoping that one of them might have picked up
Thom and the children: "A small, slender woman in her mid-
thirties, a tall boy of sixteen, a friendly boy of twelve, and three
little girls aged eight to two. . . ." Too many families looked
like that. No one could tell him anything. He counted twenty-
nine big ships that had made it to Con Son Island, plus the
Vung Tau ship that had bolted a day early, the WHEC he'd
sent back to pick up the army VIPs, and three units from Phu
Quoc that were probably running late. Still other VNN ships
had dropped off a load of passengers, then turned back; and
there were at least a dozen riverine craft drifting, abandoned,
around the bay.

In less than two hours the convoy would be regrouping and
setting sail for the Philippines. Kiem could hardly believe it—
people and ships were exhausted, and they were short of water
and food. But the ships weren't his to deploy anymore. He
radioed Rich Armitage and asked if he could be assigned to one
of the U.S. Navy ships stationed off the coastline, pulling in

refugees from fishing boats. Armitage was sympathetic, but his superiors said no. So Kiem asked the admirals if he could take an abandoned Swift boat back to Vietnam. He meant to sneak into Saigon harbor, hunt for his family, and sneak back out with them after dark. "Do what you want, but don't expect us to wait for you," they told him. Three junior officers, including Lieutenant Su, volunteered to go back with him.

Not long after they'd gotten underway, the tarpaulin over the lifeboat began to quake, and then a silver-haired head popped out like an egg hatching. "I'm sorry," said an old man none of them knew; "I knew you wouldn't have taken me if I'd asked." He explained that he'd gone down to the shipyard last night to see what all of the commotion was about. In all of the excitement, with everybody jumping onto ships, he'd jumped on, too—forgetting about his family.

The old man was a jinx. Right after he turned up, their General Motors engine broke down, and not even the mechanical officer among them could get it running again. "I hate to say this, Captain Kiem," said the junior officer, "but it looks like sabotage to me."

"Sabotage? But who'd do a thing like that to me? Who hates me that much?" asked Kiem.

"Maybe it was someone who loves you, sir," said Lieutenant Su.

They drifted for several hours, not saying much, wondering whether the sharks or the communists would to get to them first. For once in his life, there was nothing Kiem could do to control the way things turned out—and the realization brought a strangely calming peace. And it came to him then that if something bad had happened to his family, he would know it in his heart—the way his mother had dreamed that Tri was dead and he himself had dreamed about the death of his father.

"Are you thirsty, old man?" he asked, turning to the stowaway. "There's a little water in. . . ."

But the old man was peering intently at the horizon. "Isn't that a ship? I see real good far away, not so hot up close."

"A ship! A ship!" they all began shouting. "Mayday! Mayday! Help! *Au secours!*" Lieutenant Su remembered the flare gun in the bottom of the lifeboat. Soon the speck began growing bigger.

It was ex–U.S. Coast Guard Cutter HQ-17, straggling back from the reluctant rescue mission Kiem had sent it on.

"Please, please, take my stateroom," the captain kept insisting, while the rescued army generals and colonel kept bowing so low Kiem was afraid they were going to kiss his feet. But he didn't want to evict the captain's family, who were shoehorned into the tiny cabin with him, so he asked for a bunk down below with the single enlisted men.

Kiem had never seen the ocean so calm before, staying at "sea zero" conditions the entire week. HQ-17 made good time and soon caught up to the rest of the convoy. But the food and water they'd been promised by the Americans never did quite materialize. One afternoon an American supply ship pulled alongside and tossed them a half-dozen lumpy sacks, but when they slashed them open, nothing but onions and watermelons rolled out. A few brave folks tried biting into the onions like apples, only to spit them out and make a face. At least the children enjoyed the watermelons.

After dark they could see the lights of their U.S. escort ship burning like a watchdog's eyes. Then the single sailors who'd been busy all day helping widows and children would sprawl with their backs against the gun turrets, smoking and staring out to sea with tears rolling down their faces, Kiem among them.

HQ-03, with Admirals Cang and Minh on board, was the convoy's flagship; it had the code for communicating with the Americans. Kiem radioed them repeatedly, asking them to let Rich Armitage know that Kiem was still searching for his family. There was no way to tell if his messages were getting through.

On the afternoon of the seventh day, they reached the twelve-mile territorial limit offshore of Manila and found that they were not welcome. Although the U.S. government had made prior arrangements to shelter up to fifty thousand Vietnamese refugees at Subic Bay, the way hadn't been cleared for a fleet of foreign warships to come sailing into Philippine waters. To make matters worse, the new Provisional Revolutionary Government of Vietnam had just wired Philippine president Ferdinand Marcos a message claiming title to the ships.

Top-level diplomatic negotiations ensued, but it was clear that the Philippine government wasn't going to budge. Then somebody pulled out the contracts transferring the ships to Vietnam and discovered a clause: in the event that they were no longer needed for Vietnamese military service, the vessels were supposed to revert to U.S. ownership. Therefore they were now American ships, entitled to sail into Subic Bay with no interference from the Philippine government. It was a brilliant try. But, wary of offending their new Asian "neighbor" to the west, President Marcos and his minister of foreign affairs, General Romulo, wouldn't buy it. "OK," said the U.S. negotiators to the Philippine government, "feed and house those thirty thousand refugees yourselves while you thrash out the issue of ownership."

Why, said General Romulo with a sudden change of heart, the transfer of ships to U.S. control was a great idea!

But before the ships could be brought into the harbor, their guns had to be dismantled, their ammo unloaded, their names painted over, their Vietnamese flags lowered, and the American colors raised. The shame of it was almost unbearable: Kiem and his men were a bunch of losers. They had lost the long war. In all of the excitement and chaos of the past week, it was the first time the realization had fully hit them. But there was still one small thing Kiem could do to help his men save face. He could ask for a proper changing-of-colors ceremony: something to soften the blow of seeing their flag yanked down like a rag.

Late that afternoon, on board every ship, an ex–VNN officer made a speech; then a U.S. Navy officer made a speech. As the ropes creaked and the red flag with three gold stripes began to descend, the refugees broke into their national anthem: "*Nay cong dan oi . . .*" (Oh citizen of the country . . .). Their voices soared over the turquoise waters of the Pacific Ocean. Slowly the U.S. flags were hoisted into place. Then the ex–VNN officers walked to the ship's rail, ripped the insignia from their uniforms, and tossed the gold glitter into the sea with their caps. They were civilians, now, not military men. Stripped of their national identities, they could help bring another country's warships into the bay with no shame.

The next morning a launch went buzzing around from ship to ship, picking up the senior officers—from colonels on up. When it pulled alongside HQ-17, the rescued army generals and colonel lost no time jumping in. But Kiem hesitated. "What for?" he asked the launch-boat pilot.

"You senior officers can catch the next flight to Guam. You won't have to wait to be processed like everybody else."

"No thanks, then. I don't want any special treatment," said Kiem.

The pilot lowered his voice. "There are rumors you guys might be in danger from your own people." Kiem glanced over to the army VIPs; they were looking down at their feet, pretending not to hear.

"No thank you," he repeated. "I'll stay where I am."

Some time late in the afternoon they were released to go ashore. Kiem walked off the gangplank, past a row of Red Cross booths serving juice and cookies. He kept walking. But one table had *apples*—he would have traded his revolver for one, though he was ashamed to ask. Seeing the longing in Kiem's eyes, a pretty lady in a Red Cross cap handed him two.

The next stop was a clothing tent. Kiem's dirty uniform was confiscated, and he was outfitted in blue jeans and a T-shirt. "Like an American hippie," he thought.

He kept bumping into people he knew, but none of them had heard anything about Thom or his brother-in-law, Nguyen. Then he heard someone shouting his name: an old friend who'd been an officer in the IV Coastal Zone. "Captain Kiem, Mr. Phu said to tell you if I saw you that he thinks your wife and children are in Guam!"

Right behind that good news came an announcement that the camp was too full. A Military Sealift Command ship was being dispatched to divert three thousand refugees to Guam; if any former VNN sailors wished to escort her, they'd be particularly welcome. Kiem and the small group of men who'd been sticking by him signed up right away.

They were frisked along with the regular passengers before boarding the *Sgt. Truman Kimbro*. Kiem handed over his gun without a fuss, but he balked when they asked for his cigarette lighter, a gift from the CNO of the Cambodian Navy. "But it's empty," he said, flicking it to show them. Rules were rules, they said. So far that week Kiem had lost a family, a country, a home, a job, a war, a cause. But the loss of the lighter was small enough for him to comprehend. It made him want to hit somebody.

The sea, fed up with being on good behavior, began to fidget—not enough to sweep people overboard but just enough to make them good and seasick. Kiem and his men stayed busy swabbing pools of vomit from the decks or hosing it off the "latrines," which were just crude wooden boxes jutting out over the water. The sailors found a length of rope and rigged it to the boxes so children wouldn't fall down the holes into the sea. In the mornings they boiled water for breakfast and ladled out oatmeal—which the refugees didn't like but dutifully ate and dutifully threw up. At noontime they opened the supply office and counted out one orange and one C ration per person.

On the second day a widow with six children flashed seven fingers in Kiem's face. He counted out six oranges and six C rations, knowing that her baby was just a few months old. "Seven," she corrected him.

"Six," he said. "We have powdered milk and formula for the infant."

"You're cheating me," she hissed. "You were corrupt during the war, and you're still corrupt, motherfucker."

He started to say something back—"Six, and you'd better be grateful for it, bitch"—when something stopped him. She wouldn't have dared to talk to him like that in the panic of boarding the ship. She'd only said it just now because she felt safe.

"Don't ever forget that men of mine died for your right to curse me," he said as gently as he could. But six it was.

The steel hold had been converted to a dorm, but nobody wanted to stay down there where it was airless, stinking, and hot. Instead the refugees scrambled up sheets of rigging to the upper deck, where they camped out under blankets slung over ropes. One day a fat man lost his grip on the netting and fell over backward, landing on his spine. "Don't touch me!" he moaned at the first people to reach him.

"Don't worry. That man is a doctor," said Kiem, pointing to a surgeon making his way down the net.

"No! Get back! Tell him to get back!"

Heaven help him, thought Kiem, *his back must be broken*.

"Don't move unless I tell you to," the doctor cautioned, ripping open the man's shirt.

"No! No!" howled the victim.

Then everybody crowded around to see. Under his shirt the no-longer-fat man was wearing an ammunition belt studded with gold ingots. No wonder he'd lost his balance, then couldn't sit up! *"Don't touch me"* indeed!

"I'd move to the deck, if I were you," Kiem advised him. "You'll be safer from thieves in the open air."

It was late at night when they arrived in Guam. They were herded off the ship and marched like zombies up a rough jungle trail to the camp. Assigned to the same tent, Kiem and his men crawled into their army cots and passed out.

In the morning they looked out and saw one sorry mess. Tens of thousands of tents stretched in rows in every direction. There'd been little attempt to clear the terrain, which was just red coral mud and brush. They started searching for water and toilets.

"You guys are out of luck!" some of the others informed them. "The first to arrive were put up in military housing, even hotels!" They pointed Kiem's men to the single row of latrines. There were long lines for them, long lines for everything: food, water, blankets, telephones, medicine. Air trembled on top of the tents: it was even hotter than the Mekong Delta. The men peeled off their new T-shirts and went around gushing sweat, slapping at insects, and trying not to step on scorpions or snakes.

Had Rich Armitage been wrong about his family? Kiem traced and retraced every square meter of the camp, broadcast messages daily over the public-address system, stood in front of the camp's bulletin boards reading every single name on the computerized lists. But Thom and the children were nowhere to be found. Every day he wrote letters—to Armitage, Admiral Zumwalt, ex-counterparts, President Ford, everybody he could think of, asking them to please help him find his family. And every day he dropped the sealed envelopes through the slot on the side of the postal building. Then one day he opened the door into the building and peeked inside: letters were piled like snowdrifts all the way to the ceiling, those going out mixed with those coming in. None of his letters had gone anywhere.

That did it. He told the American camp commander that he and his men were volunteering to help. They appointed him a zone commander, giving him a radio and a reason to post his name outside his tent. Kiem had his men take a census and issue ration cards so that only one member of each family had to wait in line for food in the brutal sun. He had the incoming mail sorted alphabetically and placed in neat stacks. Shocked at the sight of American GIs scrubbing latrines in their uniforms, he insisted on having his own men take over the job. The camp commander tried to pay Kiem a salary, but he refused: unless his men could be paid too, he didn't think it was right.

Their days settled into a routine. The Spanish-speaking crewmen from their Military Sealift Command ship, stuck in port on a long layover, dropped by almost every day with "presents": stuff they were supposed to have given the refugees on the voyage over but welcomed now, even if late. They brought Japanese flip-flop sandals and, once, an enormous frozen beefsteak. Not knowing how to cook it, and not wanting to spoil it, Kiem gave it to his old boss Le Quang My, whom he'd found living in a nearby tent. Captain My wasn't speaking French anymore, and he seemed to have lost his pipe in the evacuation.

Gabgab Beach was too polluted for swimming, but it had the camp's only shade trees and a volleyball net. In the evenings the refugees watched Kung Fu movies in the canteen. Sometimes people even laughed in the camp—children, mostly, watching cartoons.

May turned to June, and June was halfway over when Kiem heard his name being paged. No big deal. Maurice Shine and Rich Armitage called from time to time. Captain Shine was on temporary assignment in Hawaii; he couldn't sponsor Kiem out of the camp just then, but he was looking for someone who could. Rich Armitage was keeping an eye out for jobs for Kiem in the United States.

"Hello," Kiem said, a bit irritably.

On the other end, on Wake Island, his wife began to cry. "You bum!" she said. "How could you leave your family alone? I'm so mad at you I don't even want to *speak* to you! Do you know your baby daughter nearly died on the way here? 'Don't bring any food,' you told us. Well, everybody else did, wise guy! Your children had to pick up noodles other people had dropped on the floor. And the baby had no formula—she's been in the hospital all this time and just got out. . . ."

"She's all right? Thuy's all right? And the other children. . . ."

"Fine, and no thanks to you, you bum. I should have divorced you when I had the chance, three years ago. . . ."

"I love you! I love you, Thom! I've missed you so much. . . ."

"Shut up!" she yelled. "I haven't finished yet, with the list of your crimes!"

"This call isn't free, you know," he said. "It's costing us plenty of money." He heard a *click* and then a dial tone. The love of his life had just hung up on him, and he was so happy he could have flapped his arms and flown over Gabgab Beach.

There were no flights from Guam to Wake Island just then, but there were plenty going the other way. So Thom and the children flew to Kiem, and the family was reunited in early July. Finally Kiem learned what had happened to them that final day in Saigon.

Panicking at the sound of a nearby explosion, they had raced for Kiem's friend's fishing boat and made a dash for the high seas, where they'd been picked up by the U.S. Seventh Fleet. Thom had assumed that finding Kiem at sea would be like finding someone in a room at a big party, but it hadn't been quite that easy. Taken first to Guam, they'd learned that the camp was full and land for the second phase not cleared yet, so they'd been flown to Wake Island. The baby girl, near death from dehydration, had been hospitalized just in time.

Kiem's camp in Guam was like a prison, surrounded by guards and barbed wire, but the one on Wake Island had been more like a resort. Every morning, after visiting baby Thuy in the hospital, Thom had strolled out the front gates with her children behind her, heading for the air base down the road. All day long they'd watched the planes unload, searching for Vietnamese faces or U.S. Navy uniforms. Thom hadn't been shy about marching up to strangers and asking if they knew Capt. Do Kiem. One day she'd stopped a U.S. Navy officer getting off a flight from Guam. He said he thought he remembered seeing her husband's name on a sign outside a tent. After that, the rest had been easy.

But how was Kiem going to support them, with no job and no prospects? One day at snack time, standing in the food line with the baby on his shoulder—he carried Thuy *everywhere* now, even though Thom fussed that she would forget how to walk if he didn't put her down—he placed seven cups of juice and seven pink-frosted cake squares in the bottom of a shallow cardboard lid, then wedged it under the other arm. But on the way back to the tent, he lost his grip and the box went flying. Pink chunks of cake lay in the red coral mud. "Cookie?" asked Thuy sadly in Vietnamese. She seemed to understand that not even her daddy's job as zone commander could buy her another piece of cake. Kiem wanted to cry right along with her.

Typhoon season was coming, and the camp was emptying out. There was room for them in the Fort Indiantown Gap, Pennsylvania, refugee camp, although not in the three stateside camps with climates more like home—in Florida, Arkansas, and California. So Kiem and Thom filled out stacks of papers. In mid-July the family flew from Guam to Honolulu to California in the back of a military transport plane with its seats removed, sitting on the cold metal floor and puffing on their fingers to warm them. Everybody but Kiem, Kiet, and the baby got airsick. At Travis Air Force Base, they switched to a commercial flight. This time they sank into cushioned seats and sniffed a delicious meal, although only three of them were able to eat it.

When they staggered off the plane in Philadelphia, two longhaired, bearded youths in jeans came rushing toward them, shouting their names. Kiem was frightened that it might be a protest demonstration. He stepped in front of Thom and the children to shield them.

But the "hippies" turned out to be camp employees. "We're all college students or teachers on summer vacation," the one with the black beard confided to Kiem on the way to the waiting yellow school bus. "The pay is pretty good for a summer job, and the work is really neat—especially if you like kids." Black Beard was speaking too fast for Thom to understand his English. When Kiem translated what he'd just said, she shook her head.

"Teachers and university students cooking for us, doing our wash like domestics? No way."

But Black Beard was telling the truth. What a difference between Fort Indiantown Gap and the camps on Guam and Wake Island, run by military personnel! Here the "counselors" hugged the children and laughed or winked when the refugees broke the rules. Kiem and Thom and the children shared a barracks with one other family. It was a relief to have walls around them instead of tent flaps, and a floor under their feet instead of pounded dirt, and a clean public bathroom with running water. The other family's mentally retarded ten-year-old son kept jumping into bed with the children in the middle of the night, scaring them into screaming. But they couldn't complain about anything else. There was plenty to eat, even if the rice was dry and the bread gluey in the center. The kids didn't mind about the awful rice and bread: they had discovered hot dogs, pizza, peanut butter, ice cream, and American breakfast cereal. The baby gained back all the weight she had lost, and a little more.

One of the counselors started calling the baby "Tootsie" since she couldn't pronounce "Thuy"—and the American nickname stuck. One day a metal folding cot snapped shut on Tootsie's foot, cracking the bone in her big toe. "I *knew* I shouldn't have put her down," thought Kiem. "If only I'd been carrying her. . . ." He ran with his daughter all the way to the camp's infirmary, where a medic put them in a car and drove them to a Philadelphia hospital.

"We're going to have to take an X ray," the doctor told Kiem. Then he smiled at Tootsie, trying to charm her into cooperating. "Poor little footie," he said. "Did baby hurt her little footie? How does baby's little footie feel?"

Two-year-old Tootsie sized him up with her big dark eyes. Something awful was about to happen, and she knew she didn't want any part of it. "Baby's OK," she said in perfect, accentless English. Kiem had to bury his face in the back of the child's neck so the doctor wouldn't see his emotion.

They were becoming more "American" every day. But did America want them? They couldn't leave the camp without a sponsor: someone willing to feed and house them until they could support themselves. Kiem had gone so far as to put "none" under "religious preference" on the forms he'd filled out, hoping to increase their chances, but it seemed that those who had put "Catholic" were having better luck. Some of the refugees didn't even know what their religion was: "Pssst, Mr. Kiem! What's the word for worshipping your dead parents?"

Carloads of potential sponsors kept pulling into the screening center, and Kiem's family would be put on display like goods at market. "Can you sew? Cook? Iron?" they'd ask Thom. "Can you garden? Drive a car? Change an old man's bedpan?" they'd ask Kiem. Most of the Americans drove in and out without signing for anybody—bored on a Sunday afternoon with nothing better to do, Kiem supposed. When they did make a match, it seemed impulsive, like buying a pet: "Oh, look! A boy of five and a girl of two, just like ours at home!" They didn't even think to ask if the parents could read and write.

Kiem kept placing long-distance calls to Captain Shine, who put him in touch with Ricky Petre. "Sure, I can help. I'm a very, very close friend of the mayor of Macon, Georgia," Ricky told Kiem over the phone. He had just remarried and was working for a plant that manufactured crop-duster airplanes. After making and breaking several appointments to see them, Ricky drove up one weekend in his new Lincoln Continental.

Instead of parking in the visitors' lot like everybody else, Ricky drove as close to the camp as he could and parked the Lincoln on top of a hill. He got out and came down, leaving his new wife sitting in the car. Then he made everybody march up the steep, rocky slope to meet her. Mrs. Petre rolled down the window but didn't get out. All Kiem could see was white-blonde hair and a big bosom. All five kids ran around the Lincoln, petting the hood ornament and looking at their faces in the car's black mirror-finish. "I thought you said you had *two* children," Ricky whined.

"How dare he make us climb a mountain!" hissed Thom as Ricky and his wife drove away. "I'm not going *anywhere* with him, and that's that!" But as the weeks went by and the camp's population slowly dwindled, Ricky began to look like their only hope. Kiem swallowed his pride and started dialing Ricky's house in Georgia, getting no answer. When he tried the crop-duster plant, they sounded vague. Ricky was "out"; they didn't know when he'd be back. Finally one night Ricky's daughter by his first wife answered the phone at her father's house. Ricky had been in a car accident, she told Kiem; he'd sustained a head injury, but he was getting better. He would call Kiem as soon as he got out of the hospital.

He never called.

Around the middle of August a delegation from Brazil came to the camp, looking for engineers. When they learned that Kiem was a graduate of the French Naval Academy, they wrote out a contract offering him two thousand dollars a month. "I'll let you know something tomorrow," said Kiem. Then he sought out one of the camp's English instructors and asked him, in private, how much an American teacher made per month. Depending on graduate credits and experience, around six to seven hundred dollars, said the instructor.

Kiem's next stop was the camp's library, where he checked out an almanac and a Portuguese-language book. Satisfied with what he found inside, he called a family conference. Lieutenant Su, who'd tagged along to Fort Indiantown Gap, came too.

"Surprise! We're going to Brazil!" Kiem announced.

They all stared back at him, unsmiling: Brazil?

"We'll be very happy there," he assured them. "They grow rice and sugarcane, just like home." He waved the almanac in the air. Then he began to read aloud about per capita income, gross national product, and life expectancy.

"But I don't know these people," said Thom when he'd finished. "Where will the children go to school? Who will they marry?"

"We'll be rich," said Kiem. "We can send them wherever we want for their educations."

"With all due respect, sir," said Lieutenant Su, "the government there might not be quite as *democratic* as one would wish. . . ."

"What about the language?" asked Thom. "The children are just beginning to learn English, and here you want them to start all over with . . . with . . . what do they speak down there, anyway?"

"Portuguese!" said Kiem.

"Portuguese," she echoed. "Who ever heard of it? Who are its poets?"

"We're going to be rich, rich, rich in Brazil!" shouted Kiem. But nobody else seemed very happy about it—as if they could see right through his acting performance.

CHAPTER 20

Saigon Has Exhibit of U.S. "War Crimes"

New York Times, 7 September 1975

"Dear Captain Shine: This is to let you know that I'll be leaving for Brazil in early September and so won't be needing any further assistance from you." Kiem wanted the note to sound cold, but that was a little too cold. He thought for a minute, then added: "I have lost everything, even my pride." Then he signed his name and put a stamp on the envelope.

"Cheer up!" he told his sulking children. "You'll all have new bicycles down in Brazil!" As for Thom, she had flatly refused to open the Portuguese-language book. "Four languages are enough for anyone," she snapped. "Let them learn one of mine if they want to talk to me."

As Kiem began circling the camp, saying good-bye to old and new friends, doubt and fear kept dogging his steps. Even the poor fishing families, who had escaped from Vietnam late on their junks and been routed to Indiantown Gap in a batch— who had never learned to read or write or even perch on a toilet seat, who had stolen all the chrome faucets from the camp's sinks and showers, hoping to sell them on the black market— even they were his countrymen. Even they were more like him, at heart, than Brazilians with college educations. But there would be no Vietnamese community down in Brazil.

Three days after he'd mailed the frosty letter, Kiem heard himself being paged over the public-address system. Maurice Shine was on the phone, and he was frantic: "You're going *where?* Are you crazy? You never said you were in that big a hurry! I'll get you out of there, I promise: just give me a couple more days. Stay right there and don't go *anywhere* until you hear from me. Trust me. OK?"

A few hours later Captain Shine's brother-in-law, Judge James Glancey of New Orleans, called and offered to sponsor them. The judge was going to New York on vacation that week, but he said he'd start all the paperwork as soon as he got back.

No sooner had Kiem hung up on the judge than Captain Shine's brother, a Catholic priest in California, phoned with a competing offer. Now Kiem was feeling like the courtesan in the well-known poem: her body like a piece of silk for sale in the marketplace, being grabbed from all directions.

Over the next few days Judge Glancey, Father Shine, and Captain Shine discussed the pros and cons of both places and finally settled on New Orleans. It was a port city, where Kiem should be able to find work on a ship or in a shipyard, and its climate was a lot like Saigon's. Its traces of French culture would likewise be familiar to the Do family, and its large Catholic population was already sponsoring several thousand Vietnamese, so Kiem and his family would have a community. But there would not be so many of his countrymen that Kiem would have trouble competing with them for jobs, as was the case in California.

Rereading the letter the Glanceys had sent them, handwritten on pale green paper with a spray of lilies at the top of each page, Kiem and Thom knew in their hearts that they were making the right decision: "Each of us, including our daughter, Robyn, is terribly excited about seeing you, and we look forward to a long and happy friendship with you and each member of your family. Sincerely, James and Betty Glancey."

Kiem filled out another "occupational preferences" form, listing the kind of work he thought he could do in New Orleans. One: anything related to ships and the sea. Two: teaching. Three: engineering. On the way back from picking up his "starter money" at the camp's administrative center—seven hundred dollars, the most money he'd ever had in his life—he passed by two fishermen emerging from the showers, blue-lipped and shivering.

"Why not turn on the hot water, my friends?" he asked.

"Because hot water burns, that's why."

"Yes—but it doesn't have to be one or the other. You can turn on both at the same time. I'll show you," said Kiem.

Rather than thank him for the advice, they sulked over the loss of face. *The poor illiterates, how are they ever going to make it in America?* Kiem thought. But what he was really thinking, and he knew it, was *How am I ever going to make it in America?*

On the night before they were to leave, Kiem spoke to the judge by phone. "That's right," said Kiem, "there'll be eight of us in all." Because Lieutenant Su's family name was also "Do," the judge had assumed that he was related to them—and Kiem, somewhat guiltily, had said nothing to correct him.

"Two cars should be enough," the judge estimated. "Y'all don't have any possessions to speak of, do you?"

"No, sir. Nothing but our clothes," said Kiem.

"We can't wait to see you! We'll be bringing some friends from our church to the airport," said the judge. They talked a little while longer, then said their good-byes and hung up.

Shivering a little from the coolness of the Pennsylvania night, Kiem padded on bare feet across a dirt path prickly with pine needles. The moon was a cold silver mirror; he moved toward the warm yellow glow of the barracks windows. As the screen door slammed shut behind him, Thom jumped to her feet from a squatting position on the floor. She was holding an apple-sized ball of string.

"What are you doing?" he asked, surprised.

"Packing," she said. Kiem looked around the room and counted five cardboard boxes bundled with string.

"Packing *what?*" he asked.

"Our things," she said.

"What things?"

"Oh, sheets and things. Toothpaste. . . ."

All of a sudden he understood. Thom had been hoarding their rations of soap, sheets, towels, and toothpaste, then doling it back to them with a miser's hand. One bar of soap carved into splinters had been lasting the family a week, while Thom stashed the "extras" under her cot. All five kids had been forced to share one towel, leaving four for the "kitty." When the camp officials had started rationing toilet paper because the fishing families stole it when it was hanging up, Thom had made a new rule: one square of tissue per trip to the facilities, no matter how much they begged for more.

"Em," he said as gently as he could, "those things belong to the camp. It would be like stealing."

"But I've lost *everything*," she said and began to cry.

"We have our lives, Thom. We're luckier than many."

"'Take nothing with you,' you said. 'Bring one change of clothing for the children.' Look around you! The others brought out gold, jewelry, radios. . . . We're the only ones who have nothing now, all because of you!"

"It could have been a lot worse than it was, Thom. Possessions are heavy. They slow people down when they have to run. . . ." He sighed. "Try to fit it all in *four* boxes if you can."

Thom looked happy again. But, slipping back outside to stare at the moon, Kiem worried that she no longer trusted him to provide for his family. He wasn't sure if he trusted himself. The others in the camp still looked up to him because of who he'd been—but the past was the past. *What if he couldn't make it in America? What if nobody wanted to hire him? How long would their seven hundred dollars last—and how could he bring himself to beg when the money ran out?*

In the morning, the yellow school bus took them to the airport. They flew to Chicago, changed planes, flew to Atlanta, changed again, and flew for another hour and a half—Thom and three of the children airsick, as usual. As they broke through the clouds above New Orleans, Kiem saw that the "landscape" below them was mostly water, just like home. "Metal rusts in water, grows more precious in the earth," his mother had warned when he was contemplating a career in the navy—but he'd been drawn to it, regardless.

The plane bumped down on the runway, and the other passengers began rummaging in the overhead bins. Kiem swung Tootsie up on one shoulder and grabbed his well-worn briefcase with the other. Kiet was already charging off the plane, with Lieutenant Su chasing after him. Thom and Khai and his oldest girl could hardly keep up, stopping every few steps to make dry retching noises. They walked down a long corridor lined with pictures of masks and clowns.

"Look, Daddy," Kiet called back in Vietnamese. "That sign is for us: WEL-COME DO FAM-I-LY." Kiem stood up a little straighter, smoothed the baby's dress, and turned to alert Thom. But she was down on her knees on the floor, getting sick. Then the Americans were upon them. They pumped Kiem's arm up and down, hoisted the baby into the air, and thrust bunches of flowers into Thom's arms. The smell of them made her sicker. They were all talking fast, and at the same time, so that Kiem couldn't tell who was who or which man was the leader. He rode the wave of them out the terminal door.

Thom's grip was like a parrot's on his arm. "You're forgetting my boxes," she whispered. He glared at her. She glared back.

"Excuse me," he said. Nobody could hear him. He tried again. "Excuse me! We have a few things to pick up." The wave reversed direction and surged back in the electronic door.

Kiem hoped he was looking self-assured, hauling all those cardboard boxes off the conveyor belt—seven in all. He felt like an idiot. "What should we do?" the Americans were saying. "We won't all fit in the second car, with those boxes . . . leave some of us behind . . . make a second trip. . . ." Kiem stared straight ahead as blankly as he could, pretending not to understand their English. He could have *murdered* Thom right then—except that she looked so fragile next to the hearty Americans. He wanted to kill her and hug her at the same time.

"Feeling better?" he asked in Vietnamese.

"A little. I'll take the baby now, if you want."

"You rest," he told her. They piled into a compact American car. As they eased away from the curb and Khai rolled down the window to vomit down the side of the door, Kiem saw the rest of their party standing by a second car with its trunk raised, trying to wedge all the boxes inside. Lieutenant Su was giving them advice.

Judge Glancey had rented them a three-bedroom house with a sign outside that said "For Sale / A Man's Home Is His Castle." People kept yanking Kiem's elbow and pulling him around to show him things—hot dogs and milk in the refrigerator, cereal and rice in the cupboards—when all he wanted to do was fall down on one of the beds and pass out. He did manage to shove Thom and Khai into one of the bedrooms and shut the door, though. One man in particular kept dragging him over to the dining table to show him something baffling: a music box nailed to the bottom that played a tune when the frame was pulled out to add or remove a leaf. Kiem didn't understand why anyone would need or want such a thing. "Pull it out! Touch it!" the man exhorted for the thirtieth time—as if Kiem were an idiot child.

Finally the Americans cleared out—but only after promising to come back in an hour and drag everyone to dinner at a Chinese restaurant.

"Oh, please, no," Thom moaned when Kiem told her.

Kiem started feeling a little sick himself when he saw the "Chinese" food: pink chunks of ham and yellow chunks of pineapple swimming in an orange sauce. Somehow they all managed to get through the meal without throwing up. It was after ten o'clock when they were dropped off at their "castle." They collapsed, with their clothes on, on top of the beautiful bedspreads.

In the morning, when Judge Glancey arrived to take Kiem job hunting, he found a totally different family. The children were watching cartoons and sampling all the different breakfast cereals. Thom was testing the dials on the washer, dryer, and dishwasher with a proprietary air. Even Kiem was feeling more cheerful, although he knew he wouldn't dare face his family that night without a job.

Their first stop was Avondale Shipyards, upriver from New Orleans. The sight of U.S. Navy ships in dry dock and men in uniforms scurrying around with notebooks in their hands brought a lump to Kiem's throat. It was his old, familiar environment, but he was a stranger in it. People were rushing past him like water around a stone.

To his surprise, though, they offered him a job as a "ship test engineer." The problem was that it would only be part-time, whenever a ship finished repairs. Still, it felt good to know that somebody wanted him. He told the shipyard director he'd think about it.

They drove back to New Orleans and parked near the docks. The next opening was with a maritime shipping company—but after hearing the job description, Kiem had to tell the judge no. It would have meant going to sea for months on end, at a time when his family needed him.

High-school math teacher: now, that sounded more promising. Judge Glancey had to be in court in an hour, so he suggested that they pick up his wife's car before the interview at Ben Franklin High School in uptown New Orleans. "You can follow me there, then drive home when you're finished. You drive, don't you?" the judge asked.

"Oh, yes," said Kiem. He had no U.S. driver's license, no knowledge of American traffic regulations, and no sense of direction for New Orleans. But he knew how to drive: yes, indeed!

As Kiem turned the key in the ignition of Betty Glancey's car, the judge shot out of the driveway. Kiem floored the gas pedal and took off, just as the judge disappeared around a corner. Kiem pressed down on the accelerator so hard that he was almost standing up inside the car, trying to ignore all the horns honking at him and people rolling down their windows and shouting. He knew that red meant "stop" and green meant "go"—but what about yellow? And what was the protocol for turning left or right while other cars were waiting? The judge swooped across three lanes of traffic, and so did Kiem. His speedometer said "70"—and that wasn't kilometers. They crossed a bridge, barreled down an exit ramp, barely missed being chopped in half by a streetcar, and screeched to a halt in front of Ben Franklin High School: a gracious, white-columned mansion on a palm-tree-lined boulevard.

The principal looked awfully young for his position, in Kiem's view. But once the two of them started talking, Kiem was impressed. The man's ideas on education sounded a lot like those of Kiem's father. Before the interview was even over, the American was smiling and saying, "I know that the students of Ben Franklin would be thrilled to have you as their teacher." Kiem was touched by the democracy of his phrasing, not yet realizing that an interview by student leaders was coming up next. He was nervous until he realized that the half-dozen juniors and seniors were on his side. They asked him a few questions about homework and discipline, which he answered as truthfully as he could.

The job was his if he wanted it, but he'd have to teach biology as well as math. That worried him because, while math was a universal language, science would mean crossing a language barrier. "Would it be possible to look at a biology textbook?" he asked. The principal went to get one from the library. Bean plants, amoebas, body parts: the pictures looked pretty much the same as he was used to. The English terminology scared him at first, but the more he looked at it, the more he realized that it came from the same Latin roots as the French.

He signed a one-year teaching contract.

The principal apologized for making Kiem start work the next day, but the semester was already underway, and the students were falling behind. Kiem suggested that he be allowed to sit in the back and observe a more experienced teacher on his first day. The principal said that was a good idea and that he'd try to arrange it.

Judge Glancey was outside waiting for him, already finished with his court business. "I was worried you might get lost," he told Kiem. "You can follow me back across the river." Rocketing home behind the judge, Kiem wished he could have chosen to get lost.

Everybody at home was happy about his job: they hadn't doubted him the way he'd doubted himself. But later that night, after the kids had gone to bed, Kiem confided his fears to Thom.

"I can help," she said. "I was good at biology in high school."

"Really? I didn't know that," he said. "Not me. I was good at math and art."

"I can type, too," she said. "And I know where there's a typewriter in this house."

"I didn't know you'd learned to type," he said. "Did they teach you at Shell Oil?" She nodded. "If we could type up my outlines and mimeograph them, it might help the students understand my pronunciation. . . ." He and Thom hauled out the typewriter and sat up the rest of the night typing lesson plans and handouts. They grabbed two hours of sleep; then Thom got the children ready for their new schools while Kiem showered and drank a cup of tea. He stuffed his briefcase with papers and books and walked to the bus stop the judge had pointed out the night before.

A bus came right away, but when Kiem gave the driver his dollar, he shoved it back in Kiem's face and said, "Change!"

Change what? thought Kiem. *His behavior? His clothes?* He'd borrowed his jacket and tie from the judge: surely they were the appropriate attire for bus-riding.

He held out his dollar bill again. "Change! Change! Change!" the driver yelled at him.

"Where are you going, dear?" an elderly black woman asked him.

"I'm going to teach," he said.

"Change! Change!" bellowed the driver.

"Hold on now, Son," the lady told the driver. "I'm giving him change." She seized Kiem's dollar, gave him back a handful of coins, and showed him how to feed the coin machine. So that was it: he had known what "coins" meant, but not "change."

He rode the bus across the river, got off at the right corner, found the streetcar stop, and boarded a car with the correct "change." *So far, so good.* But when the scenery started looking familiar, he realized that he was already several blocks past Ben Franklin. Not knowing how to make the bus stop, he waited until it slowed down; then he jumped off.

Despite all his mishaps he arrived on time. The school secretary gave him directions to the math classroom, but the senior teacher hadn't arrived yet, and Kiem didn't want to breach protocol by going in first. Students were already arriving and taking their seats—but some were hippies with beads and long hair! He knew that hippies hated the South Vietnamese people. The student leaders who had interviewed him yesterday had worn dresses and suits.

A bell rang. The senior teacher was definitely late. The hippies had begun peeking out in the hall at him, and Kiem was stealing nervous glances back at them. Two or three more minutes ticked by. Then, shaking all over, he made his way into the room and to the blackboard and picked up the chalk: "Mr. Do Kiem," he wrote. *Oops.* He found an eraser and rubbed it out: "Mr. Kiem Do," he printed—the American word-order. He thought he heard laughter behind him, but when he wheeled around, they were just looking at him expectantly. A brown-haired girl with glasses smiled at him, and he smiled back.

For no more than a minute, he was back at his grandfather's school in Phu Tai, sitting cross-legged on the ground in a ring of children. He knew that, if he tried, he could still chant all the way through to the end of the "Three Thousand Words," though much more slowly now and not without hesitation. First *thien, troi:* heaven. Then *dia, dat:* earth. Then *cu, cat:* to carry a burden. Then *ton, con:* to remain—but not to re-main *behind,* exactly. To persist, to endure, to abide: though the sea rolls in and drowns the mulberry field, or mulberry trees begin to grow on the floor of the vanished sea.

He took a deep breath, and then he began to teach.

About the Authors

Kiem Do was born in Hanoi, Vietnam, in 1933, and served for twenty-one years in the South Vietnamese Navy. At the time of the fall of Saigon in 1975 he was a captain and the deputy chief of staff for operations. His previous naval positions included district commander, chief of staff of the Mobile Riverine Force, and commandant of the Vietnamese Midshipman's School.

After settling in the United States he taught high school math and science, studied in the MBA program at the University of New Orleans, and completed a second twenty-one-year career as a cost engineer with a Louisiana utility company. Since his retirement in 1997, he has been active as a leader in the New Orleans Vietnamese community and has lectured frequently on the Vietnam War at local universities and before veterans groups. He and his wife of thirty-nine years, Thom Le Do, have five children and six American-born grandchildren.

Julie Kane is a native of Boston and longtime resident of Louisiana. She holds a B.A. in English from Cornell University and an M.A. in creative writing from Boston University, and she is presently finishing work on a Ph.D. in English at Louisiana State University in Baton Rouge. She has published three collections of poetry in the United States and Great Britain, and her poems have appeared widely in literary journals and anthologies. Past writing awards include first prize in the Mademoiselle Magazine College Poetry Competition, the George Bennett Fellowship in Writing at Phillips Exeter Academy, and the Academy of American Poets Prize. She has worked as a nuclear technical writer, science journal editor, and college English instructor.